A MILE OF STRING

FORWARD

I initially sat down a few years ago to write a story of my life for my children and grandchildren. I wanted them to have a written record of some of my experiences to give them an idea of the amazing and unprecedented cultural and technological changes that have occurred during my generation. I was also aware of my unusual career change in middle age from practicing physician in a small town in northern Idaho to flying large passenger jets up and down the west coast of the United States as an airline pilot for a major airline. Between these two careers, I had lots of good stories to tell and wanted to get them down on paper. What I didn't realize when I started out was how interesting my childhood was. I opened this project with my birth in 1945. As I started writing, I began to recall things I had not thought about for many years. Each experience I wrote about seemed to trigger memories of other things, and the words began to flow in a continuous stream. I now think my childhood and teenage years may have been the most interesting segment of my life. So this book is about my life from birth to graduation from high school. The more recent stories from college, medical school, life as a doctor, and experiences as a pilot may come as a sequel at some time in the future.

In this narrative I recall experiences from my life as a boy growing up in and around Kansas City during the 1950s and early 1960s as I remember them. Nothing is fabricated. The names of people in the story, however, may or may not be their real names. I have inserted some historical references at various places in the book to add some perspective to the story. I hope you enjoy reading my story as much as I enjoyed writing it.

Dedicated
To
Martha

My Best Friend and Partner in Life

A MILE OF STRING

A Boy's Recollection of His Midwest Childhood

By

David B. Crawley

A Memoir

May 26, 1963

1:30 AM

I wasn't sure whether I was dead or alive or just having a bad nightmare. I was looking out through a shattered glass windshield and could see only tall grass and what looked like a muddy creek bottom. It was pitch-dark, but the vehicle's headlights projected their yellow beams on this eerie scene. I could hear only the faint ticking of my wrist watch, which seemed to be wedged between the left side of my face and the side window. Otherwise there was complete silence. The perspective of what I was looking at was all wrong. Everything in view was turned sideways.

I couldn't move. I couldn't remember what had happened or how I got there. I must have had a terrible wreck. My eyes focused on some closer lights. I could see lighted instruments. They seemed vaguely familiar. It was my own car. Yes, I was in a terrible wreck.

I tried to move. I couldn't move. Someone's knee was against the right side of my head, and another heavy weight was squeezing down on the entire right side of my body. I thought I must be severely injured—even paralyzed. Something was pushing hard on the side of my neck, and there was a foot sticking up just under my chin. I felt a warm liquid dripping onto the right side of my face.

My head slowly started to clear. I felt like I was waking up. We had been on our way to a party at a farm—I and two of my classmates. It was high school graduation week. I was not ready to die in a ditch next to a Kansas farm road. I was supposed to be celebrating my graduation from high school this week, and my life should be just beginning, not ending.

I was thinking this when I heard Buzzy say, "Let's get out of here! It may catch fire any minute."

Chapter 1

Mom and Dad enjoyed telling the story of my mother's trip to the hospital when she was in labor with me. My father was working at the time, and my mother did not have a car and didn't even know how to drive. She called my Uncle Kenneth Crawley, my father's older brother, a lifelong bachelor. He owned an interior decorating business, near their apartment, on the Country Club Plaza in Kansas City. Kenneth drove her to St. Mary's Hospital in his dark blue, sporty 1938 Buick convertible. It was a bright sunny day, 80 degrees, and humid. All the windows were down on Kenneth's car. Uncle Kenneth was so nervous during this excursion that his driving was erratic, and he killed the engine several times due to uncontrollable spasms of his left foot on the clutch pedal. Each time this happened, the car came to a shaking stop, and Kenneth's trembling hand stabbed frantically toward the starter button. There was heavy afternoon traffic, and there were times when they were completely stopped for several minutes. My mother was laughing at Kenneth the entire way. Mom always had a whacky sense of humor and was actually enjoying the crazy scene despite the painful cramps of labor.

Dad's family was opposed to their marriage because Mom was a Catholic, and they all hated Catholics. Dad's mother had grown up as a Methodist but had converted to a Christian Scientist. Dad wasn't religious at all, but his brother and two sisters were still Methodists. I think they all kind of liked Mom, but none of them ever really admitted it. The religion was a big issue. Mom never seemed to let it bother her much though.

Dad met Mom through his sister Emily. She probably would never have introduced them if she had known my mother was a Catholic. Dad asked her out on a first date to hear the Jimmy Dorsey Band play at the Meuhlebach Hotel in downtown Kansas City. Mom was impressed that Dad was taking her to this since she assumed it was quite an expensive first date. It was a double date in Bill Catron's roadster with the top down. Bill was one of Dad's best friends. Mom and Dad sat in the rumble seat. Mom got all dressed up for the occasion, but when Dad escorted her out to the car, she noticed the other three were dressed casually. When they arrived downtown, Bill pulled into the alley behind the Meuhlebach, and they whipped out a

1

bottle of booze and four glasses. The windows of the hotel opened onto the alley, and the four of them sat back and enjoyed the smooth jazz of the Jimmy Dorsey band as the evening cooled and the breeze from the Missouri River flowed gently down the alley and wafted over them. When the band played "Blue Moon," Mom and Dad were feeling mellow, and they climbed out of the rumble seat and danced to the music in the alley. The year was 1938.

Mom's zany sense of humor went right along with her free, adventurous spirit. She was always coming up with new ideas for her and Dad to do together or fun activities for us, the kids. She and Dad were teenagers when the Great Depression of 1929 started, and they both had toughed their ways through it. Mom was no stranger to hard work. She had an incredible work ethic. By the early 1940s she had established herself as a successful fashion model. She had worked in the stockroom of a classy, upscale women's clothing store and had peeked through a curtain to watch the runway models during a fashion show. She knew the pay was good and decided she could do that. She practiced the walk, the poses, and the twirls and bluffed her way into a job as a model. As it turned out, she was a natural, and her career took off. She was in fashion shows and did photographic modeling for newspapers and magazines. She was even the model for the heroine in an illustrated detective series that was published in Saturday Evening Post nationwide for several years. She was invited to appear in an occasional stage show. We have a photo of her on stage with Bob Hope, just the two of them standing together looking at each other. He has a microphone in front of him and is smiling at her, and she is looking at him with a shy smile and a demure tilt to her head.

Dad and Mom were very different. I think their personalities complimented each other though. Dad was reserved—Mom was outgoing in social situations. Dad was messy—Mom was neat. Dad was cautious—Mom was adventurous. Dad was a bit of a pessimist—Mom was an optimist. Dad hated physical work of any type—Mom was a workaholic and didn't mind getting her hands dirty. One trait Mom and Dad shared was a wonderful sense of humor. They both were bountifully endowed with funny bones.

Dad had a lonely childhood. His parents were older when he was growing up, and his nearest sibling was nine years older than he. He never had much sense of family. Dad was always quite reserved and conservative. There was little spirit of adventure, and he didn't

2

like doing anything new or different. But Mother had a way of dragging him into activities he never would have done on his own, and he then often had a wonderful time in spite of himself. Dad wasn't lazy by any means, yet he didn't have the work ethic Mom had. He was a little sloppy in his personal habits, but accurate with numbers and figures. Dad was always scrupulously honest and never tolerated anyone who he thought might be lying or cheating. At the time of my birth, he was working as a bookkeeper while he took some accounting courses at a junior college. He later took the CPA exam and became a certified public accountant.

The only son of this union turned out to be an occasionally optimistic pessimist, an extremely cautious seeker of adventure, a scrupulously honest person who likes to play zany practical jokes on his friends, and a neatness freak who is good with numbers and figures.

They made it to the hospital, my mother's labor progressed throughout the afternoon and evening, and I was born in the wee hours of the morning on July 14, 1945. I was the second of five children and, as it turned out, the only son. My older sister, Judy, was four years old at the time of my birth.

I was born in Kansas City, Missouri, at St. Mary's Hospital. My 1945 birth made me an early member of what became known as the "Baby Boomer Generation," named for the surge in birth rate following World War II. My folks named me after my great-grandfather, David Crawley, of Sullivan, Indiana (b. 1831, d. 1910). He was a master cabinetmaker by profession, and it is interesting that I have always had an avid interest in tools and woodworking. If it is possible that such skills and interests can be passed on genetically, it seems to have skipped two generations in between. My dad and his father had no interest in tools whatsoever.

We lived in a cozy little second-floor apartment at 4542 Jarbo in Kansas City, Missouri. The apartment was just a few blocks from the Country Club Plaza, a beautifully designed shopping, restaurant, and entertainment section of the city. All the buildings of the Plaza were copied from Spanish architecture, and the area remains a beautiful Kansas City landmark today. Our apartment itself had a nice, large central courtyard which opened toward a steep set of concrete steps to the street. As a toddler, my mother allowed me to race along the sidewalk in the courtyard in my light blue steel "Taylor Tot" stroller with the foot tray removed from the bottom. I propelled myself and my vehicle at a breakneck speed by rapidly churning my bare feet on the pavement. As soon as my mother released me, she tore out ahead in order to reach the top of the concrete steps and arrest my careening carriage before it became an airborne projectile. We have actually preserved some old 16-millimeter home movies which recorded this activity. The movies were taken by my mother's cousin, Mary Virginia Bird. She was an expert cinematographer and had state-of-the-art equipment. She was employed for most of her life as a film editor by Fox Studios in Los Angeles, making her a semi-professional

4

behind the camera. We were lucky to have Mary Virginia recording those memorable times for us. She amused and entertained us over many years by always bringing her camera, projector, and screen on her visits from Hollywood. On one of her visits she played the movies backwards for us. We laughed hysterically as we watched them, and, from that point on, we never wanted to even see them played normally.

My maternal grandmother and grandfather, Tom and Bernadina Fearon, lived in a nearby apartment, just a couple of blocks away, also on Jarbo. My grandmother took care of Judy and me when my mother worked as a fashion model.

My grandmother, whom we called Namo, was a German immigrant. She was a skillful seamstress and made dresses and did alterations. We still have several of her beautiful handmade quilts. When I was a young boy and she asked me what I wanted for my birthday, I invariably told her I wanted a new shirt; she then always made one for me, usually out of corduroy fabric.

My grandfather, Thomas Michael Fearon, was a policeman for the Kansas City Missouri Police Department. He was an Irishman, born of Irish immigrants on a farm in Edina, Missouri. He grew up on the farm in a family of seven girls and seven boys. He was a devout Catholic. He always carried a rosary in his pocket and frequently had it out, fingering the beads as he silently recited his prayers.

Tom Fearon, always speaking in a bit of an Irish brogue, liked to tell stories about his three best friends: Duke Hardsocks, Reddy McAtee, and Charlie Gooch. We never saw any of these friends and always wondered whether they were real or not. In his later years, my grandfather loved to play dominos with my dad. When he was winning, he would look across at my dad and say, "Snyder's on the roof and Sullivan's gaining ground."

We called my grandfather "Dabo." Dabo was out on foot patrol in Kansas City one Christmas Eve. His beat was along a business section of Main Street. He stopped off and checked on each of the businesses as he patrolled, and all of the owners knew him well. They each offered him a little sample of "holiday cheer," so he got a little nip at each stop. His last inspection along the route was at Quirk and Tobin Funeral Home. He got another little sample there, and the undertaker wisely determined that Tom probably needed to go home. They delivered him horizontally to their apartment in a big black hearse and carried him in. Dena Fearon, my grandmother, was not happy and never let him forget that night.

1945 – Franklin D. Roosevelt dies in office – the world's first computer is built – the Germans surrender, ending the war in Europe – the first microwave oven is invented – the United Nations is founded – the U.S. drops the Atomic Bombs on the Japanese cities of Hiroshima and Nagasaki – Japan surrenders, ending World War II -

1946 – The Central Intelligence Agency is formed –Dean Martin and Jerry Lewis form a musical/comedy team – Average gasoline price is 15¢ per gallon - 12 high-ranking Nazis are sentenced to death by the International War Crimes Tribunal in Nuremberg and hung – The price of the average American home is $5,600 –

Chapter 2

Sometime in 1947, my father bought a newly constructed house at 1287 West Gregory in Kansas City, Missouri. We moved out of our tiny apartment when my mother was pregnant with her third child, my sister Martha; she was born in October that year. The house was a white two-story of frame construction, had a stucco exterior, and was located in a large suburban neighborhood of similar homes. It had a nice yard with a paved driveway leading to a one-car detached garage toward the back of the lot. Ours was the second house from the corner of Gregory and State Line Road. There was a wooded area on the other side of State Line Road, and we referred to that area as "over in Kansas." I was over in Kansas one day (where I was never allowed to go) with several of the older neighbor boys (whom I was not supposed to be with) when the boys started a fire from dried leaves by focusing sunlight through a magnifying glass. The fire mushroomed into a full-blown brush fire and spread to some trees. We all scampered back across the street into Missouri, sat on the curb, and watched as the fire trucks arrived to battle the blaze. It was all very exciting, and I remember worrying my mother might find out I was over in Kansas when all of this got started, but I don't believe she ever got wind of that fact. The firemen extinguished the blaze without difficulty and life went on.

At some point, a wonderful old stray dog began showing up at our house on a daily basis, and we started feeding him. He would spend the day with me, and I remember he enjoyed napping on the grass in the backyard just behind the screened porch and next to the driveway. We didn't know his name, but, since he slept so much, I named him "Snoozy" and considered him my own dog. Snoozy was a medium-sized dog with a thick, furry coat, mostly black in color, but with some patches of brown and white. He was some type of sheep dog—possibly an Australian Shepherd. He wandered over from Kansas almost every morning, we fed him, and then he took his nap. Sometime toward the end of the day he'd go back over into the Kansas woods to spend the night. One day he stopped showing up at our house, and we never found out what happened to him. If he met some tragic demise that my parents were aware of, they probably sheltered me from that news. I still miss my dog Snoozy, even to this day.

ater in my life when I had a family of my own, we had
hepherds in sequence followed by a Border Collie. I
ᴄ an attraction to sheep dogs as a result of my love for
child.

ᴧy mother had a friend who lived in another area of Kansas
who had a son named Andy Kinzer. Andy was one year older
ᴄnan I was, but he was a nice boy, and his mother brought him over to
play every once in a while. We always had fun. One day my mother
told me Andy couldn't come and play with me anymore because he
and his sister had gotten polio, and he might even have to go into an
"iron lung" machine. No one seemed to know back then exactly how
polio was spread, but it was known that it was a contagious, infectious
disease. There was a terrible fear of this crippling (and sometimes
fatal) disease, and my mother was constantly warning us of all the
things we needed to avoid that might cause us to get polio. She
stopped letting us play outside in the hose spray and wouldn't let us
dip in our little rubber wading pool during the summer anymore. Also,
we liked to collect Lady Bugs, and she wouldn't let us do that anymore
because they "might carry polio." My little friend Andy finally
recovered, but the next time I saw him he walked with little crutches
and braces on his legs because of paralysis in his lower limbs. Andy
seemed to eventually completely recover from the paralysis, and when
he grew up he became a successful veterinarian.

Every Monday was "wash day" at our house, and Tuesday was
ironing day. I think most families of that time had the same schedule
we did. This must have been an old custom originating on the farm.
The whole day was set aside for this chore because it was quite a job.
We kids all brought our dirty clothes from the week down to the
basement early in the morning. My mother spent most of Monday
morning in the basement washing the clothes and then spent the
afternoon in the backyard hanging them out to dry. Automatic washing
machines were in the early stages of development then, and there was
no such thing as an electric or gas clothes dryer.

Our washing machine was a round tub with four legs. Each leg
had a hard rubber castor at the bottom so the machine could be
wheeled to a position near the floor drain. It had a white enameled
finish, and there was a "wringer" attached to the back protruding
above the rim. The machine had an agitator inside powered by an
electric motor. (Machines for rural areas without electricity had

gasoline engines for turning the agitator.) The dirty clothes were placed in the tub and the tub filled with warm water from a hose attached to the laundry sink. Soap was added to the tub, and then the agitator was turned on and allowed to run for 10 or 15 minutes. The soapy water was then drained. There was a hose attached to the bottom of the tub, and the other end was clipped up to the top near the rim of the tub. To drain the tub, the upper end of this hose was unclipped and lowered to a position near a drain in the concrete floor. The soapy water ran out onto the floor and down the drain. The residual soapy water in the clothes was then wrung out with the wringer at the top of the tub. The wringer consisted of two hard rubber rollers which abutted one another and were turned by an electric motor. Earlier versions of the wringer, and ones on machines destined for homes without electricity, had a hand crank instead of the motor. The wet soapy clothes were fed manually between the rollers on the wringer and then returned to the tub for rinsing. The fill, drain, and run procedure was repeated, and the clean clothes were fed through the wringer a final time.

The wet clothes were then placed in a bushel basket which was made of thin wooden slats woven together with wire. These baskets were previously used as containers for fruit and vegetables from the farm. Every household had a few of these around. There were no plastic laundry baskets like we have today. My mother took the basket of clothes and carried it up the steps to the backyard. Every yard had clothes lines. We had two "T" shaped steel clothesline trees set into the ground in concrete about 50 feet apart. There were several parallel clotheslines strung between the horizontal bars of these two supports. My mom placed the basket on the ground and hung the clothes one at a time on the lines to dry. She used clothespins to secure the clothes to the lines and prevent them from blowing off in the wind. There were two types of clothespins, both made of wood. There was a simple clip type that basically looked like a short length of dowel with a slot in it. The other type was a pinch type with a metal spring. There was generally a baby in the laundry basket with the clothes. With a family of five kids, it seems there was always a baby to care for at the same time all of the other chores were being accomplished.

After the clothes were on the lines, Mom kept a close eye on the weather. If a strong wind came up, the clothes could end up scattered all over the neighborhood. This actually happened a few times. If it started to rain, we all ran out and helped get the clothes down and inside. They were then hung on lines which were strung in the basement to finish drying. This was less than ideal. It took much longer for the clothes to dry in the basement. Also, if it was raining to start with and the clothes had to be dried the entire time in the basement, we did not enjoy the unique, fresh, sun-dried smell our clothes had when they had been hung outside. I still remember how wonderful our clothes smelled after being dried outside in the sunshine and fresh air.

The electric ringer on the washing machine was a potentially dangerous contraption. The operator had to be careful not to have any body parts pulled into the rollers with the wet laundry. Women had to be careful not to get long hair caught in the mechanism and, of course, had to keep their fingers clear at all times. Wringer injuries were not uncommon and could be quite severe and debilitating. The usual result was fractures of bones in the hand and/or forearm associated with crushing soft-tissue injuries. My maternal grandmother had a wringer injury to one of her forearms that caused painful episodes most of her life.

I haven't seen wooden clothespins for many years. I don't know if you can even find them in a store anymore. We kept our supply in a peck-sized produce basket made of thin woven wood slats with a bent-wood handle at the top. We found lots of uses for these little gadgets besides clipping clothes to the line. We kids used them to make little toys and crafts—sawing them, painting them, gluing them together. The pinch type could be converted into guns that would shoot rubber bands through the air. We also used them to attach playing cards to our bike fenders so the spokes made a putt-putt sound like a motorcycle as we rode. We used these handy little things to clip all kinds of things together. I usually had a clothespin or two in the pocket of my jeans just in case I needed one.

We always ate meals together at home. Breakfast (and lunch on weekends and during the summer months) was at the kitchen table. Dinner, the evening meal, was always a more formal affair in the dining room. My mother cooked all the meals, and the older girls helped with the preparation and serving. I was never involved with the cooking but was required to set the table though and take my turn at washing or drying the dishes. We were all expected to take a rotation at that job as soon as we were old enough. Automatic dishwashers did not start appearing on the scene until the late 1950s or early 1960s. I don't remember having an electric dishwasher in our kitchen until I was in my teenage years. So one of us washed and rinsed the dishes, and the other dried them and put them away in the cupboards. When we made up the wash water, we put a bar of soap in a little wire cage-like contraption that had a handle on it and swished it around in the dishwater to make the suds. I never really minded doing the dishes except on nice summer evenings when we were all anxious to get outside and play as long as possible before dark.

One day my mother and I were in the front yard and we saw a kid yelling down into one of the street drains which led to the storm sewer. He apparently had a friend who was spelunking his way through the sewer system with a flashlight and was yelling at the top of his lungs: "Louie, Louie where are you?" I thought this activity seemed fun and exciting. I asked my mother if I could go play "Louie, Louie where are you" myself. She discouraged this, but I must have kept this vision in my mind because, when I was a little older and we had moved to our next house, I became a regular storm-sewer spelunker myself. My mother never forgot the "Louie, Louie where are you" line and repeated the story over and over again throughout her life.

1947 – Chuck Yeager breaks the sound barrier in the X-1 Rocket Plane – The Marshall Plan for rebuilding Europe is introduced – Polaroid Cameras go on sale – The greatest production was recorded in the peacetime history of this country or any other country –

11

Chapter 3

Our first family car was a Plymouth sedan. It was probably about a 1946 or 1947 model. The car was light blue in color. It had "suicide doors" in the back which opened backwards. The design of the doors became a significant factor one day when my father drove the car into the garage with one of the rear doors open. The door caught on the frame of the garage door and was seriously damaged. My father was quite upset about this and was mad at himself. Our neighbor next door was a nice man named Mr. Lark. He was good with tools, and, since I knew my dad was not good with tools and didn't know how to fix anything, I told him I would run next door and get Mr. Lark. This suggestion seemed to make my dad much madder than he already was.

Our next car was a black Packard—a 1948 or 1949 model—and the one after that was a light green 1951 Packard Clipper. The Packards were pretty fancy cars. The black Packard had wide white-sidewall tires which was an option when you bought tires in those days. Another option to dress up a car then was fender skirts. These were panels fastened onto the body to partially cover the rear wheel wells, but they could be removed for cleaning the white-sidewall tires. I helped my dad wash the car on Saturdays, and we spent a lot of time scrubbing the white-side walls with Brillo pads.

Gas stations were called "service stations" in the 1950s and early 1960s. When you pulled into a service station, your car ran over a rubber cable strung across the entry which rang a bell in the office and in the garage. This signaled the owner and employees that a customer had arrived and prompted the team to a flurry of activity. It wasn't uncommon to have the owner and one or two of his employees, all in crisp uniforms with neckties and "officer hats," arrive at your vehicle before you had gotten stopped at the pump. Their uniforms were generally in the colors of the associated oil company and always displayed the company logo on the chest or back. Two of the team members immediately began washing the windshield, one on each side. The third, often the owner of the station, positioned himself by the driver's window. After a smiling, cheerful greeting he would ask, "Fill her up with Ethyl?"

There were two grades of gasoline: "Ethyl" (now "premium") and "Regular." Gas prices were in the range of 15 to 20 cents per gallon, and Ethyl was usually a penny or two more than Regular. Many cars then had large V-8 engines and didn't run well on the lower octane Regular. Even if the car ran okay on Regular, the oil companies had us all convinced the pricier Ethyl ran much cleaner and was better for the engine. There was actually some truth to that. I clearly remember my mother complaining about the high price of gasoline when she had to pay four dollars to fill up the big tank of the family station wagon.

While one of these natty professionals was pumping the gas, the other two, after washing all the windows, checked the oil and all of the other fluid levels under the hood. They then checked and adjusted the pressure in the tires. All of these services generally happened automatically while the fuel was being pumped, without a request by the customer, and were expected whenever fuel was purchased. It didn't matter whether you asked for a dollar's worth or for a fill-up.

Pumping your own gas was not an option. There was no slot for a credit card, and the numbers on the pump were mechanical. Before the attendant started the pump, he rotated a crank on the side that made a little pinging sound as it turned, and all of the numbers (gallons and price) would spin to zero. Then, as the gas flowed into the vehicle, the numbers increased with a soft ticking sound as they rotated on an internal wheel. Since gasoline was pretty cheap, the price window on the pump turned much slower than the gallons window. Payment at the pump was usually in cash, but most stations accepted personal checks too—and always did if you were a regular customer.

The attendant often had, attached to his belt, a shiny chrome change dispenser with vertical cylinders for quarters, dimes, nickels, and pennies. Each cylinder had a little lever at the bottom to dispense the appropriate coin. If he didn't have one of these slick little devices, and the customer was paying cash, he had to run to the office to get change from the cash register. And, yes, he ran. The whole team seemed dedicated to providing the best service in the shortest possible time. They all performed like a practiced and polished drill team.

Almost everyone had a favorite oil company and even a specific local station they "traded with." Dad liked Skelly for some reason and always went to the same Skelly station near our house in the suburb of Fairway, Kansas. Service stations didn't have mini-markets then. The building had an office with a desk, a cash register, and a rack of oil cans of various viscosities. There were often rubber fan belts of various sizes hanging by nails around the top of the wall. The office commonly had a large front window with a view of all of the pumps. There was also frequently a display of new tires somewhere along the outside of the building. A side-door from the office led to a service garage with one or two bays equipped with hydraulic lifts. The walls of the typical garage were usually papered with a few "girly" pin-up posters (to keep up employee morale, I assume), but these were always much less revealing than the ones published today. In any case, they were always discretely placed so female customers were not likely to be exposed and thus lower their esteem for these fine professionals.

When a car broke down or just needed routine maintenance, your local service station was where you took it. Whether it was points, plugs, condenser, timing adjustment, a brake job, oil and lube, or tire repair—the corner station did it all. Almost everyone who worked there was a mechanic. The owner was usually the expert and was often on a first-name basis with his customers. Having a favorite station you always went to for these services engendered trust, and it also helped the mechanic because he got to "know" your vehicle.

Gas prices in those days now seem so low compared to the prices today, but there were times when the prices plummeted. This happened during "gas wars" when all of the competing stations in an area were trying to attract new customers by having the lowest price. A "war" started when one station lowered the price by a penny or two. Then the station down the street dropped their price a penny below

15

that. After a few days, prices per gallon were ridiculously low, but I'm pretty sure the only winners in these wars were the customers. People hopped around like puppets to the station with the lowest price until the gas war was over. They generally then returned to their favorite neighborhood station.

All of the big oil companies were in fierce competition. It was hard to watch a television show without seeing an advertisement by one of them. They each had a logo and some kind of catchy slogan. I can remember the red Texaco star emblem, and their line was, "Trust your car to the man who wears the star." Esso's slogan was, "Put a tiger in your tank," and for Conoco, "Hottest brand going."

I was sorry to see the demise of the full-service gas station. I am quite nostalgic about it and consider it an American icon. Those were the days!

On Sundays we often went out for an afternoon drive—usually into the country. These drives, in the days before home air conditioning, were a great way to escape the summer heat. Cars did not have air conditioning either, but with all the windows down, we were much cooler speeding down a country road than we were sitting on the porch at home. The cars had no seatbelts in those days, and one of us kids usually climbed up and lay on the deck in the rear window as we cruised along. I have a memory of seeing a long train chugging along a track parallel to the country road we were driving on one Sunday afternoon. The train was pulled by a steam locomotive with black smoke puffing out of its coal-fired boiler. The engineer saw us waving from our car, waved back, and then, to our delight, pulled on the rope hanging from the ceiling of his cab sounding the shrill whistle.

Sometimes on these Sunday drives, we ended up at Aunt Frances and Uncle Frank Miller's farm in Lenexa, Kansas. We sat on the porch swing in front or went into the parlor to visit. Aunt Frances was my mother's aunt, her mother's sister. They grew various types of produce on the farm and had a productive hen house. Frank was a carpenter most of his life and built the old farm house they lived in. It was a white frame, two-story clapboard house, and the rooms inside had high ceilings. The kitchen had a hand-pump next to the sink to pump water from the well. The light switches on the walls were round, black, knurled knobs that you twisted in order to turn the lights on or off.

When we were at Uncle Frank and Aunt Frances's farm, one of my favorite activities was feeding the chickens. I went to the chicken yard with a bag of dried corn kernels and tossed out handfuls onto the ground. If it was cold outside, I had on my little tweed overcoat which had a matching tweed cap. Feeding the chickens was great fun until I ran out of corn; then the chickens became aggressive and vicious. My mother was usually standing by to rescue me from their attack at this point.

Uncle Frank sold chicken eggs he delivered to homes in Kansas City in his Model T Ford. He kept this car in a barn behind the house, and I can remember him starting it by turning the crank on the front end. It did not have an electric starter. This was a very old car to be driving in the 1950s, and Frank kept a roll of bailing wire in the back seat of the Model T to make jury-rigged repairs while on his delivery route.

I went with Frank on his egg delivery route in Kansas City a couple of times. He seemed to lose control of his Model T when we were going downhill, and it was a little unnerving. The brakes were only on the rear wheels, as with all Model T's, and were probably completely worn out as they seemed to have little or no effect in slowing the car. I bounced up and down in the right passenger seat as we careened wildly down the hills with Frank laughing maniacally as he jerked the steering wheel back and forth and the car bounced sideways to the right and then the left. At one point his corncob pipe flew out of his mouth and hit the windshield. Dabo, my grandfather, made one of these trips with Frank, and afterward suggested to Mom and Dad that being Frank's assistant on his delivery route was probably not the safest activity for me. That ended my Model T trips with Uncle Frank.

Frank was actually quite an old man to still be driving at all in the 1950s. He was born in 1869 and was 90 years old when he died in Lenexa in 1960. He was quite a character, and I remember that he made homemade wine and frequently invited me to try it when I was a small boy. He always called me by the nickname "Nussbaum." I have no idea why. He was hard of hearing, and we had to yell for him to hear anything we said. He held his hand cupped up to his ear as we spoke.

Frank loved to tell stories and regaled us with one about the time his goat Bucky ran around the tree he was tethered to and tied Frank up tightly against the tree. He didn't get loose until Frances ran out to help him after hearing his screams. We were never quite sure how true this was, but it made a hilarious story, and Frank told it over and over again.

We took a drive to another farm one Thanksgiving Day, probably in the late 1940s. The farm belonged to Aunt Anna and was in Edina, Missouri. Aunt Anna was my mother's aunt, her father's sister. Dabo, my grandfather Fearon, grew up on that farm near Edina in a family with fourteen children, seven boys and seven girls. Aunt Anna's house was another old clapboard farm house with a hand pump for well water at the kitchen sink. I remember helping with the pump when we washed the dishes after the Thanksgiving meal. I also recall that the bathroom was an outhouse behind the house and that we city kids were quite disgusted with the odor we had to endure when we had to use it.

At some point that day, either before or after the meal, I was out exploring and became acquainted with one of the Billy goats on the farm. I had a leather jacket with fringe on it which the goat took a great interest in. The goat backed me up against a fence and started chewing on the point of the collar, right next to my chin. When the goat got tired of the collar, it discovered the fringe on the sleeves and began pulling off the leather strips with its teeth and swallowing them. I was afraid to move a muscle during this episode, fearing it might decide to chomp into me next if I riled it in any way. I don't recall how I finally escaped from this predicament, but I suspect I was eventually rescued by one of the adults at the party. I saved my leather jacket, which still bears the scars from that day—a chewed collar and missing fringe. I recently gave the coat to my grandson, Will Griset, age two. The coat was a perfect fit.

18

1948 – The Big Bang Theory for the origin of the universe is formulated – Harry Truman is elected for a second term as President of the United States – The state of Israel is founded – A game called "Scrabble" is invented – The transistor is developed – A daring new swim suit called the "bikini" is introduced in Paris -

Chapter 4

When we lived in the house on Gregory, there was a boy named Ray Molitore who lived in the house behind us on the next block. Ray was a year or two older than I was, but we played together frequently. Ray was always getting us into trouble, and he was probably involved with the fire that started in the woods over in Kansas. The reason I think that is I can recall another incendiary incident. I was at Ray's house one day when Ray brought a can of gasoline out of their garage, poured some on the driveway, and tossed a lit match on it. My father was in our backyard and came rushing over to the Molitore house and put the fire out with a garden hose. Maybe Ray's last name should have been Molotov instead of Molitore.

Ray and I spent many hours together playing cowboys. We had almost identical black cowboy outfits with black hats, black western shirts with shiny imitation pearl buttons, black jeans, and black cowboy boots. We each had double leather holsters for our cap gun revolvers, which had imitation pearl handles. Ray and I loved our cap guns. Some of our guns took rolls of caps. We loaded the rolls, and the caps then fed into the hammer for a loud pop each time the trigger was pulled. Some of the fancier, more realistic cap guns had individual bullets into which we loaded single round caps. The bullets were then inserted into the revolving cylinder of the gun, and each cap fired in sequence as the cylinder moved each bullet in line with the hammer when the trigger was squeezed.

Besides loading the caps into the cap guns, we discovered at some point we could make a much louder bang by stacking up a whole bunch of caps on top of one another on the concrete driveway and then striking the stack with a hammer. The caps themselves were just globs of black gunpowder affixed to a paper backing, so it made sense that the larger the charge, the bigger the bang.

The interest Ray and I had in guns could have gotten us into serious trouble one day when the two of us handled a loaded revolver Ray had gotten out of the nightstand drawer in his parents' bedroom. We each took it in our hands and admired it before replacing it in the drawer. None of our parents were ever aware of this activity. Toy guns are not considered appropriate toys today, but when I was a little kid, it seemed practically every kid had a pair of guns on.

We also had other cowboy paraphernalia, such as "Lone Ranger" masks, handcuffs (hanging from our belts), bandanas, western belts with fancy buckles, sheriff's stars, spurs that attached to our boots, and lariats. Our horses were either broomstick horses or we pretended our bicycles were horses. We made a stagecoach by tying a cardboard box onto our red wagon and cutting out windows and doors. My younger sister, Martha, was the usual passenger, and I was the horse for the stagecoach. Martha somehow survived a number of stagecoach wrecks on her wild rides, and, although she sometimes crawled out of the overturned coach crying after an upset, she often amazingly calmed down and climbed right back in to do it again. When the stage coach box got to the end of its useful life, we found another big box and made a new stagecoach.

1949 – China becomes communist – NATO is established – The Soviet Union has the Atomic Bomb –

Chapter 5

At some point in the early 1950s, we got a television set. I had seen television a couple of times at a friend's house. Most of the early models were large pieces of furniture. These console models sat on the floor and had tiny round screens which were eight or nine inches in diameter. The one we got was a table model with a square screen having a black and white picture. Color TV hadn't been invented yet.

TV programs were broadcast over the air only. Cable and satellite TV were many years away. As a matter of fact, the only satellite at that point was the Moon. To get the best reception, an outside antenna had to be installed on the roof or in the attic, but we got along with a "V" – shaped antenna called "rabbit ears" that sat on a base on top of the TV and was connected to terminals on the back by a wire. We were always fussing with the rabbit ears, moving them around and putting them at different angles in an attempt to improve the picture. Mashing a piece of aluminum foil onto the antenna arms also sometimes helped. Later model sets actually had built-in rabbit ears that telescoped out of sockets at the back of the unit and could be swiveled around after they were extended.

There were many hours of the day when there were no programs being broadcast. During those times, there was sometimes a "test pattern" broadcast which was a grid-like display by which we could make various adjustments of the set in order to be ready when the next scheduled program started. I don't remember how many stations we received in Kansas City on that first set; it may have only been one. When we wanted to watch TV and there were no programs on, we frequently lined up on the couch and stared at the test pattern until something did come on. This got a little boring after a while, so, if we weren't rewarded in a fairly short time, we usually headed outdoors.

Everyone in our family was fascinated with the TV. When there were shows being broadcast, they were all family-oriented. When my father was at home on weekends, he and I spent a lot of time on Saturdays watching Westerns. These shows were usually a half-hour long and filled with exciting action. There was a lot of fancy riding tricks and plenty of shooting, roping, and fist fights. The good guys always won in the end, though, and almost every episode had some kind of a moral lesson to impart.

The early Westerns I especially liked were *Hopalong Cassidy, Wild Bill Hickok, The Cisco Kid,* and *Roy Rogers.* A few years later, more good Westerns appeared, some of them showing in the evening during prime time. The most popular included *The Rifleman, Maverick, Gunsmoke, Rawhide, Zorro, How the West Was Won, Have Gun Will Travel, Bonanza, Death Valley Days, Sky King*, and a few others. Another show we always watched on Saturday mornings was the *Howdy Doody* show featuring (besides Howdy, the puppet himself) Buffalo Bob, Mr. Bluster, and the clown Clarabelle. We occasionally watched shows in the evening and, besides the Westerns I have mentioned, I remember watching *Dragnet* and *Westinghouse Presents.*

There were few advertisements on TV, and often the whole show had only one sponsor. So in that case, the only ads were for the products of that company. *Westinghouse Presents* was a weekly evening drama, and all of the advertisements were for the latest Westinghouse appliances, which were sure to make our lives better. Home appliances were demonstrated by a happy homemaker who seemed to be dressed for an evening out on the town rather than to do housework.

Kids were usually the target of advertising on Saturday mornings between cartoons. We were encouraged to eat Kellogg's Cereal and Wonder Bread and to wear only Buster Brown Shoes. The cereal box often had a surprise inside. If it didn't, we could save box tops until we had enough to send in for a prize. Wonder Bread didn't offer any prizes, but we all wanted to eat it because "it builds strong bodies 12 ways." If you bought Buster Brown shoes, you could look inside and see a picture of Buster Brown and his dog, Tige. The slogan was, "Hi, I am Buster Brown, I live in the shoe, that's my dog Tige, he lives here too."

The early television sets were not very reliable. Vertical flipping of the picture was common, and we all got adept at running up to the set and stopping it with the "vertical hold" knob. That was one of the many controls, all of which were quite touchy. But it was also not uncommon for the picture or the sound to go out completely while we were watching a program. My father possessed almost no mechanical skills and never seemed inclined to jump into any do-it-yourself home repair projects. So it seemed totally out of character when he pulled the TV out from the wall, unplugged it, and took the back off the chassis.

Dad and I then peered into the mysterious tangle of wires to see if we could identify a suspicious looking vacuum tube that might have failed. This was long before the days of transistors, diodes, and other components of solid-state circuitry. There were many vacuum tubes in every TV, they got hot during normal operation, and they all eventually burned out like light bulbs.

If we couldn't see a discolored tube, we tried plugging the set back in, turning it on, and then seeing if we could see one that didn't light up to a normal orange glow. If this procedure didn't identify the culprit, we simply pulled all the tubes out of their sockets and took them up to Crown Drug where they had a tube tester, located just to the left inside the front door. We made a little diagram of the sockets as we pulled them out and wrote down the tube numbers. Some of them had different numbers of prongs on the bottom, from four prongs up to 10 or 12 prongs. So it was impossible to put some of them in the wrong sockets, but there were also some that had different tube numbers with an identical number of prongs. This necessitated the diagram.

When we got to the drug store with our brown paper bag of tubes, we hoped we would not find another customer already using the tester since it took a bit of time to analyze all the tubes. If someone was already there, we might have to wait quite a while for our turn. The tester was like a small, rectangular table top, approximately 30 inches by 20 inches, and covered with numbered sockets, dials, knobs, and meters. Some of the tubes required hooking up a wire to a terminal on the top of the tube after it was plugged into a socket. Dad and I waded through the complex instructions attached to the tester and tested, one by one, each tube. We frequently found the bad tube by this procedure. There was a cabinet filled with hundreds of new tubes nearby, and there were more on a shelf under the tester. If we were lucky, they had the tube in stock, and we'd be on our way home to get the TV up and running again.

Most of the time we were able to correctly diagnose and repair our television ourselves in this manner, but occasionally a bad vacuum tube was not the problem and the culprit was a hard-wired component that couldn't be simply pulled from a socket. In these cases, we would have a house call by one of the busy TV repairmen. When a repairman

27

came he often "camped out" in our living room for several hours trying to find the problem. The carpet would be littered with tools, gauges, meters, and testers of every description. He often ended his visit by announcing he would have to take the unit in to the shop.

Color television sets were first introduced in the early 1950s, but they didn't start showing up in most homes until the late 1960s and early 1970s. My uncle Kenneth was way ahead of everyone else though. He bought one in the mid- '50s. There was only one show broadcast in color then—the western, *Bonanza*. All the other programs on his fancy new set remained in black and white. *Bonanza* came on every Sunday night at 8:00 PM and Kenneth frequently invited us over to watch it so he could show off his color TV. The colors on the screen were pretty basic, limited, and not very realistic. But we all loved the novelty of it and thought it was so much better than black and white.

Besides the TV, we also had an old Victrola. It was a console model radio/phonograph. It was a fairly large piece of furniture made of mahogany with a dark glossy finish. It had a hinged top to access the controls for tuning the radio or accessing the turntable to play records. There were only AM band stations then—no FM. Even after the advent of TV, there were still stories and serials on the radio. My sister Judy and I sat on the carpet in front of the Victrola and listened to *The Adventures of Hopalong Cassidy*, *The Amos and Andy Show*, *Gunsmoke*, *George Burns*, *Kukla Fran and Ollie*, and a few other shows on the radio long after we got a television.

Chapter 6

When I was about five years old, my father, who was an accountant, had to go on a three-day business trip to Chicago, and he decided to take me and my mother along. We went to the Union Station in Kansas City, Missouri, to board the train. The Union Station was a magnificent stone building with ceilings that were several stories high inside. We checked our baggage and then went to our gate to await boarding. The waiting area reminded me of a church because of the wooden benches, which looked like pews. The Stationmaster called our train number over the loud speaker in a sing-song voice, and it echoed through the cavernous waiting area. We went through the boarding door and down a long flight of steps to the tracks. We walked along a raised concrete walkway between two trains. My father and mother took me to the front of the train to show me the engine because it was one of the new diesels which we also referred to as a "Streamliner." It was sleek and modern looking compared to the steam locomotive at the front of the train on the next track. As we turned to walk back to our car to board, the steam locomotive suddenly released a puff of steam, which they periodically did in order to keep the pressure in the boiler from getting too high. This action caused a loud hissing noise, and the steam shot up all around us and clouded the air. My father and mother seemed to be used to this and took it in stride, but it scared the daylights out of me. My mother, relating this incident years later, said I practically walked up her side and jumped into her arms.

Our quarters on board the train was a "roomette." There was a couch that converted into a bed, a second bunk above it that pulled down to open, and a small bathroom that had only a commode in it. There was a small metal sink in the room itself. I don't know how long it took us to get to Chicago, but I remember eating at least one meal in the dining car. I don't recall what we ate, but the table was fancy with white tablecloths, and the waiters were all black men who wore white coats with black bow ties. When we walked through the coupled area between cars, it was noisy and cold, and the floor of the walkway moved to and fro. I found this a little frightening.

In Chicago we stayed at the Drake Hotel, which was right across the street from Lake Michigan. I recall a tunnel under the street connecting the lobby of the hotel with another hotel lobby—or possibly with another tower of the same hotel. One morning my mother and I were in the lobby when a bellman came over to us after he had spotted me in my cowboy attire. He informed us that Hopalong Cassidy was checking out at the desk in the lobby at the other end of the tunnel, and, if we hurried, I might be able to meet him before he left. My mother and I raced through the tunnel, but by the time we arrived, Hoppy had already left the hotel and I didn't get to see him. I was so disappointed I had to press my fists against my eyes to hold back the tears.

While my father was busy with his clients in Chicago, my mother kept the two of us busy seeing the sights and shopping. Mother was always "dressed to the teeth" on these excursions. She wore a hat and long white gloves and always had on high-heeled shoes. She was a fashion model and always looked classy. I certainly didn't appreciate such finery as a five-year-old boy, but now, as I look back, I remember how she looked.

One of the days we were in Chicago, my mother took me to the Museum of Science and Industry. I was most fascinated by the farm machinery and railroad exhibits. There was something about these big, powerful machines that attracted me. I haven't changed in that regard. I still whine to my wife Martha, "I never got to be a train engineer." I do have a lot of experience on tractors though—but it never seems to be enough. I can't drive past a John Deere or Massey Ferguson dealership today without feeling a magnetic pull sucking me in. I hope to go back and tour that magnificent museum in Chicago again someday.

Another thing we did one day was go to the famous Marshal Field's Department Store. While we were there, we found a little log-cabin playhouse with walls and a roof made of real split logs. My mother let me play in the cabin on display and had a hard time pulling me away from it. She later ordered the cabin from Marshall Field's as my Christmas present that year and had it shipped to the house on Gregory in Kansas City. My grandfather Fearon and Uncle Frank Miller helped my father assemble it in our backyard after it arrived. The cabin became a fixture in our cowboy and Indian activities and was often considered "the fort." It had a large open doorway in the front, but my sister Martha and I usually got in and out of the cabin by climbing through one of the windows. When we later moved from our house on Gregory, the log cabin was moved with us to the new house and got many more years of use.

One night in Chicago, my mother took me out on the beach of Lake Michigan, across the street from the hotel. It was after dark, the wind was blowing hard, and there were breaking waves crashing in— just like the ocean. I had never seen anything like that before, and it impressed me so much that I still remember it, over 60 years later.

❖   ❖   ❖

Travel by railroad was the most common means of public transportation for long distances in the late 1940s and early 1950s. When the golden spike was driven at Promontory, Utah, on May 10, 1869, the Union Pacific Railroad was connected to the Central Pacific Railroad and the final link for transcontinental public transportation was complete. The age of rail travel in the United States lasted in its full glory for almost 100 years. From that day in 1869 forward, the railroad served as the backbone for public transportation in our country. It accelerated the occupation and development of the American West to a frenzied pace.

By the late 1940s and early 1950s, air travel was becoming more popular and available, but travel by train was still the norm. Commercial air service did not have the safety record it has today, and many people had a justifiable fear of flying. The technology required for instrument flying was in its infancy during that period, so relatively good weather was required for a flight to depart and arrive on schedule. Also, the aircraft used for public transportation were piston-driven propeller planes which lacked the speed, mechanical reliability, and passenger load capacity of the turbojet-powered aircraft coming in the dawning jet age. With the advent of reliable, high-speed, high load-capacity jet aircraft (the Douglas DC-8 and the Boeing 707) in the late 1950s, rail travel began a gradual decline over the next two decades as air travel replaced it as the favored mode of mass transportation.

Chapter 7

My mother was a devout Catholic and wanted all of her children to receive a Catholic education. My father remained a non-Catholic, and, in those days, it was difficult for a Catholic and non-Catholic couple to obtain approval for a Catholic church wedding. For a "mixed marriage" to be sanctioned by the church, the non-Catholic partner had to agree that all the children would be raised Catholic, which meant educating them only in Catholic schools. So my father had gone along with all this, and, back in 1940, they were allowed to be married by a priest. The wedding ceremony, however, was not allowed to be inside the church itself. So the priest had performed the service quietly in the rectory adjacent to the church. My father eventually became a convert to Catholicism when he joined the church many years later after we were all grown. I always thought he only did this to please my mother though, knowing she had prayed for this all her life.

When I was five years old, I started kindergarten at St. Elizabeth Catholic School in Kansas City, Missouri. My sister Judy was in fourth grade. Judy and I rode the school bus every day. The bus picked us up each morning in front of the house on Gregory. The kids on the bus were pretty much out of control all the time. It was sheer bedlam with screaming and yelling and objects flying through the air. There were, of course, no seatbelts, and kids were running up and down the aisle and climbing over the backs of the seats. There was an occasional fistfight among some of the more rambunctious older boys. Several bully types rode our bus, and one morning one of these monsters leaned over the front rail and spit all over the top of Judy's head as she climbed up the boarding stairs. This was a big issue with our parents when we arrived home that day, but I don't recall what the consequences, if any, were for the young perpetrator.

Our school bus driver was a middle-aged man named Ray, who might have shaved once a week, probably didn't bathe that often, and his huge belly rubbed against the steering wheel as he maneuvered the vehicle. Ray had a perpetual scowl on his face and seemed to be in a trance-like state of detachment most of the time. Every once in a while, however, some particularly violent outburst summoned him from his reverie, and he would yell in an extremely loud, gravelly voice, "SIT DOWN AND SHUT UP." This was always a bit of a shock to the rioting passengers, but I don't recall it having much of a calming influence for more than a few seconds. Other than this one phrase, I don't believe Ray ever said much else to any of us.

St. Elizabeth's didn't have a cafeteria or serve any food for the kids, so Judy and I brought our lunches with us in lunch boxes. Our lunch boxes each had a glass-lined, insulated thermos, which was usually filled with milk. Occasionally my mother didn't have anything to send for lunch, or she didn't have time to pack it. On those occasions Judy came to my classroom during the lunch break and fetched me, whereupon we walked to a nearby cafeteria-style restaurant called *Lavo's*. I don't know how this restaurant got its name, but I assume Mr. Lavo and his family must have been the owners. In any case, it seems to me now that the name does not seem particularly appetizing, and, as I recall, the food at *Lavo's* left a lot to be desired. I never liked to go there—mostly because of all the choices I was required to make. I was also afraid I might make some giant faux pas, like forgetting to pick up my silverware or napkin at the beginning of the line. Judy always took care of me though, helped me through my uncertainties, and paid for our meals from her little coin purse when we got to the cashier at the end of the line. Despite her help and assurances, I seem to have somewhat of a phobia for cafeteria style meals to this day.

When I finished kindergarten at the end of the school year, we had a formal graduation ceremony with caps and gowns and diplomas. It must have been hilarious for our parents and relatives. In our graduation photo, one of the girls in my class was dressed as a nun and one of the boys was dressed as a priest. The rest of us appear in our caps and gowns.

Chapter 8

I got my first bicycle when I was six years old. It was a dark red two-wheeler with big, wide fat tires and fenders. There were no gears on bikes then; it was a "one-speed." You just pedaled, and it went forward. The brakes were applied to the rear wheel when you stepped on the pedals in the reverse direction. Bikes did not have caliper hand brakes as they do today, and the brakes were not as effective as they are on modern bikes.

The only accessory I had on this first bike was a horn, which was chrome with a flared front and a rubber bulb at the back that I squeezed to make it honk. Training wheels were mounted on the back, and my father gradually raised them as he instructed me and my confidence increased. After he finally removed the training wheels, he ran alongside and steadied me until I could balance myself. I had a few crashes and wound up with a few skinned knees and elbows before I figured it out.

Ray Molitore was happy we could go out riding together. I now had a horse when we played cowboys and Indians. My sister Martha was two years younger than I, but she learned to ride a two-wheeler not too long after I did. It wasn't long until she was riding with Ray and me. The neighborhood had concrete sidewalks, and we rode our bikes on those sidewalks. We never went far on the bikes, usually staying within one block of our houses.

Besides imagining our bikes were our horses much of the time, we also occasionally pretended they were motorcycles. We tried to make this seem realistic by attaching playing cards to the fender braces with clothespins in such a manner that the cards were struck by the spokes of the wheels. When we pedaled our bikes, the cards made the "putt-putt" sound of a motorcycle. The more cards we attached, the better the effect. The main limitation of this activity was the procurement of playing cards. Our parents weren't willing to provide us an unlimited number since this activity seem to be pretty hard on the cards.

Chapter 9

A telegram was a common method of sending messages in those days. We had a telephone but rarely made a long distance call as is it was quite expensive. One Christmas my father gave my mother the gift of a phone call to her sister in California. She was only allowed to talk for about three minutes, and I believe the charge for this call was over $10—much more than our entire phone bill for a normal month. Mom said it was the best Christmas present she had ever received. This seemed kind of odd to all of us since there had always been a lot of friction between her and her sister, and they didn't seem to even like each other much.

When we received a telegram, a Western Union delivery boy in uniform appeared at our door to make the delivery. This was always somewhat worrisome since a telegram did not often contain good news and was, in fact, a common way to notify relatives of a death or serious illness in the family.

I went to the Union Station once with my father to send a telegram. I don't know to whom he was sending it or what the message was about. We stood in the station lobby at a window surrounded by fancy wood trim and watched the Western Union telegraph operator tap out the message in Morse code with his key. This seems so archaic today in this world of cell phones, text messaging, email and the internet.

We always had a telephone as far back as I can remember. The phones were all black metal with a round base and a round dial with the numbers and letters on it. The receiver sat in a cradle (also called the "hook") on top of the base. The receiver was fairly heavy. To call someone, you first picked up the receiver to see if someone else was talking on the line, since we had a "party line" and there were several homes on the same line. If the line was clear and there was a dial tone, you would stick your finger in the hole of the dial over the number or letter you wanted to dial and then turn the rotary dial until your finger hit the stop. You then pulled your finger out of the dial and let it spring back to its original position, dialing each number in sequence in that manner. All of the phone numbers were a prefix of two letters followed by four numbers. For example, our phone number was Delmar-5299. To call our house you dialed D E, followed by 5299.

There were no area codes. If you needed to make a long distance call, you dialed zero to contact the operator and then told the operator what city you wished to call and the telephone number. You could request a "station to station" call or a "person to person" call. The long distance rate was much cheaper for station to station, but you had to pay for the call regardless of whether the person you wanted to talk to was there or not. The person to person rate was higher, but there was no charge if the person was not home. I believe this is still the way operator-assisted calls are handled today, although I haven't made a call through the operator for many years.

There were, of course, no cordless phones, and a coiled, springy cord connected the base to the receiver. The wire from the base of the phone went into a small, square, electrical terminal box usually mounted on the baseboard of the wall. There were no phone jacks, so the phone could not be unplugged or moved to another location without calling the phone company repairman to do it. Most homes only had one phone in the house, and it was often placed on a table in a hall near the front room. There was only one giant phone company then—Bell Telephone—and any repair service on the phone, inside the house or outside, was included in the one low monthly service charge. The telephone itself was owned by the phone company, not the customer, so if you needed a new phone it was provided.

1950 – The first modern credit card introduced – The first Peanuts cartoon strip appeared – The Korean War began -

The short interval of peacetime for the United States ended on June 25, 1950, when the North Korean Army invaded the Republic of South Korea. Early in the war, President Harry Truman committed American forces in an effort to check communist aggression. My mother's sister's husband, Gus Roy, was a Navy doctor and was sent with the US Marines to South Korea. We received a telegram from my mother's sister, Gertrude, informing us of Gus's deployment. The bloody war ended on July 27, 1953, when a cease-fire agreement was

38

signed with North Korea. There were an estimated 54,246 U.S. military personnel killed during this war and an estimated 8,142 reported as missing in action. Our Uncle Gus came home from the war unscathed and was assigned to the Naval Dispensary at Camp Pendleton, California.

Chapter 10

My sister Betsy was born on March 27, 1951. After that event, the three-bedroom home on Gregory began to seem a little crowded, and my mother started showing signs of stress. She was now raising four children in a relatively small space.

Whenever we needed some type of discipline or correction after we had disobeyed or gotten into a scuffle with each other, a spanking on the behind was the normal punishment. The spankings were normally done by my mother when we were young. She usually used her open hand and used a sharp slapping technique which hurt by causing a sting, but it was never hard enough to produce any significant injury. When we got a little older and it was harder to drape one of us over her knee, she used a "switch" from a tree branch or the yard stick to slap us on the butt or on the backs of our legs. She broke the yard stick over me on more than one occasion.

I can only remember getting a spanking from my father once, and it was after he had taken me down to the basement. He used his leather belt on me then. I must have done something mean to one of my sisters to warrant that. I don't remember feeling I was being mistreated when I was spanked, and I probably deserved it each time.

Virtually all kids got spanked when they were naughty, and it wasn't unusual to get a swat or two from the teacher at school if you misbehaved. It is amusing to me to see how attitudes have changed regarding this type of discipline. Most mothers and fathers today would be considered child abusers if they treated their children the way most parents did when I was a child. A teacher would likely end up in court. I don't recall ever feeling like I was being abused though. I'm not advocating bringing back this disciplinary measure for children, but I will say the spanking always let me know my behavior was unacceptable and I needed to change it. It provided a clear message and seemed to be fairly effective.

We were generally pretty good kids, but there were times when the four of us bickered with each other and got severely on our mother's nerves. Mother was in tears on several occasions and even threatened to run away and leave us at one point. I think she was coming apart at the seams that day, but we talked her out of leaving us as she stood at the door with the car keys in her hand. We all promised

41

to be good from that point forward. We were all crying hysterically and so was she.

She later must have decided she needed some other type of threat to levy on us the next time we got out of control, and she came up with a story about a fictitious Mrs. Camel who was extremely mean and was in the business of taking care of bad kids. She made vague references to some of the horrible tortures Mrs. Camel performed on the children, whom she kept in cages at her house. After that, all my mother had to do was threaten to put us in the car and take us to Mrs. Camel's house, and we immediately all turned into perfect angels.

We never questioned the reality of Mrs. Camel, but after a while, we suspected taking us to Mrs. Camel's was an empty threat, and the tactic became less effective in subduing the bedlam. Then one day when apparently my mother felt she could no longer take it anymore, she actually loaded us all up in the car for Mrs. Camel's. We screamed and begged for forgiveness until she finally shut off the engine and released us. This maneuver was quite effective in revitalizing the Mrs. Camel threat.

In our home, we ate all of our meals together as a family. My mother was an excellent cook (which I probably didn't sufficiently appreciate as a young child). She always had a hot breakfast ready for us and for my father each morning before we went to school and he went to work. One rule enforced in our family, and almost every other American family at that time, was: you had to sit at the table until you had finished everything on your plate. We were told it was a sin to waste food, and no food should be thrown out since there were millions of starving children in China. I now believe that was not a good rule to enforce on little children and likely contributed to a generation of obese adults.

One morning my sister Judy had not finished her fried egg, and it was almost time for the school bus to arrive. My mother must have gotten up on the wrong side of the bed because she was not about to put up with anything from any of us that morning. Just before the bus got there, she picked up Judy's plate of eggs and turned it upside down on the top of Judy's head. Judy ran, crying, into the bathroom and wiped as much of the egg yolk out of her hair as she could with a towel. She then put a scarf over her head and ran out and got on the bus with me. I'm sure if a mother was reported to have done such a thing today, it would warrant a visit from the Child Protective Agency at the very least. No such agency even existed in those days as far as I know. Judy got over it and didn't seem to hold any grudge against our mother, although she remembers this incident in vivid detail to this day.

My sister Martha, who was two years younger than I, was my constant companion when I was a child. She was somewhat of a tomboy, and I always thought she was tougher than I was, at least when we were quite young. We played together a lot, and if I had a friend over to play, she was usually hanging around and frequently joined in our games.

The people who lived next door to us on the corner were the Camels (not to be confused with the mean, fictitious Mrs. Camel). They had a son named Gregory Camel, who was younger and smaller than I. I believe he was actually about the same age as Martha. Gregory was kind of an obnoxious kid, and he liked to push me around and hit me, and I seemed to let him do it even though I was bigger than he. Martha had a strong dislike for Gregory and actually beat him up pretty badly on several occasions after she had seen him pushing me around. Martha sent Gregory home with a bloody nose one day, and she got in a little trouble after his mother came over to our house and complained. He continued to come over and visit us after that but seemed to have a great respect for Martha.

Gregory's family was Jewish, and when he came to our house, he almost always had a bagel he was munching on. Martha loved those bagels and sometimes took his bagel away from him and ate it. This usually resulted in him going home in tears, but then he started showing up at our house with an extra bagel for Martha. I think his mother must have come up with the idea in hopes it might prevent him from getting beaten up so badly all the time.

I never tried to take Gregory's bagel away like Martha did. He often had a big glob of yellow snot hanging from one or both nostrils on which bubbles formed when he started crying about something. This made the bagel he was munching on seem not very appetizing to me, but it didn't seem to bother Martha.

I was pretty sure of myself around Gregory as long as Martha was around. One day when Gregory was over, we stuffed him into a large cardboard box that was left over from some delivery and still sitting in our backyard. We closed him up in the box so he couldn't get out, and we both sat on it for a long time and listened to him scream with sadistic pleasure. We finally got tired of this activity and went into the house, leaving Gregory in the box. He was in there quite a while longer before he realized we weren't sitting on it anymore and he could easily get out.

In the summer of 1951, there was a flood in Kansas City, Missouri, and Kansas City, Kansas, when the Kansas and Missouri rivers overflowed their levies due to three months of torrential rains. There was enormous damage to the low-lying areas of the two cities in the flood plain. The area we lived in was not in the flood plain, but we were without running water at our house during the flood due to the fact the water treatment plant and all of its pumping stations were under water. We were warned ahead of time this might happen, and we filled every available container with water, including our bath tubs. My dad took an old, steel army Jerry Jug container down to Brush Creek, which was near our house, and filled it with water on several occasions. He brought it home to fill the toilet tanks with water so we could flush them.

After the flood waters receded, we took one of our Sunday drives down into the flooded areas of the city to view the damage. I specifically recall my father pointing out the high water line which was way up on the side of a row of concrete grain elevators. I recently reviewed a news story about the 1951 Kansas City flood and discovered 28 lives were lost and the estimated property loss was over one billion dollars (in 1951 dollars). There were many other smaller communities in Kansas and Missouri affected by this flooding as well, including the two state capitals, Topeka and Jefferson City.

1951 – Color TV Introduced – Winston Churchill again Prime Minister of Great Britain –

Chapter 11

I finished kindergarten and first grade at St. Elizabeth's. Then in 1952, when I was seven years old, we moved to a house in Fairway which is a suburb on the Kansas side of the state line. The address was 5424 Mohawk. The house was a big, old colonial that had been built in the 1930's. It had three finished floors and a partially finished basement. There were four large bedrooms and two bathrooms on the second floor and one enormous bedroom with its own private bath on the third floor. This third-floor room eventually became my quarters for the remainder of my life at home.

One of the features of the house my mother particularly liked was a clothes chute. In the wall of the second floor hallway, there was a little wooden door we opened and stuffed our dirty laundry into. The clothes slid down the chute to the basement and landed in a pile in a large open cardboard box that was just a few steps from the washer. Shortly after we moved in, we got an automatic washing machine and a gas dryer. This made laundry day much easier. Even after we got the dryer, my mother preferred to hang the laundry outside to dry on nice days.

This house was four blocks from a Catholic School, St. Agnes, where we attended school and went to church. We generally walked or rode our bikes to school every day. I was quite intimidated with starting a new school in second grade and initially didn't like it at all. We were mostly taught again by nuns, but there were a few Catholic lay teachers at the school as well.

My first teacher at my new school was Sister Lucille. She walked with wooden crutches or propelled herself along with an electric wheelchair, but none of us knew exactly why. She supposedly had some debilitating neurological disease, but no one seemed to know exactly what it was. We did observe that she could pick up the crutches and practically run when she was in a hurry which made a few people question whether her disability was real.

Sister Lucile was not a nice person, putting it kindly, and if I am a little more candid, I'd have to say she was downright mean. She used her crutches as a weapon and struck us on the backs of our legs if she felt we were misbehaving. She did this to me once when we were practicing for a school play and I wasn't doing my part right. Before recess, we were all required to stand in a single-file line at the door of the classroom in readiness for the bell. Sister Lucile ordered us into the line and then walked up and down the aisle whacking any student on the legs who was not standing perfectly behind the person in front of him or her. When the bell rang, we marched out and down the hall to the door to the playground. We then charged out the door to play.

We had a 15-minute recess in the morning and in the afternoon. There was a longer outdoor recess associated with the lunch hour. If the weather was bad outside, we had recess in the classroom or the gymnasium. I don't think we had much in the way of organized sports activities at recess until we were in the upper grade levels. In second grade, we may have had a soccer ball we kicked around a bit, but I remember mostly just chasing around on the playground. We probably played tag sometimes, and there was also a period of time where a lot of the boys were into playing marbles. We each brought our marbles in a bag with a drawstring, and then "shot" marbles on the playground at recess.

I was somewhat shy and tentative during the recess activities. I was small compared to many of the boys in my class, and some of the rougher ones teased me and push me around a bit. I had transferred from St. Elizabeth, and most of the other kids already knew one another from kindergarten and first grade. I was the new kid. The isolation I felt from this, fear of the class bullies, and fear of Sister Lucille caused me to be "ill" on many mornings when it was time to go to school. Sometimes I was probably just feigning illness in order to avoid school, but, at other times, my anxiety caused me to be genuinely physically ill. My parents let me stay home on some of these occasions, but sometimes, on the days they successfully encouraged me to go, they got a call from the school nurse and had to come pick me up. I think my parents knew what was going on, coaxed me along, and sort of met me halfway on most of these occasions.

My mother encouraged the development of friendships to help me get over this. I eventually teamed up with a couple of nice boys— Gordon Bennett and Steve Hudson. Gordon and Steve and I became a threesome on the playground at recess, and our mothers got us together after school and on weekends. We played and rode bikes together and became good friends. I recall one time I was at Gordon's house and we were running around in his yard playing Sir Lancelot with swords we had made out of yardsticks and shields we had fashioned from cardboard. We had a lot of fun together. I hadn't known Gordon long when his family moved to Texas. I never saw or heard from Gordon again.

Steve Hudson had a wonderful family, and he and I went all through grade school and high school together. On one of my first visits to Steve's house when I was in second grade, the ice man was making a delivery of ice for their "icebox." Many people did not yet have electric refrigerators. Our family had an electric refrigerator as long I can remember, but we called it the "icebox" throughout my childhood, as did everyone else. I still have to catch myself sometimes from saying, "I'm going to get myself a snack from the icebox."

Steve's mother was like a second mother to me over the years, and Steve has remained a life-long friend. We keep in touch to this day.

1952 – Dwight Eisenhower was elected to President of the United States with his running mate Vice-President Richard Nixon - Car seat belts were introduced – The polio vaccine was invented by Jonas Salk -

Chapter 12

One day my father sat down and talked to me about sticking up for myself, probably after one of the boys in my class had picked on me a bit. He told me if anyone ever hit me, I shouldn't just take it, but I should haul off and hit him harder than he'd hit me. He told me he was also quite small when he was a young boy and encountered similar situations many times. When he was older, he faced more problems like this, and from what I gathered, he was in a lot of fights and was one tough little kid. My dad's little talk instilled a surge of self-confidence and was sort of a turning point for me.

It was not too long after this talk with my father that I actually got to try out this new confidence. We were all streaming out the door onto the playground for recess when Frank Egan came running past the line of kids whacking each person on the head with a cylindrical cardboard tube he had in his hand. After he hit me with it, I took out after him, chasing him across the playground. I brought him down with a flying tackle. Frank was a stocky kid who was much bigger than I, but I rolled him over in the dirt and sat on him, straddling his chest. I then began pummeling his face with my clenched fists until his lips and nose were bleeding. The other kids were crowded around in a circle cheering. By the time one of the teachers arrived to pull me off of him, Frank was crying.

I went all through grade school and high school with Frank. There were many times in grade school when he had to sit on a stool in the corner of the classroom, facing the wall, as punishment for some infraction. Frank continued to cause trouble for several years, but he never again messed with me. I don't think he was actually afraid of me, but he did seem a little wary of me after that episode on the playground. Frank eventually changed for the better, and he actually transformed, from a poor student and class troublemaker who was always being disciplined, into a likable guy. By the time he was in high school, he was a good student, a good athlete, and had lots of friends.

This scrap with Frank was the first of quite a number of fist fights for me. I was "tested" on more occasions than I can remember, and I always responded to any physical challenge by following my dad's advice. I didn't always come out the winner, but I always stuck up for myself and wouldn't be intimidated by anyone regardless of how big or how tough. I came home on quite a few occasions over the years with a bloody nose, a cut lip, or a black eye. When I was unable to hide my injuries at home, my parents wanted to know what happened, but I rarely enlightened them.

1953 – DNA discovered – Sir Edmond Hilary and Norgay summit Mount Everest – Joseph Stalin dies – Cease-fire agreement with North Korea -

Chapter 13

St. Agnes School and the church were both beautiful stone buildings built from limestone quarried in the local Kansas City area. All of the classrooms in the school had large, wood-framed windows. The rooms were pretty much the same, with a slate blackboard at the front behind a big oak teacher's desk. There was a "cloakroom" (as the nuns all called it) down one side where we stored our coats, book bags, and lunch pails.

The student desks were made of wood, usually oak, with cast-iron legs. Each desk had a slanted top for writing with an inkwell at the top and a horizontal groove to put a pencil in, preventing it from rolling down the slanted surface. The top was hinged at the front and opened up to a space just above your lap to store workbooks and supplies in. Just about all the desks had some initials or etched pictures carved into the wood, some more artistic than others. Carving anything into the desk was absolutely forbidden, but it was apparent the rule was flagrantly violated. The seat for the desk folded down and up and was actually attached to the front of the desk behind you. This feature gave you the option of jiggling the person in front of you for amusement when the teacher's back was turned. This type of student desk had probably been a standard design for schools for at least 100 years. As a student progressed through the grades, the desks found in each successive class were larger and larger in order to fit the growing child. I did not see any other design for a classroom student desk until I entered high school where we had more modern chrome and laminate desks. There are probably a few small country schools today in which you could find the old wooden desks with inkwells, but probably very few. You can still find one of these desks once in a while in antique stores.

I mentioned that our desks had inkwells. We started out using only pencils for printing in first and second grade. In third grade we began learning cursive writing and were introduced to ink pens. The ink pens we used were modern fountain pens. We never used the ink wells on any of our student desks in grade school. They were used in an earlier day, before the invention of fountain pens, when the tip of the pen or quill was dipped in the ink before each stroke. I was always a little disappointed we didn't use the inkwells since I had heard that if

51

a girl was sitting in front of you, a fun thing to do in the inkwell days was to dip the end her braid or pony tail in the ink.

Each student starting third grade was required to have a small jar of ink, and it was kept in the student's desk compartment. These glass ink jars had a little reservoir at the top from which you filled your fountain pen. To get ink into the reservoir, you turned the bottle upside down, then turn it back up and opened the lid. You stuck the point of the pen into the reservoir and held it there while you pulled up on a little lever on the side of the pen causing the ink to be sucked up into the pen. A few years later, the fountain pens were further developed, and you could buy disposable cartridges of ink which fit into the pen making the jar of ink unnecessary.

Sometime during the mid- to late 1950s, the modern ballpoint pen was invented. I know that all of our mothers were eternally grateful for each of these improvements in ink pens and especially for the invention of the ballpoint pen. During our days of using the ink jar and fountain pen, most of our school clothes were permanently stained with ink. Some of the kids in the class had a harder time with the ink filling procedure than others. Those kids went home every day looking like they had been working in a print shop without an apron, with ink all over their clothes and skin.

The girls at St. Agnes were all required to wear uniforms. They were navy blue jumpers over white blouses. The boys were expected to wear slacks and a sport shirt with a collar. Most of the kids in our class were generally clean and neat. There were a couple of girls and a couple of boys in the class who were exceptions. The worst was a girl I will call Lucy Duncan (not her real name). Her personal hygiene left something to be desired, and no one wanted to be near her. Her greasy blond hair was always tangled and matted. The worst thing I could imagine when seating was assigned at the beginning of a new school year was to sit in front of or behind Duncan. Lucy got teased mercilessly, and some of the kids touched her on the arm, and then chased around after other kids, threatening to contaminate them with Duncan's "cooties." I always felt sorry for her, but she handled her notoriety quite well and even initiated the game herself sometimes, threatening to touch us and give us her cooties. She had a toothy grin, and when she was on the attack waving her arms with outstretched fingers, it was quite frightening. After we had started using our bottles of ink, Duncan's white blouse was always covered with ink, and she also had black ink all over her hands, arms, face, and even in her hair. This added to her already-frightening appearance. Every so often, she picked out one of the boys she considered her new boyfriend and made sinister advances toward him. I was always on my guard to avoid being the object of her affections. Whoever happened to be the unfortunate Romeo suffered non-stop teasing from the other kids despite his no-doubt totally passive role.

In November of 1953, my sister Helen was born, expanding the size of our household to seven. My father hustled my mother out to the car with a small suitcase on her way to St. Mary's Hospital in Kansas City, Missouri, for her fifth childbirth. We kids had no idea how a baby had gotten into our mother's tummy, and whenever we asked questions along those lines, we got some pretty vague answers. There wasn't even the slightest hint our father might be involved in the process in any way. Sex education didn't exist in those days—either at home or at school. In fact, no one was ever allowed to utter the word "sex" in any context whatsoever. It was many years before I pieced together bits of information to arrive at a proper understanding of the mystery of conception.

With a family of five kids, it seems like at least one of us was sick all of the time with one thing or another. When I was a young child, there were few immunizations available to prevent the common viral diseases of childhood. But actually suffering through these illnesses was considered a good thing (with the exception of smallpox and polio) because acquiring the disease generally conferred lifetime immunity. This was good because some of these diseases, which generally ran a relatively benign course in childhood, had the potential of being much more serious, or even fatal, if contracted as an adult. Rarely, a child could also develop a serious complication from one of these viral illnesses and die, but such an event was much more likely in an adult. There was no vaccine available at the time for polio, measles (rubeola – also known as "hard" measles or two-week measles), mumps, chickenpox (varicella), or German measles (rubella—also known as three-day measles). Immunizations were available at the time to prevent smallpox, diphtheria, pertussis, and tetanus. Public health immunization programs, generally administered through the school systems, were in their infancy, and the incidence of these diseases remained significant in the population.

All of my sisters contracted the measles at the same time. This disease generally ran a relatively benign course, but complications could include meningitis, blindness, and even death. The major concern in our family at the time was that my father had never had measles as a child, and all of these serious complications were much more likely in an adult who contracted it. Dad carefully avoided contact with my sisters for those two weeks, apparently never exposed himself to the virus, and remained well. On the other hand, my mother tried to expose me to the infected girls as much as possible so I would contract the illness as a child and have immunity from then on. For some reason, I never got sick with measles and somehow avoided it. Some years later, I received the measles vaccine when it became available. During that same outbreak of measles, my third grade teacher, Sister Monica, contracted the disease. She was hospitalized in critical condition and almost died. She finally recovered, but her eyes had been infected, and she was blind after that.

The German measles (otherwise known as three-day measles) was, on the other hand, generally a fairly mild disease. However, if a pregnant mother contracted this illness, it had the potential to cause horrible congenital defects in the unborn fetus. So despite the benign course of this disease, it was equally dreaded due to this consequence.

The mumps was another common viral disease of childhood, and it caused an inflammation and swelling of the parotid salivary glands in the cheeks. Mumps presented with a comical picture which almost anyone could diagnose. It caused the victims cheeks to puff out on both sides as if the kid had stuffed two tennis balls into his or her mouth. Again, this was a disease that generally ran a mild course, but the virus had an affinity for other glands in the body which it could less commonly infect as well. The testes in males could be infected, and, if severe, this complication could result in sterility. Again, this and other complications were more likely to occur when an adult got the disease.

The mumps was another disease my father never had during his childhood. But when there was an outbreak of this disease in our area, Dad wasn't as lucky as he was when my sisters had the measles. He got the mumps at the same time I did. I moved into my mom and dad's bedroom, which became our sickroom. So he and I propped ourselves up on pillows in twin beds and, for a few days, entertained one another while my mom waited on her two puffy-cheeked boys. Dr. Walthall,

54

our pediatrician, made a house call and checked us both over on one of those days. He joked that my dad was the oldest kid he had ever had in his pediatric practice, and Dad enjoyed recalling the old doctor's comment for many years later. The worry for my father with mumps was that the infection might "go down." This is the way they referred to the complication of mumps orchitis, which could result in sterility. Dr. Walthall did a thorough exam on Dad and gave him the good news that there was no evidence of testicular involvement. We both recovered without any complications.

Dr. Walthall made many house calls during my childhood. Dr. Damon Walthall was everything you would picture an old-time horse and buggy doctor to be. He had white hair and bifocal glasses and was always dressed in a fine, if somewhat rumpled, suit which included a vest and pocket watch on a chain. At least one of us kids was always watching for the doctor to arrive with a nose pressed to the window. When he came to our house, he was not in a horse and buggy but arrived in a big Cadillac sedan. He always parked at the curb and hurried up the drive with his black bag in hand. All of his rushing stopped when he got inside the house and came to the bedside of the sick kid (or kids). He reviewed the symptoms with Mom and then began a methodical exam. When I was the sick one, the big question on my mind was whether or not I would get a shot. And it seems a shot of penicillin was the treatment more often than not. During my early childhood, penicillin was known as the "wonder drug" and used for almost every infectious illness. It was the first and only antibiotic for quite a few years, and it seems it may have been used a little indiscriminately in those early days. In any case, I liked Dr. Walthall, but I didn't care much for his shots.

The old doctor didn't always come when we were sick. My mother had a number of home remedies she frequently applied before calling the doctor. She may have been instructed in a few of these by Dr. Walthall himself, but some of these "treatments" I believe must have been passed down intact from witchcraft manuals of the middle ages. An example of the latter was my Mother's practice of giving each of us an enema when we became ill. You might think this could be a possible remedy for severe constipation, but I don't remember that ever being the affliction for which this torture was dispensed. Someone must have made my mother believe that immediate and complete evacuation of the bowels was the treatment of choice for a whole host of illnesses, often including (but not limited to) a sore throat. Whenever she got it in her head that one of her kids required this treatment, it frequently turned into an operation resembling an assembly line.

It was hard for any of us to understand why the kids who were not showing any signs of illness should be included in this process. Her logic may have been that the ones who weren't showing any signs of illness yet should have one too since it might prevent them from getting sick, and getting all of those bad germs out of the gut certainly couldn't hurt anything. She likely thought it should probably be done every once in a while anyway.

So she lined us all up in front of the bathroom door and, one at a time, we took our turns. When I entered the bathroom, my mother was appropriately prepared with an oil-cloth apron and long rubber gloves on to protect her clothing and her hands and forearms from the possible airborne body fluids and/or solids. There were times when she probably should have had a mask and goggles on as well. The routine was for the patient to first take off every stitch of clothes and then position himself/herself face-down on a large bath towel in the knee-chest position with the head down and buttocks straight up. Mom then began the process of injecting what seemed like gallons and gallons of some mysterious liquid concoction up into her offspring's colon using a glass bulb syringe. Whatever the stuff was, it was powerful. Each time she removed the syringe from the anus to refill it she screamed, "HOLD IT...HOLD IT...HOLD IT" at the top of her lungs. The siblings standing outside the door always cringed, knowing from past experience the meaning of this exhortation. The idea was to remain totally anal-retentive during the entire procedure and not release a drop until securely seated on the toilet and commanded to do so. Each time she refilled the syringe using her right hand, she would use the gloved thumb of her left hand as a firm stopper to prevent any uncontrolled release. With each refill of the syringe, this became more and more difficult, and after a number of these injections, the kids outside the door would hear the victim crying, begging her to stop, and warning her about what was about to happen if she did not. My mother was pretty good at judging when she had pushed the envelope to the limit and when she should give the command to jump on the toilet before things could get too messy. But even at that point, we were always told to sit there and hold it all in as long as we possibly could and that if we let it all go too soon, she would have to start over.

At some point during my childhood, enemas seemed to go out of vogue—either that or we all got a little too big and rebellious about this treatment for her to handle us. There was one other thing about this experience that bothered me. Every Thanksgiving I noticed that my mother basted our turkey with a glass syringe with a red rubber bulb on it that looked exactly like the one she used for our enemas. I never got up the courage to ask her about this, but to this day, I'm not a big fan of turkey dinners.

I'd like to put the enemas behind me, so to speak, and talk about another favorite home remedy—Mentholatum Ointment. My mom used it for colds and coughs. She stuffed it into our nostrils with her little finger as she instructed us to snort it up. She put the final touch on this by running a little bead of ointment across our upper lips so we couldn't avoid breathing the healing vapors. If a chest cold was the problem, then she rubbed the Mentholatum all over our chest walls—front and back. An "inhalator" was then placed in the sick room. The inhalator produced steam that was routed through a little cup on the top of the unit which was filled with—you guessed it—Mentholatum. I actually liked the strong smell of the aromatic Mentholatum, and, if nothing else, it did slow down a runny nose since the thick ointment did a pretty good job of plugging up the nostrils.

For scrapes and abrasions, I think every household of the 1950s had a vial of mercurochrome, tincture of iodine, or tincture of merthiolate. All of these antiseptics were generously dripped onto a fresh wound before a bandage was applied. And all of these stained the skin varying shades of orange, purple, or red. The color eventually wore off as the wound healed, but I had orange knees and elbows most of the time during my early childhood years. Whenever anyone in the family sustained a burn, the treatment was to apply butter to the skin. It did seem to make it feel better.

Dr. Walthall's miracle drug was penicillin. But my mother's miracle drug was Paregoric. Paregoric was a medication my sisters and I were frequently treated with. It was administered to control diarrhea and also used as a cough suppressant. It was commonly dispensed in the 1950s in practically every household and was used for a number of other symptoms including calming of infants who were teething. I recently looked this medication up to find out what was actually in it.

It turns out it has been in use since the early 1700s and is a complex mixture of various pharmaceutical agents, but the main active ingredient is OPIUM. Amazingly, it wasn't regulated as a controlled substance by the Controlled Substances Act until 1970. Before that, it was available in most states without even a prescription from a physician. I remember, when taking a spoon full of Paregoric, that it had an unpleasant taste of strong licorice. My sisters and I, after being dosed, were totally zonked out. It is no wonder parents loved this drug so much. Instead of a teary, whining little runny-nosed, hacking kid to deal with, they had a happy and quiet little zombie.

I'm not sure my parents realized they were hitting us with narcotics almost every time we got sick, but I'm pretty sure most of the other parents of the 1950s were doing the same thing. They did try to keep us from getting sick in the first place though. We were all required to take a full teaspoonful of cod liver oil every morning. Cod liver oil was supposed to be full of essential vitamins, and so it was part of our daily ritual. It was truly disgusting, and I never got used to taking it. There were mornings when I somehow managed to swallow it, and then it came right back up. I think it would be easier to swallow a golf ball than a teaspoonful of Cod liver oil. We were all required to take it, all the way through our early teenage years. When we each reached that age, I think my mother retreated permanently from the battle required to force it down us. I got to the point where I "just said no."

1954 – The first atomic powered submarine is launched – A report is published indicating cigarettes may cause cancer – Roger Bannister runs a four-minute mile -

Chapter 14

Our Catholic education at St. Agnes School was steeped in religion at all times. After we arrived at our respective classrooms each morning, we assembled and marched across the parking lot to the church where we attended Mass. One rule for receiving Holy Communion at Mass prohibited eating or drinking anything (including water) after midnight. So after Mass, we all went to the cafeteria for a breakfast pastry (usually a "Long John") and milk before class. Communion was not mandatory though, and many times my sisters and I ate breakfast at home and then skipped communion.

As I mentioned, most of the classes were taught by nuns. We had catechism class every day in which we were taught things deemed essential for all good Catholics to know. We learned a lot about Heaven and Hell and had a pretty good picture of what each was like. It was clear Heaven was where you wanted to end up and Hell was not. We learned more about what might send you to Hell than what would get you to Heaven, but this information was nonetheless helpful. We memorized the Ten Commandments and also memorized rote answers to hundreds of questions found in our catechism textbook, and each student stood and recited the answer to a question when called upon. We rehearsed and polished our answers in preparation for a visit of the pastor, Monsignor Koch, to our class. This occurred about once per week, and we were expected to be on our best behavior for him.

We learned about Jesus, Mary, and Joseph and studied the lives of the saints and martyrs. We were taught all about sin—venial sins and mortal sins. Committing a venial sin would result in going to a place like Hell when you died, but it was called Purgatory. After a number of years went by and you had atoned for your venial sins, you would then ascend into Heaven. But committing a mortal sin and dying with it still on your soul was an entirely different matter. If you did that, you went to Hell and burned in the eternal fires forever. It became apparent that it was extremely important to be able to distinguish between venial sins and mortal sins. The nuns taught us this by basically itemizing all of the mortal sins, and the rest were venial sins. Mortal sins included skipping Mass on Sunday without a valid reason, killing someone, committing adultery (whatever that was), and a few others. Whenever a student asked what adultery was, the teacher usually gave some vague, unclear answer or changed the subject. I think all of us kids were a little worried about unknowingly committing adultery and inadvertently going to Hell for all eternity because we didn't know what adultery was. There were also some gray areas in distinguishing mortal sins from venial sins. For example, a lie was generally a venial sin as long as it was only a little white lie. But if it was a great big serious lie, then it could be a mortal sin. It was always difficult to find out the specifics about this because if you asked whether or not a certain sin was a venial sin or a mortal sin, then your teacher might get suspicious as to why you wanted to know.

Fortunately for all of us, we had the safety of the Holy Sacrament of Confession. As long as we went into the confessional and told the priest all of our sins, mortal or venial, then they were forgiven and the flames could be avoided. So as long as you went to confession regularly, and you didn't forget anything, and you didn't get hit by a car and killed before you got to the confessional, you'd be okay. So if all of this worked out, you really didn't have to worry about the distinction between mortal and venial sins. I, and I think most kids, felt the safest and most conservative approach was to avoid committing any mortal sins if at all possible. When we did go to confession, we were assigned a penance. We were told we were forgiven the moment the priest granted us absolution in the confessional, but regardless of that, you still had to do your penance when you came out. The penance was typically to say some prayers and it was practically always a few "Our Fathers" and a few "Hail Marys." If your sins were particularly bad or numerous, you might have to say a whole rosary (I have heard).

It was possible, even though you went to confession and got your sins forgiven, you could still end up in purgatory due to some omission or other technicality. I never completely understood this, but in such a case it was still possible to have your sentence in the fires of Purgatory removed or partially removed by means of indulgences. This was really a good deal! Most of the information about indulgences was found on the back of holy cards. The card always had some sort of religious picture on the front, but on the back there was often useful information about a specific indulgence.

There were basically two types of indulgences—plenary indulgences and temporary indulgences. The plenary indulgences removed all of the time you had coming to you in Purgatory, whereas the temporary indulgences were just worth a certain amount. The card told you what you had to do and the amount of time that would be credited for it. For example, it might say you would receive a temporary indulgence of three weeks if you said three Our Fathers and three Hail Marys, or it might say if you said a whole rosary you would have three months removed from your time in Purgatory. The plenary indulgences were harder to come by. They were quite difficult and involved a serious commitment—like going to Mass and communion seven days a week throughout Lent. I don't think I ever worked on one of the plenary indulgences, but I did lots and lots of the temporary ones. I added these up for a while and tried to figure out how many years, months, weeks, and days of purgatory credit I had. But the real problem was that I didn't have any idea how much time in Purgatory I had racked up already from being a little sinner, and there was a rule that you couldn't get ahead on this—like savings in a bank. It only worked to offset the time in Purgatory you had already had coming. So you didn't want to overdue the indulgences because it was of no advantage to you, but there wasn't any way of knowing your exact score. I never really thought much about who had figured out all this stuff about indulgences, but it was obviously a good deal, and I certainly tried to take advantage of it.

Somewhere along the line we were taught about making a "Novena" which rewarded you sort of like an indulgence. The reward for this Novena was almost too good to be true. It required going to mass and communion for nine first Fridays of the month in a row. If you did this, you would remain in the state of grace for the remainder of your life on earth, and you were guaranteed to go to Heaven when you died—no matter what else you did. Once the word on this was out, practically every Catholic kid I knew tried to do it. Although it sounded like it would be easy to do since we went to Mass at school every day anyway, it wasn't actually so easy. It seems I never got started in time to coordinate with the school year masses and would end up with one or two of my first Fridays falling in the summer. Riding my bike up to church on a warm, beautiful summer Friday morning was not appealing to me by the time I had gotten into my vacation routine, so I'd end up skipping it. Another thing that would happen is that I would miss one of the nine first Fridays along the way for one reason or another. You couldn't miss one. You had to do them all consecutively or you had to start over at the beginning again. When this happened, I never worried about it too much, figuring I had plenty of time to get the whole sequence accomplished.

I never did complete the nine first Fridays Novena, and I never talked to a single kid who did. It's hard to believe I couldn't discipline myself to do such an easy thing to assure I would go to Heaven, but I never got it accomplished. I did have some questions in my mind about this Novena though. If you actually did this, could you then go out and become a serial killer and still go straight to heaven when you died, or did the grace you received just make you so holy after doing the nine first Fridays that it was simply impossible for you to sin again? If this latter was the case, then I'm not sure I would want to do it anyway because what if you decided later there was some sin you really wanted badly to commit, and then you couldn't because you were in a state of perpetual grace? That would certainly limit what you could do with the rest of your life, so maybe it was better that I never actually accomplished this one. Sinning when you needed to and then going to confession afterwards seemed like it would give you more flexibility.

There was a lot of talk throughout grade school about religious vocations. This started early and continued throughout grade school and high school. The boys were encouraged to grow up and join the seminary, and the girls were encouraged to enter the convent. Besides frequent pep talks in this regard, we also prayed for religious vocations. They made it seem appealing. I doubt if there was a boy in my class who didn't have aspirations of becoming a priest at one time or another as this was put forth as the highest calling. And I doubt if there was a girl in my class who hadn't considered becoming a nun at some point.

Sometime around fifth grade, the boys had an opportunity to become trained as altar boys and serve Mass. I don't know whether this was really an option or not, but I can't think of a single boy in my class who didn't become an altar boy. One of the older altar boys trained us in the church. There was a room in the sacristy on the right side of the altar which had closets with our vestments in them. This is where we suited up. We wore floor-length black robes called cassocks which we put on over our street clothes and buttoned down the front. Then, over the cassock, we wore a white linen blouse with short, puffy sleeves that was called a "surplice." Women who were members of the Altar Society inspected these costumes on a regular basis and, when they needed attention, took them home to wash and iron them, so that we always found them clean and fresh.

As soon as I was trained, I was placed on the schedule for serving Mass. There were several priests, besides the Monsignor, assigned to our parish, and there were several Masses each day—starting at 5:45 AM and continuing through mid-morning. A couple of these services were for the students after school started each day. The altar boys were assigned to serve a certain Mass each day for a week at a time, and it usually ended up being one week each month. On the week you served it meant going to Mass twice each day unless you happened to be assigned to serve the Mass you normally went to with your class; Mass was mandatory regardless of whether or not you had attended or served an earlier Mass. I sometimes rode my bike in the dark to serve 5:45 AM Mass, rode back home on my bike for breakfast, then rode my bike back to school and went to Mass again as soon as I got there. This routine was not uncommon at all.

There were all kinds of other regular church services besides daily Mass. It's a wonder we Catholic children had time to do anything outside of church. There were "Stations of the Cross" one afternoon a week. I always kind of enjoyed being one of the altar boys for that service because you got to march around the church saying a prayer in front of each of the stations. The "stations" were wooden carved depictions of Christ's arrest, trial, his march up Calvary as a condemned criminal, and finally his crucifixion. I liked the Stations of the Cross service for several reasons. The carved stations were interesting to me because they told a story. It had more meaning to me than the Latin Mass because of that. I also liked the fact that we got to move around the church as we proceeded from one station to the next and were able to see what was going on. When we stopped abeam each station, we were in the center aisle of the church, facing each carving in turn, and were close to the kids at the end of the pew. On the boys' side of the church, I could amuse myself by surreptitiously making a funny face at one of my classmates. On the girls' side, I put on a pious face and did my best to look holy and priest-like in my vestments. I also carefully looked around for my favorite "girlfriends" to see if I could detect a furtive glance or coy smile directed my way. When we finished the circuit of the Stations, we would end up at the front of the church again, proceed to the altar, and then we served the priest as he performed the Benediction service.

The Benediction service was short but dramatic. The priest removed a consecrated host from the gold doors of the tabernacle on the altar and then placed it into a round, glass compartment in the center of a large gold apparatus that I can't remember the name of, but which had long gold spikes sticking out of it all around the host compartment. He would pick it up, turn to face the worshipers, and then hold it up for adoration while he said some sacred words in Latin. We altar boys would swing a little gold, lantern-like incense boat suspended by a chain up toward the gold-spiked thing the priest was holding. The incense burning in the lantern-like vessel smoked like crazy, and the smoke had a distinct, sweet smell. We tried on occasion, for our own amusement, to direct as much smoke as possible into the priest's face to see if we could make him cough or choke. Whenever we were successful at this and reproached later, we always proclaimed our innocence and explained how the direction of the smoke was totally out of our control.

Besides daily Mass, Stations of the Cross, and Benediction, we also had formal rosaries in the church, evening Novenas, and Saturday confessions. And if these formal church services were not enough, we had private prayer at home. My mother made sure we said "Grace" before every meal and that we each got down on our knees next to the bed and said morning and evening prayers. We also said a family rosary together once or twice a week at home and sometimes in the car as we rode along. We said a family rosary together too whenever there was a bad thunderstorm or other threatening weather in the area. If we ever happened to pass a Catholic church anytime we were out in the car (or walking), we were all expected to make the sign of the cross, and if I had a hat or cap on, I was supposed to remove it.

We celebrated the feast days of all of the saints at school. For really big ones, like the Feast of Immaculate Conception for example, we would have several church services to honor the saint or, as in the case of this feast, to honor the Blessed Virgin Mary. Any feast day that honored the Blessed Virgin Mary was celebrated to the fullest. There was often a formal procession in the streets of the neighborhood around the church. The Fairway Police Department generally closed the streets to traffic during this march. We sang hymns at the top of our lungs as we marched, and some of the older students carried lit candles. Some of these processions occurred at night, and the combination of candlelight and singing was quite beautiful and impressive. It was always a problem keeping the candles lit, and it amazes me, with all of these flames and matches and flammable clothing and vestments, that no one actually caught on fire and burned up. I have often wondered what the non-Catholic segment of the population surrounding our church thought of all of this activity. I never heard that any of them complained, but maybe most of the neighbors were Catholic anyway and were into it as much as we were.

There were a couple of times during the year when our normal religious fervor was propelled into its highest gear. This occurred during the Advent Season leading up to the celebration of the birth of Christ on Christmas, and it occurred again during Lent, the time for penance and abstinence leading up to Good Friday and Easter. I would venture to say the busiest time for church services of all was the three days encompassing Good Friday, Holy Saturday, and Easter Sunday. Activities at our church and school were at a fever pitch during this time. Monsignor Koch, all of the other parish priests, and the nuns seemed totally stressed as these three days drew near toward the end of Lent. For us, as Catholic School children, these were three days of nonstop processions, rosaries, Stations of the Cross, Masses, Benedictions, Holy Communions, confessions, fasting, prayers, and hymns. It all culminated with attendance at a grand High Mass on Easter Sunday with the altars splendidly adorned with tons of fresh, spring flowers and the air filled with the magnificent music of a practiced and polished choir. All of the kids, I believe, felt holy and full of grace at this point. I think we were all proud of whatever role each of us played in all of this. But when I got home from Easter Sunday Mass, I ripped off my coat and tie, jumped into my play clothes, and felt thankful this season was over for another year and things would get back to normal for a while.

Most of us Catholic kids had been baptized as infants, but there were other sacraments we had to receive as part of our maturing Catholicism. We had preparatory classes for each of these which included First Communion, First Confession, and Confirmation. There was usually a Mass associated with each of these and a celebration of some sort. As an altar boy, in addition to all the regular services, I would often be a server for these special masses as well as for the occasional wedding or funeral.

Chapter 15

Summers in Kansas City were great. I always looked forward to that last day of school before summer vacation. I felt sheer exhilaration as I pedaled my bicycle at full speed toward home with the long hot summer before me. For me and for my sisters, the summer was filled with outdoor play activities.

Cowboys and Indians remained a favorite for many summers, and our bicycles were our horses. I was always decked out and equipped as a cowboy with a hat, boots, guns and holster. I even had a pair of handcuffs, which came in handy when I had to take a prisoner—usually one of my sisters. I had a star I wore on my shirt when I was a sheriff and a bandana I tied across the lower half of my face as a mask when I was an outlaw. The log cabin in the backyard was either a jail or a fort. We put lots of imagination into these games and had a wonderful time.

We had a swing set in the backyard and occasionally had "swing shows" on summer evenings for which we sold tickets to our neighbors. My sister Martha and I spent hours practicing. We started a show by running out in our bathrobes with music playing from a portable record player operated by one of our "stage hands" (our little sisters, Betsy and Helen). One of us ran to one end of the swing set and the other ran to the opposite end. As we approached the swing, we dramatically cast off our warm-up robes, dressed in our swimming suits beneath. We usually started our routine by each of us hopping up on the end crossbars and symmetrically hanging out, facing the audience, with one arm and one leg extended in midair to each side. We then turned and moved hand over hand along the top bar toward each other, crossing in the center, and finally leaping onto the opposite crossbar at each side. We would then hang out to each side again as we had started, but on opposite sides. At this point applause was expected from the audience.

We had a number of routines we performed on the bars and rings. There was one maneuver, called "skinning the cat," in which we hung by our hands from the top bar (or the rings), turned upside down and put our legs through the space between our arms, then flipped to the ground as our legs dropped through. Our repertoire was limited, so the show didn't usually last long. When it was over, the neighbors were generally served liquid refreshments by my parents, which may have been a reward for humoring us by dutifully attending. As years went by, Martha's and my interest in the swing shows declined. Our younger sisters, Betsy and Helen, became the trapeze artists and continued the tradition for many more warm summer evenings.

Roller-skating was another favorite pastime. We skated a lot during the summer, but also sometimes after school during the school year. The skates were all metal with steel wheels with ball bearings. A leather strap at the heel came up over the top of the ankle and metal clamps at the front held the toe of the shoe in. The clamp at the front was tightened against each side of the shoe's sole plate with a steel key that served as a wrench. It was imperative to wear shoes with sturdy leather soles for this apparatus to grip. Tennis shoes did not work. Wearing the correct shoe, putting the skates on correctly, and tightening them with the key until your fingers turned blue was important. The steel key was on a string, and you always hung the string around your neck so you could stop and tighten up the skates whenever they loosened. Even when everything was done correctly, the skates sometimes came off. This was a dreaded occurrence since it always resulted in a terrible fall.

We frequently looked for the steepest hill around to skate down for maximum velocity or, if we really wanted to go fast, one of us would ride a bicycle and pull the skater along behind. There were lots of accidents, often a result of the skates separating from the skater at a breakneck speed. Since we were always skating on concrete, every fall resulted in skinned knees, hands, or elbows at the very least. These abrasions were painful and took weeks to heal. I don't think we ever put those skates on without one of us getting hurt. There was a lot of wailing associated with each spill, but my mother did a patch-up job on the victim, and he or she was back on his/her skates in a short time.

The skating we did in those days was similar to the rollerblading of today, but our equipment left a lot to be desired. Not only were the skates themselves inferior and dangerous, but we didn't have any of the safety equipment skaters have today, such as helmets and wrist, elbow, and knee guards. The skates we had were all we knew and all that was available, and we had a great time roller-skating.

My sisters and I played together a lot in the summer, but we also played separately with our individual friends, either at our house or their houses. If I went over to another kid's house it was usually within a few miles, and I rode my bike. I rode to Steve Hudson's house a lot. His house was a pretty long ride, but even after that long ride, we frequently took off on our bikes together as soon as I got there. There was a public swimming pool near Steve's house that we liked to go to on hot summer days, and it was always packed with kids. Sometimes I stayed over at Steve's house for the night, and other times he, or another friend, came to our house for the night. We always had a great time doing this, but our mother's usually had a hard time getting us to settle down and go to sleep when it was bedtime.

Another thing we did during the summer was go to the "Wednesday Morning Movies" at the Fairway Theater. We bought the tickets at the beginning of the summer; the price was $1.00 for a book of 12 tickets. They came on a long card, and you tore one off for each movie. The tickets could only be used for the "Wednesday Morning Movies," and not for any other shows. It was a great deal! Most parents, including mine, made us save up our allowances and pay for the season pass out of our own funds. This did not hurt a bit since it was one of the highlights of the summer and probably the best entertainment value I have ever encountered to this day.

I rode my bike to the theater with my sisters, and sometimes a few of our friends, every Wednesday morning. We parked our bikes behind the building with what appeared to be hundreds of other bikes. We'd hand our ticket to the ticket taker at the door and then press ourselves into a compact mob of screaming kids in the lobby who were all trying to make their way to the concession stand and, once there, try to get the attention of one of the frazzled servers. If any of us had brought a little extra allowance money, we joined in to push and shove our way to the counter. A bag of popcorn cost either a nickel or a dime. A Coke (in a glass bottle) was a nickel. My sister Martha usually bought herself a box of "Jujubees." These were chewy candies of different colors that came in a little box. I think she liked them because she always saved a few for rationing out to herself during the week. I never thought much of the Jujubees, but I did occasionally buy a "Holloway Bar," which was a chewy chocolate candy on a stick in the form of what we referred to as an "all-day sucker." The Holloway Bars were wonderful.

After we had purchased our treats, we headed into the theater and tried to get a good seat. Everyone wanted to sit in the front row, so these seats always were taken first. While waiting for the show to start, the atmosphere in the theater was sheer bedlam. I think some of the delinquent kids bought Jujubees just to have something to throw at people, because the atmosphere was so saturated with flying Jujubees you could hardly take a breath without inhaling one. Once the theater was essentially filled to capacity, everyone suddenly became impatient for the curtain to open and the show to start. Someone would somehow get this disorderly mob coordinated enough to start chanting "We Want The Show," accompanied by a rhythmic clap. I don't think any of us actually knew whether the show was late starting since no one had a watch to see what time it was, but that didn't matter, we were ready for the show.

The show always started with a newsreel (in black and white of course) which lasted a few minutes. I don't think many of the kids really got too much out of the newsreels, but we did get to see some exciting scenes of our American soldiers shooting their machine guns on the front lines in Korea. We all knew the newsreel wouldn't last long and the *Looney Tunes Cartoons* would follow shortly. The cartoon characters included Bugs Bunny, Daffy Duck, Goofy, Pluto, Porky Pig, Donald Duck, The Road Runner, Mickey Mouse and Minnie Mouse, Sylvester the Cat and Tweedy Bird, and a few others. The cartoons were always ushered in and ushered out with the same loud music that I can't describe but is etched into the memory of every kid of my generation. There were usually several cartoons, which were then followed by a double-feature—two full-length movies back to back. The movie was usually either a Walt Disney animated film or some type of adventure movie which involved cowboys and Indians, kids and horses, kids and dogs, or pirates. We watched *Black Beauty, Shane, Old Yeller, Snow White and the Seven Dwarfs, Alice in Wonderland, Lassie Come Home, My Friend Flicka, The Black Stallion, Peter Pan,* and many more.

As soon as the curtains opened and the first cartoon started, the rhythmic clapping and chanting stopped immediately and was replaced by peals of raucous laughter. Once the cartoons were over and the main feature started, the kids generally quieted down. The theater ushers became less tolerant at this point, and if you got a flashlight in the face, it meant you had to leave. The kids who liked to whap someone with a Jujubee had to do it a little more discreetly after the main show started.

Every movie theater then had several uniformed ushers on duty. During the movie, there was usually one stationed at the head of each aisle to scan the crowd and look for trouble-makers, each equipped with a flashlight. If anyone was being noisy or causing a disturbance, he or she would be given a verbal warning or would be ejected. These guys were the enforcers, and their authority was generally respected.

During the main presentations, the child audience reacted openly in unison to the drama unfolding on the screen. There were squeals of glee during happy scenes and moans of disappointment when a tragedy unfolded; during especially sad moments, crying sobs could be heard.

Occasionally during the movie, the film broke and had to be spliced, or the projection bulb burned out and had to be changed. This immediately brought on more chanting and clapping. The problem was usually resolved after a short delay, and the show would go on. It seemed we had been in the movie theater forever by the time we emerged several hours later, squinting in the bright sunlight, to jump on our bikes and head home.

One summer weekend my dad had a number of errands to run and took Steve Hudson and me with him. As I have mentioned, there were no seatbelts in the cars in those days, and Steve and I were clowning around and lying on the floor of the back seat as my dad maneuvered the car through city traffic. We had a bunch of small toys of some sort with us—I don't remember exactly what they were—and we started throwing them over the top of the seat into the front of the car. My dad was turning his head around and trying to peer over the back of the seat to see what we were up to when suddenly we heard a screech of brakes and then a tremendous crash. My father had crashed into the rear end of a car stopped at a stoplight. Steve and I were slammed against the back of the seat in front of us, but no one in either vehicle was injured. We were both in a little hot water with my dad for the next few days though since we had caused the distractions leading to the wreck.

Around that same time, I had been working on my mother to get me an army tent to put up in the backyard. I told her I wanted to leave it up all summer, sleep in it every night, and make it my summer quarters. I was really excited about it, and my mom seemed to be warming to the idea—but that was before the car wreck. She had

71

talked about taking me downtown to an army surplus store to look for a tent, but, during our quiet ride home with Dad in the car with the front end all bashed in, I suspected I might as well forget about the tent. When Dad told her how Steve and I caused the accident, it would surely cancel our planned shopping expedition.

When we got back to the house, Steve decided to stay outside while Dad and I went in. We found Mom in the kitchen, and he told her the story through clenched teeth. His anger seemed to have been building all the way home and had reached a peak. She stood at the stove stirring a pot of chili and calmly listened to his description of what had happened. When he finished his tirade, I decided the cancellation of the tent purchase was probably the least of my worries. I wondered what punishment the two of them might come up with. Mom didn't say anything for a minute or two and just kept stirring the pot of chili with a thoughtful look on her face. Finally, she turned to Dad and said, "Hubert, it sounds to me like you weren't paying attention to your driving. This wasn't the boys' fault, and you can't blame the accident on them."

After Dad stormed from the room, Mom said, "Do you think Steve would like to go when we go shopping for your tent?" At that point, you could have knocked me over with a feather. The relief I felt is beyond description, but, regardless of that, I continued to feel considerable guilt about the accident for some time afterwards.

Not long after that, Mom and I made our trip to the army surplus store. We bought a big, olive green, canvas wall tent, two folding army cots, and a red kerosene lantern. Steve didn't go with us, but he came over to help me and Dad set the tent up. Mom found a little wood cabinet, which was painted white and had two doors on the front of it, that I used as a table between the cots. I set the kerosene lantern on top and filled the shelves inside with books and old issues of Boys Life Magazine. Every summer for the next several years, that tent was my sleeping quarters and room for the summer. My little sisters, especially Martha, frequently begged me to let them sleep in the tent with me. I let them on occasion, but I usually required they trade something or do something for me in exchange for the privilege. Whenever I had a friend over to spend the night in the summer, we always slept in the tent, but most nights I slept there alone and I loved it.

I enjoyed many hot summer nights in the tent with the flaps tied back at both ends—hoping to get a little breeze through—listening to the soothing sound of cicadas as I drifted off. On the nights there was some breeze, I listened to the sweet rustle of leaves in the thick canopies of the giant surrounding elm trees. There were also nights of thunderstorms when I had the flaps tied tightly and, lying on my back, watched the lightning flashes through the canvas, listened to the pounding of the rain, and felt the tent shake and flap with the wind gusts.

I moved all my stuff out there on the first day of summer vacation every year. At the end of the summer, I carried everything back up to my attic room in the house and would then strike the tent, fold it, and put it in the basement for the winter.

After several summers of being out under the hot Kansas sun, the tent began to deteriorate. While lying on my back on one of the cots during the day, I began to notice the light coming through between the threads. The canvas was starting to look like gauze. On rainy nights it was beginning to leak. One morning, after a stormy windy night, I awoke to see the sun shining in through a giant tear in the canvas. That was the last night in the tent, and it was stuffed into one of the trash barrels later that day. We didn't replace the tent. My summer nights after that were in my attic room, but I always slept with my bed pushed up against the wide-open window. With my pillow on the sill and my head against the screen, the sounds and smells were the same, and I imagined I was still in my wonderful tent

Chapter 16

My "allowance" was a little different than a lot of other kids' allowances. Some of my friends got a set amount each week in return for routine chores he or she was expected to do around the house. Mine was set up a little differently. I had regular chores I was required to do—like making my bed every day, keeping my bedroom straightened up, and occasionally washing the dishes after a meal—but I didn't receive a regular allowance for these jobs. These were things I was just expected to do. My mother did pay me by the job, though, for certain tasks such as cleaning out the garage, mowing the lawn, waxing the kitchen floor, or washing the family car. I earned a dollar here and a dollar there and carefully saved it all. I don't think my sisters ever had any arrangements like this. This was probably because none of my assigned jobs were considered ladylike. I don't recall whether or not the girls received an allowance for the household chores they performed.

I credit my mother with instilling a strong work ethic in me which I have carried throughout my life, and it started with these jobs around the house. Paying me was a good motivator, but these assignments also provided me with some self-satisfaction and a sense of accomplishment. I saved my money initially in a piggy bank, but later my mother opened a savings account for me. I then regularly rode my bike to the bank, made deposits, and then dutifully updated the register which I kept in the top drawer of my dresser.

My mother didn't just make me work all the time. She also came up with creative ideas for me and my sisters to have fun during the long summer days when we were out of school. One of her more imaginative ideas—one we all loved—started with taking me up to a furniture store located in the Fairway shopping center, just a few blocks away. We went behind the store to the loading dock, and I picked out a large empty cardboard box from their rubbish pile. We tied the box to the top of the car, brought it home, and put it in the backyard where my sisters and I began drawing on it and cutting into it with a knife until we had transformed it into a playhouse, or stagecoach, or ship, or submarine, or railroad car, or whatever else our imaginations envisioned it to be. We carved doors and windows that we opened and closed so many times that their "hinges" eventually tore through and the moving panels fell off.

When our creation was a house, we painted shutters next to the windows and flower boxes under them. If we decided it was something other than a house, our artwork was adjusted accordingly. When a "house" was finished, we put an old blanket down for a carpet inside, and my sisters moved their children's table and chair set in for a tea party with Kool-Aid. Armloads of dolls and stuffed animals were carted from the big house to the little cardboard house.

We got a lot of mileage out of a cardboard box, and my mother's ingenuity in this regard freed her from dealing with bored and restless children most of the time. These various creations eventually came to ruination from an afternoon or evening thunderstorm, but that just opened the opportunity for another trip to the furniture store with ideas for creating a new project which would be bigger and better. The "bigger and better" sometimes involved multiple boxes, tied or taped together, to make a multi-room dwelling or to serve as a row of train cars. What fun we had!

Our three-month-long summer vacations from school seemed to last forever. It was almost as if time stood still as summer day followed summer day. Eventually, though, September and a new school year approached. Sometime in late August, my mother took me out to shop for school clothes as I had outgrown the clothes from the previous year. She had to practically drag me kicking and screaming to get this done. I hated it.

My sisters didn't have to shop for new clothes since they were required to wear uniforms to school and only had to be fitted for new shoes. All five of us usually needed new school shoes. When we watched the Howdy Doodey show on TV at this time of year, there was an ad for Buster Brown shoes at every commercial break. So when we did our shopping, we wanted to get Buster Brown shoes. When you look inside you could see a picture of Buster Brown and his dog "Tige".

After being outfitted, we went to Crown Drug at the Fairway Shopping Center where we bought our school supplies—pencils, erasers, rulers, notebook paper, etc. When we got home from the store, we begged our mother to let us try out all of these new art tools at the dinette table. She would not allow this initially, but we eventually wore her down until she conceded to let us each test out one or two of the items. This helped to get us all looking forward to starting a new school year and accepting the fact summer was over.

Chapter 17

I was eight years old when I started third grade at St. Agnes. My teacher was Sister Monica. Within the first couple of weeks of starting school, I came home with a sheet of information about Cub Scouts. Eight years was the minimum age to join. I knew nothing about what this was all about, but my mother decided right away it would be good for me and signed me up. This meant another shopping trip to buy the uniform and books. There was a boys clothing store in Prairie Village that carried all the stuff, so she took me there and got me all outfitted.

The school's Cub Scout Pack was Pack 391. I was assigned to Den Four, and on the day of a den meeting, I was required to wear my uniform to school since the meeting was right after school. My first den mother was Mrs. Key. She was a pretty young mother who was soft-spoken and very nice. She had two boys. Jed was a year older than I and was in Den 4 also. Billy was younger and not old enough for Cub Scouts yet. Billy watched our meetings from the sidelines. Mr. Key was a Braniff Airline pilot, and this impressed me. I saw him come home from a trip in his uniform a few times and thought he had the coolest career anyone could possibly have. I hoped I could be an airline pilot someday like Mr. Key.

I wore my uniform to school for the first den meeting. I walked into class that morning in my navy blue uniform with the yellow kerchief and beanie cap, not realizing it was the first of many uniforms I would wear throughout life – Cub Scouts, Boy Scouts, Medical Intern, United States Naval Officer, and Airline Pilot. I think I have worn a uniform for more days of my life than I have worn regular clothes. At any rate, I was self-conscious that day. I was upset that I was the only one in class in uniform. There were other new Cub Scouts in my den, but none of them had their uniforms yet. The girls seemed to all be impressed by my uniform and either stared or made eyes at me. Most of the boys, though, teased and poked fun at me mercilessly throughout the day. As far as the boys went, I seemed to be the laughing stock of the class. The day seemed to last forever, but I made it through the day, and when school was out, Mrs. Key was there to pick us up and drive us to her house for the first den meeting.

Cub Scouts and Boy Scouts are wonderful organizations which teach high moral standards, codes of conduct, and achievement of goals. Cub Scouts gives younger boys an introduction to scouting and encourages them to continue on into Boys Scouts. As a Cub Scout, each scout is initially the rank of Bobcat. The ranks that follow are Wolf, Bear, Lion, and finally Weblo. There was a book for each badge outlining the requirements for attaining it. The Weblo is like the Eagle rank of Boys Scouts, and after attaining the Weblo and reaching 11 years of age, a Cub Scout is allowed to move on to Boy Scouts. Mrs. Key explained all this to us and helped us get started in earning the first badge – the Wolf.

Our Cub Scout Den meetings generally involved some simple craft activity. There was a carving exercise in which we created little sailboats out of bars of soap. Mrs. Key was careful to buy Ivory soap since, as the advertisement of the time said, "it floats." Maybe the point of this was just to teach us a new skill, but I suspect the real reason for this exercise was an attempt to encourage some of our scouts to get into a bath tub a little more often.

I recall another den meeting at which we made candles by melting old broken candles in a pot in Mrs. Key's kitchen and then pouring the hot wax into empty milk cartons which served as the molds. After cutting them out of the molds, we decorated them with sequins and took them home as Christmas candles. Another time, we made Christmas wreaths from evergreen boughs we tied onto a heavy wire ring. In addition to the crafts, we worked on the requirements for our next badge at the den meetings.

Occasionally the den went on some type of educational field trip. My dad worked as an accountant for a chemical company and agreed to take Mrs. Key's Den Four on a field trip to the Spencer Chemical Company Plastics Plant. This facility was located in the Fairfax industrial area of Kansas City, Kansas. For this excursion, my father was planning to be home by the time I arrived home from school, and all of the little scouts were to meet at our house. One of the other scouts in my den was a kid I will call Arthur Finkley (not his real name). Arthur didn't have a bike, and so I "rode" him on the back of my bike from school to our house that afternoon. I picked up quite a bit of speed going down our sloped street and lost control of the bike as I turned into our driveway. We had a bad crash, and I landed on my head and was knocked unconscious.

Unbeknownst to me, my father was in his car right behind us all the way down the street and witnessed the crash. Arthur got up from the crash unscathed, but my dad carried me into the house and laid my limp body on the sofa in the family room. My mother was there also and called my Aunt Emily who had allegedly been a nurse's aide at some point and lived just a few blocks away. I was unconscious for about 30 to 40 minutes I am told, and when I awakened, my Aunt Emily was there putting iced towels against my forehead. I had some amnesia for the previous few hours but, otherwise, apparently appeared to be okay.

When I finally remembered about the plastic plant tour, I begged to be allowed to go. We ended up all piling into my dad's car (no seatbelts) and heading down to the industrial area. We were about halfway there when I asked my dad to pull over. I opened the door and threw up on the gravel shoulder of the road. When we got to the plant, I got out of the car and promptly threw up again in the parking lot. My dad decided I had better just lie in the car while he took the kids on the tour, and at that point I agreed without a fuss. I was feeling pretty awful.

The tour probably lasted about an hour, and then my dad drove all the kids to their respective houses. It was after dark when we finally got back home. I obviously had suffered a moderately severe cerebral concussion and remain amazed to this day that my parents never took me to an emergency room or to see our family doctor. I recovered with no apparent damage or residual effects though, proving again "all's well that ends well." I was back in the saddle the next day, but I still don't know how plastic is made. When I applied for a job as a commercial airline pilot many years later, there was a question on the application asking if I had ever had any kind of a head injury. I answered it, "No." But since I had suffered a concussion, I didn't think I should be expected to remember that I actually did have a head injury. In any case, I believe it should only be considered a white lie, and that is only a venial sin.

Mrs. Key was a great den mother and remained at her post for the entire school year. I was disappointed in fourth grade when I found out she wouldn't be our den mother that year and that Mrs. Finkley, Arthur's mother, had taken over. She turned out to be another good den mother, and we all liked her. But Mrs. Finkley had one distracting physical characteristic she had obviously passed on genetically to

Arthur. Arthur was probably the only kid in the fourth grade who should have been shaving every morning. It appeared he had inherited his mustachioed countenance primarily from his mother's side, and it was always hard at den meetings for me to concentrate on not staring at Mrs. Finkley's upper lip or her hairy legs.

My younger sister Martha met Mrs. Finkley one day when my mother was dropping me off for a den meeting. That night at the dinner table, Martha looked at my mother and said, "how come Mrs. Finkley has a mustache and none of the other mothers do?" My mother was unable to come up with a good answer for that.

Having made all of these rather unkind observations about the Finkleys, I must say they were wonderful people. Arthur was a nice kid, and his mother turned out to be a good den mother. We had a good year and I enjoyed my time with the Finkleys
.

Chapter 18

Iwas nine years old when Dabo died. He was 65. Dabo always seemed very old to me. When he was still actively working as a Kansas City, Missouri, policeman and all decked out in his uniform, he, even then, looked old to me. He was a big man and looked like he was strong, but his face showed the wrinkles of time, his hair was thin and gray, he wore wire-rimmed bifocal glasses, and he had false teeth he took out at night.

I don't think we kids realized Dabo's health had been deteriorating for some time, and I couldn't have imagined losing my grandpa. Namo and Mom had talked about his high blood pressure, his memory problems, and his confusion at times, but to me and my sisters, he was the same old Dabo.

When Mom was working and Namo came over to stay with us, she started bringing Dabo along. Namo was afraid to leave him alone. Namo and Dabo didn't have a car, so Mom always picked them up at their apartment and drove them to our house. In the early 1920s they had owned a Model T Ford for a short while, but they had a bad wreck in which the car rolled over and was totaled. When my folks told me about this accident, they said Namo was driving the car at the time and that she had always been a horrible driver. My mother's sister, Aunt Gertrude, was in the car, and she told me Namo stepped on her neck while she was climbing out of the wreckage. It seemed she had never forgiven her mother for that and told the story whenever she got the chance. They never got another car after that, and I'm not sure Dabo ever learned to drive. This seems odd for a man who was a policeman, but he was a foot patrolman and often talked about walking his beat.

At our house, he sat in a big easy chair in our living room most of the day. My sisters and I were always trying to get him to play some type of game with us, and he went along with it most of the time. One of our favorite things to do was to tie him to the chair he was sitting in. We had several lengths of thick hemp rope we brought in from the garage for the purpose. We started with one piece and tied his wrists together and then took a longer piece and wrapped it around and around the chair. Martha and I worked together on this, pulling each piece as tight as we could get it and then tying a knot. We tied lots of knots, thinking the more knots there were the harder it would be for

Dabo to escape. He sometimes pretended he was asleep until we tied the last knot. Other times he let us just get started tying his hands, and then, before we got the knot tied, pulled loose and started twirling his hands around one another in the air in front of him and laughing as we tried to pull his wrists back together and start over. We always said, "Dabo, THAT'S NOT FAIR....THAT'S NOT HOW TO PLAY." At times like this when he was not cooperating, I sometimes sent Martha off to find Judy to come help. Even when he was cooperating and pretending to be asleep through the whole process and we successfully got him all tied up, he quickly got himself free. I was always amazed he could do this and didn't believe Houdini himself was any better as an escape artist than my own grandpa.

Another thing we liked to do with Dabo was to get him to extend his legs out in front of his chair, and then we took turns sliding down his legs to the floor. He complained the game was destroying the crease in his slacks, but my sisters and I thought that was a weak excuse. I think, in retrospect, he was trying to get us to just stop bugging him so he could enjoy a little peace and quiet.

One of Dabo's favorite things was to listen to boxing matches every Friday night on the radio. If he was at our house on a Friday night, we watched the fights on our television. He got really excited during some of these bouts, shouting and swinging his fists in the air. Rocky Marciano was the heavyweight champion for several years, and we never missed one of his fights. Namo didn't like boxing at all and left the room whenever he started listening to a fight or watching one on our TV. She didn't like it when I watched a fight with him, but he overrode her objections, and I always got to stay.

Dabo liked to smoke a cigar when he listened to a boxing match on the radio or when he was playing Dominos with my dad. He preferred Roi-Tan cigars, and everyone knew a box of Roi-Tans was a great gift for him on Christmas or his birthday. I loved the smell of his cigars when he smoked them. Each cigar had a little red paper band around it that he would carefully remove and give to one of us to wear on a finger as a ring. I also looked forward to him finishing the last cigar in a box since he always gave me the empty box. The boxes were sturdy cardboard with hinged tops and had colorful ads pasted on the outsides. An empty cigar box was handy for storing all kinds of things – like spare change, my pocket knives, nuts and bolts, a yoyo, or my marble collection. I usually had one cigar box on top of my dresser in my room and several of them under my bed.

I don't remember seeing Dabo drinking alcoholic beverages much. I don't think Namo approved of it and wouldn't let him keep a bottle of anything at home. But he and my dad occasionally enjoyed a whiskey before dinner when he was at our house. Namo always warned him at times like this that she didn't want to have to call Quirk and Tobin to cart him home like they did on that famous New Year's Eve. She never let him forget that incident. When talking about whiskey, Dabo always said, "it's all good, but some of it's better than others."

One day when Dabo was at our house, he started confusing my sister Judy with his long-deceased sister, Alice. When Namo came into the living room to check on this, she noticed one side of his face was drooping. Dabo had suffered a stroke.

Kids weren't allowed to visit patients in hospitals in those days. So Mom took me to the hospital and showed me from the parking lot which window on the side of the big brick building was the one for Dabo's room. I could wave at Namo, standing in the window, and she could tell Dabo I was there. We repeated this several times over the next few days.

Dabo never got to come home from the hospital. He had several more small strokes, and then, on about the fifth day of hospitalization, he had a massive cerebral hemorrhage. He lost consciousness and was in a coma after that until he finally died on October 8, 1954.

Tom Fearon's funeral was held at 9:00 AM at Guardian Angel Catholic Church on October 11. The church was filled to capacity, all of the pall bearers were in police uniform, and it seemed the entire Kansas City, Missouri, police force was there. Following the funeral mass, a procession of police cars followed the hearse with motorcycle escort to St. Mary's Cemetery where Tom was laid to rest. The entire service and burial was formal and proper. It was a sad day for me, for the rest of our family, and for the entire law enforcement community of our city. Everyone who knew Tom Fearon loved him.

Chapter 19

One spring afternoon, when I was in the fourth grade, we had two visitors to our class. They were both young brothers of the Benedictine Order of priests who were there to give a presentation about Camp Saint Maur, a Catholic summer camp for boys ages nine through twelve. The two brothers were dressed in priestly black slacks, black belts, and black shoes, but above the waist, they each wore white T-shirts with *Camp Saint Maur* and the camp logo imprinted. These two novitiates were both on the staff of this summer camp located in Atchison, Kansas, about 50 miles from our home in Kansas City. Their job on that particular day was to recruit campers for the upcoming summer sessions. I listened to their marketing efforts during which they described the camp activities, and it seemed these included almost every recreational opportunity available to mankind. At the end of the presentation, they passed out camp brochures for each of us to take home to our parents. The flyers provided more information about the camp and included fee schedules for each of the three two-week summer sessions. At the top of the brochure was their catchy camp slogan: "Sun and Air for Your Son and Heir." It all sounded like fun, but I definitely felt a little uneasy about living away from home for a two-week camp session. I had never been away from home other than to stay overnight with a friend on occasion.

When my parents looked over the brochure, they immediately decided this was *just the thing* for me. My mother filled out the application and sent it off to Atchison along with a check for the first two-week camp session. Later, when I was older, they explained their enthusiasm to ship me out at the first opportunity. They had been concerned for some time about the fact that I was somewhat shy, hesitant, and lacked confidence—especially in any new or different situation. They thought being away from home on my own for a while might be the perfect antidote for this perceived problem.

Throughout my life, I have regarded their decision to send me to Camp Saint Maur, in the spring of 1955, as the best and most important decision my parents ever made concerning me. I not only gained the self-confidence I was lacking, but the camp provided me with a platform of skills and moral values that have served me well throughout my entire life. In fact, I had the time of my life there. For four consecutive summers, 1955 thru 1958, I was a camper at Camp Saint Maur, and I have always considered that experience my favorite part of childhood. For my second, third, and fourth summers at the camp, I attended double sessions (four weeks) each summer and would have preferred to have attended for the full six weeks if my parents had allowed it.

On Sunday, June 6, 1955, we loaded up our new Buick and headed for Atchison. My older sister, Judy, and one of my younger sisters, Martha, went along. Betsy and Helen, the little ones, stayed home with Namo.

Atchison is a typical small mid-western town with modest, neat homes along streets shaded by mature elms, pin oaks, and maples. We navigated our way to Camp St. Maur, which we found on the south edge of town. The camp was located on the campus of Maur Hill, a boys "preparatory" boarding school, also run by the Benedictine monks. The campus consisted of a number of beautiful red brick buildings, generously spaced apart and surrounded by large, tree-shaded, open, park-like spaces. There were also several athletic fields.

As we drove into the main drive, the administration building was on our left and the refectory, or dining hall, was on our right. The entrance led to a circular drive surrounding a central flag pole adjacent to a parking area.

The main building housed the administrative offices and also the living quarters for the students during the school year and for the campers during the summer. These living quarters for us at camp consisted of a large open dormitory on the second floor which was furnished with enough bunk beds to sleep approximately 120 kids—all in this one large room. The beds looked like they may have been purchased from Army Surplus of World War II. There was a large lavatory with toilets, sinks, and showers. On the first floor of the building, there were lockers for our clothes and personal items.

The refectory, as the monks referred to the dining hall, was located across the main drive from the administration building. The dining room was a long room with hardwood floors and long, dark, oak tables placed end to end. The dining chairs were simple straight-backed wooden chairs. The refectory building also housed the infirmary which was staffed by a nurse who was dressed in a starched white uniform, white shoes, and a white cap at all times.

On the same side of the drive as the refectory, there was another smaller brick building sitting back a little farther from the main drive. This was the student union building for the boarding school, but it served as a snack bar for the campers. A camper's parents could, if they chose, leave some money on account for their son to use at his discretion. The monk who ran the snack bar, Brother Herbert, kept track of all of this, and when a camper's prepaid account was exhausted, that was it—no more snacks. The snack bar was also where the Camp St. Maur T-shirts were purchased and where the stamping equipment was located to imprint the shirt with various awards as they were earned during the camp session.

The last building, fronting the central flag circle and on the same side of the drive as the snack bar and refectory, was the nature and crafts building. I assume this was the main classroom building for the students of Maur Hill during the school year. For the camp sessions, the classrooms had been converted to a nature room, a leathercraft shop, a ceramics shop, and a woodworking shop.

Other buildings on the campus included a gymnasium and an indoor swimming pool. These two buildings were located to the east of the administration building.

On a corner of one of the athletic fields, there was a large fire pit for evening campfires. The fire pit was surrounded by a wooden circular bench to seat all 120 campers. There was also a tall, carved, wooden totem pole near the fire pit and an Indian tepee. Down a slight hill behind the nature and crafts building, there was a riding stable, a corral, and a herd of horses. In front of the administration building, in a large, grassy open area, there was an archery range.

My parents registered me in the director's office of the administration building. Father Edwin was the director that year, 1955. I was assigned a "squad" and introduced to my camp counselor who would be in charge of that group of campers for the next two weeks. He was a young Benedictine brother by the name of Matthias Schmidt. He beamed a huge smile as he introduced himself to me and my family. He gave us a little orientation to the camp, showed me where to stow my clothes and other personal articles for the next two weeks, and stood by my side as I watched my mother, father, and sisters drive off.

I stayed close by Brother Matthias's side that afternoon as more boys arrived and our squad, Squad Eight, gradually grew to a full complement of 10 campers. By late afternoon, all of the parents had gone, and at about 5:00 PM, everyone responded to a loud bell by mustering around the flag circle. We assembled by squad for a welcome address by the camp director, a brief evening prayer, and then a short march to the refectory for the evening meal.

Once inside the refectory, we took our places with our respective squad counselors but were not allowed to talk until we had all said the traditional Catholic blessing together, known as "grace." "Bless us, oh Lord, and these, thy gifts, which we are about to receive from thy bounty through Christ, Our Lord. Amen." After that, the dining hall turned into sheer bedlam; maybe not that first night so much when we were all a little shy, but after that, I remember it being quite noisy. We were required to exhibit good table manners, however, and the counselors enforced this. The food was served family style in large serving bowls that were passed around. There were stacks of white bread, and you could spread as much butter on as you liked. Milk was on the table in pitchers but wasn't popular because there was also colored Kool-Aid; it was referred to as "bug juice" by our counselors, and the name was quickly adopted by us, the campers.

After the evening meal, we had free time for a couple of hours. Then, in the twilight hour, we grouped again by squad and walked around the campus while reciting the rosary aloud. We did this each evening of every day at camp.

That first week was a little rough for me. I had a hard time enjoying much for the first few days as I was extremely homesick. I even went and saw the camp nurse in her office a couple of times, hoping if I appeared to be sick, I might get to go home. Brother Matthias took me under his wing that week and got me involved in all kinds of fun activities, apparently quite aware of my uncertainty and homesickness. By the end of the week, I was having a wonderful time and my homesickness had evaporated. Earlier in the week, I had written a letter home during an afternoon rest period. In the letter I told my mother I was very sick and "had to see the nurse." Well, all of this had the desired effect, and my parents showed up Saturday morning to bring me home. Of course, by that time, I was having an absolute blast. When they located me, I was totally engrossed in some wonderful activity and was irritated and embarrassed they had shown up and were interrupting my fun. They had a short discussion with my counselor, Brother Matthias, and headed back out for the highway to Kansas City.

I never got homesick again and returned to camp in the summers of 1956, 1957, and 1958. That first year, 1955, I attended camp for a two-week session, but for each of the next three years I signed up for four weeks.

Brother Matthias became a lifelong friend to me and my family. We kept in touch throughout his life, and he continued to have a positive influence on me. I followed his progression from Brother to ordained Priest to Bishop. He spent most of his life as a missionary in Brazil, but he wrote frequent letters to me and my family and arranged to see us whenever he returned to the United States. Bishop Matthias died suddenly of an apparent heart attack in Brazil in1992 at the age of 61.

Attending Camp St. Maur was the highlight of my childhood. The activities there were fun and educational. There was an enormous array of events each day to choose from, and all of these revolved around an award system that was similar to earning badges in Cub

Scouts and Boy Scouts. When a camper arrived at camp for his first session, he was a "pioneer." He would then set out to become an Indian and work his way up to Brave, Medicine Man, and finally to Chief.

There were quite a number of skills to be learned and tests to pass to become a Brave. Every requirement was carefully tracked and recorded. When all of the requirements for Brave had been accomplished, and all tests passed and signed off, you were allowed to have the sleeve of your camp T-shirt stamped with an insignia indicating your rank, and you were allowed to wear the headband of a Brave with a single feather in it. You were also bestowed with an Indian name at that point. The counselors chose the name for each new Indian and tried to pick a name which fit each kid. "Paka"—Whitehead—was an easy choice for me since I was such a little towhead in the summer. After a few days out in the summer sun, my hair was white as snow.

Each level of the Indian hierarchy became more difficult to achieve. To pass all of the requirements for Medicine Man and Chief required attendance at camp for several years, so most campers never got beyond the level of Brave. Requirements for brave included passing tests of horsemanship, beginner's swimming, plant and tree identification, animal tracking, ropes and knots, woodworking, leathercraft, ceramics, camping skills (such as fire-building and cooking), lanyard weaving, riflery, archery, etc.

By the end of my second year at camp I was a Medicine Man, and by the end of my fourth summer session, I had completed (just barely in time) all of the requirements for Chief. The final required project was quite tedious and occupied me for almost every waking hour during those last four weeks of camp in the summer of 1958. It involved making a full Indian war bonnet. I did the beadwork on a loom for the portion of the bonnet across my forehead. The beadwork spelled out my Indian name, "Paka". The beadwork portion alone took many hours to complete.

Various levels of swimming proficiency were required to be demonstrated at Camp St. Maur by passing standardized American Red Cross tests. Swimming was one of the many requirements that had to be signed off in order to be designated a Brave, Medicine Man, and, finally, a Chief. A higher level of proficiency was required for every stage of advancement up the Indian hierarchy. When I first arrived at

92

camp I could not swim at all and actually had quite a fear of the water. I had never taken any previous swimming lessons, but my father had tried to teach me himself at Lake Quivera, near Kansas City. That was a bad experience, and it had seemed more like he was trying to drown me than teach me how to swim. My dad subscribed to the "sink or swim" method of instruction, and that method did not work for me.

It was somewhat embarrassing that I didn't know how to swim because most of my friends and most of the other campers were swimmers by the age of nine. So I started out in the Red Cross Beginner Swimming class. As luck would have it my buddy, Brother Matthias, was the swimming instructor for the class. My parents had warned him of my fears and that I might be a difficult student, and so he approached his task with the utmost care giving me extra attention when needed. He was a wonderful instructor. He was extremely patient, took things one step at a time, and never pushed me beyond my comfort level. Once I got over my fear and passed Beginner Swimming, I rocketed through all of the other Red Cross courses and tests. By the time I left camp, four years later, I had completed every swimming course offered and had passed every certification. In my final year at camp I completed "Junior Lifesaving" and, finally, "Senior Lifesaving."

There were approximately 120 boys at each camp session. We all slept together in the big dormitory room in bunk beds. There were always a couple of counselors quietly patrolling the aisles between the army bunk beds during the night to make sure there were no shenanigans going on. We each had a stool next to the bunk to sit on while we took off our shoes and then to lay our folded clothes on for the night. There were many occasions when a sleeping camper would roll out of a top bunk during the night and come crashing down onto his stool. You would hear a loud crash, then hysterical crying. One of the counselors on duty would rush to the scene and check the poor kid for injuries. I amazingly never heard of anyone actually sustaining any significant injury.

There was a secret society at Camp St. Maur known as *The Golden Thunderbirds*. Members of this group had to be Indians—no pioneers were admitted. The kids who were Golden Thunderbirds were usually only campers who had been returning to camp for a few summers. Of the 120 campers at each session, there were usually about six to 10 Golden Thunderbirds. The other campers could identify members of this special group by the Golden Thunderbird emblazoned on their camp T-shirts and by the Golden Thunderbird lanyards—with a hawks claw woven in—that each of them wore. When a camper was selected to be a member of this elite society, he was "struck by the Golden Thunderbird" in the middle of the night. Other campers woke up in the morning to find the kid who was struck missing from his bed and the image of the Golden Thunderbird emblazoned on his pillow. The new member would not be seen at the camp for the next 24 hours as he underwent an initiation into this brotherhood.

My third year at camp, 1957, I was spirited away late one night. I had been struck by the Golden Thunderbird. As part of the initiation, I normally would have been dumped off in the woods with three provisions—two matches, a Snickers candy bar, and a can of beans. Those plans went awry because of severe thunderstorms throughout the area that night associated with torrential rain and wind. Instead, I was blindfolded and taken to one of the other buildings on the campus and led to a recessed corner at the bottom of a stairway. I was left there with the three provisions and instructions not to come out of hiding until late the following afternoon.

I slept on the floor in the corner of the stairwell. It was a long night! The matches were of no use since I was inside of a building. I had no way of opening the can of baked beans since they had emptied my pockets and I no longer had my pocket knife. If I had been in the woods as originally planned, I would have opened it on a rock. I did eat the candy bar, but I was really hungry by the time I emerged from hiding and went to dinner the next evening. I was also extremely bored from sitting under the stairs all day with nothing to occupy my time but my own thoughts.

I waited until I heard the dinner bell ring to be sure I didn't come out too early. I then joined my fellow squad members for dinner, but I was not allowed to talk or communicate with anyone for the next two days. If this rule was violated and I was caught, I would be removed from the initiation and not be allowed to become a Golden Thunderbird.

The next two days were difficult. All of my buddies were trying hard to get me to talk. The only easy part was when we had our mandatory two-hour rest period in the dormitory each afternoon. No talking was allowed then anyway. I became aware, during the next two days, that there was another camper who was not talking and was also being taunted. I learned, by listening to what was being said, that he had been "struck" the same night I had been. It was one of my best friends, Charlie Crawl.

On the evening of the third day after being struck, I was pulled aside, after evening prayer and taps at the flag pole, by two members of the Golden Thunderbirds. While the rest of the campers marched to the dormitory to go to bed, I was escorted behind the nature and craft building and blindfolded. I was then pushed down behind some bushes where I was instructed to stay until called for. After what seemed like an eternity, my two escorts returned and led me away blindfolded in the dark. They poked long pine needles up into my arm pits to hurry me along. After walking a few hundred yards, I was told to bend down and crawl through an opening, then maneuvered to a place on the ground where I was ordered to sit with my legs crossed, Indian style. I could see flickers of flames through my blindfold and feel the heat from a campfire. The air was smoky, and I started coughing. Someone said "Ugh, weakum lungs, Ugh." My blindfold was then removed and I could see I was sitting inside the large Indian tepee located near the bonfire ring used on Saturday nights. There was a small campfire burning in the center of the tepee. Brother Matthias, Brother Herbert, and Brother Owen were sitting across the fire from me. All three of them were Indian chiefs and completely decked out in feathered war bonnets, beaded vests, and Indian jewelry. Their faces were all painted with war paint. All of the Golden Thunderbird campers were crowded into the tepee as well, about six in number. There was no light except for that of the campfire, and it was eerie. I suddenly noticed, sitting next to me, was the other camper who had been struck—my friend, Charlie.

"Chief" Matthias began our indoctrination with a prayer and then an explanation of what it meant to be a Golden Thunderbird and whose leadership and guidance we should always follow—The Grand Sachem. Charlie and I were told we now had special privileges none of the other campers had, but we also had new responsibilities. We were expected to help with indoctrination of new campers and serve as assistants for the camp counselors when needed. As Golden Thunderbirds, we were always expected to set the highest example for behavior so that all of the other campers would look up to us at all times. We were also sworn to secrecy with respect to all Golden Thunderbird doctrines, meetings, and activities. After we both agreed and accepted the conditions and responsibilities of membership, an Indian Peace Pipe was passed around for everyone to take a puff. I coughed uncontrollably after my puff on the pipe, and one of the chiefs again said: "Um....Ugh...Weakum lungs." After everyone in the tepee had smoked the Peace Pipe, a ceramic crock with some kind of thick liquid in it was removed from the fire and stirred with a spoon by "Chief" Matthias. He then ladled out a portion of the broth for each of us. He said Charlie and I would officially be Golden Thunderbirds after we each swallowed a spoonful of this most sacred potion. He handed me the spoon, and when I put it in my mouth, I experienced a most vile taste. The mixture tasted as if it was almost 100% black pepper with just enough water or other liquid added to make it all glob together. Everyone was chanting, "you must swallow, you must swallow...." I swallowed it quickly, but immediately started retching, and the contents of my stomach from dinner were on the ground in front of me in short order. One of the chiefs said, "Ugh, weakum stomach too!" Charlie was horrified as the spoon was passed to him. He immediately began retching as well but did not throw up his dinner as I did. The initiation ceremony ended promptly at that point, and everyone exited the tepee as quickly as possible. Once outside in the fresh air and moonlight, away from the stench of vomit, congratulations were passed around, and Charlie and I were welcomed as the newest members of the Golden Thunderbirds. We were then each presented with a hawk's claw, which we would each weave into our Golden Thunderbird lanyards and wear around our necks. I had pretty severe diarrhea for the next 24 hours until I had expelled all of the pepper. It all seemed well worth it though, and I was ecstatic because I was now a member of the most elite organization in the entire world! The morning following the completion of my initiation, I got all of my Camp St. Maur T-shirts stamped with the Golden Thunderbird emblem. I then started to work on an eight-strand braided yellow lanyard with the hawk's claw woven into it.

My first responsibility as a Golden Thunderbird came later that week when Brother Matt asked me to help him set up for the annual Pioneer-Indian campout. We left the campus Friday morning in an old, beat-up pickup truck. We first went into town to Brother Matt's boyhood home where we briefly visited his mother. We then drove out of Atchison and followed a country road to one of the Benedictine farms. The Benedictine monks are known for their self-sufficiency, and there were several farms the order owned and worked to raise produce and livestock for their subsistence. When we arrived at the farm, we rounded up a large lamb and herded it into a corral, and from there, maneuvered it up a ramp and into the pickup bed, which was equipped with high stock racks. Brother Matt then drove us to another farm, also owned by the order. This would be the location for the Pioneer-Indian campout. I opened a gate leading to a beautiful, green rolling pasture. Brother Matt drove the truck through the gate and then asked me, 11 years old at the time, if I would like to drive. I told him "I sure would," although the only thing I had ever driven was my toy tractor and my two-wheeler bike. I got behind the wheel, and Brother Matt got into the passenger's seat. I think our fluffy passenger in the truck bed already had ominous misgivings about this little excursion and seemed not to care who was at the wheel. Brother Matt sat in the middle of the seat and operated the clutch and the brake since my feet wouldn't reach any of the pedals. We lurched comically across the field as I controlled the old truck with one hand on the steering wheel and the other on the hand throttle. We climbed to the top of a ridge where a pretty valley came into view. There was a shady grove of trees next to a creek bed in a depression at the bottom of the hill. Brother Matt directed me to steer down the hill toward the grove. He maneuvered his foot over to my side and helped me brake the old truck to a stop as the terrain flattened out. We stopped next to a large old cottonwood tree, and he said, "This will be a good place to tie up our little friend."

We had a length of sturdy hemp rope with us. We opened up the back of the truck and trapped the lamb in a corner of the truck bed. With one end of the rope, we tied a bowline around his neck, a good knot which wouldn't allow the loop to tighten around the lamb's neck and choke him. We then dropped the tailgate and coaxed the little guy out. We tied the other end of the rope around the big cottonwood tree. There was enough rope so the lamb could do a little grazing on the plentiful grass around the tree. We left a bucket of drinking water next to the tree. We then jumped back in the truck, with me again behind the wheel, and followed our tracks back up and over the rise to the gate by the road.

On the way back to camp, Brother Matthias told me I was not to tell anyone about what we had done before the upcoming campout.

97

When I asked him why we had taken the lamb out there and left it, he was evasive. He said I would know soon enough.

When we got back to the campus, Brother Matt drove us to the riding stables where all of my fellow-Golden Thunderbirds were gathered. By then, the afternoon rest period had started, and all of the other campers were in the dormitory. We saddled up eight horses, mounted, and with Brother Bruce leading us, rode out of town toward the country road which Brother Matthias and I had just driven in on. It was about a 45-minute ride back to the meadow where we had left the lamb tethered. The rest of the "pioneers" and "Indians" would hike there on foot to set up their respective camps for the weekend later that afternoon. When we, The Golden Thunderbirds, arrived there on our horses, we set about building a temporary corral for the horses for the weekend using ropes and poles which we cut from the woods.

When the rest of the campers hiked in later that afternoon and the supply trucks arrived, two encampments were established on either side of a rise, making the pioneer camp out of line-of-sight from the Indian camp. There were separate games and activities at each encampment, but the horses were shared for rides. There were also "wars" all weekend between the pioneers and the Indians with sneak attacks, some after dark, and lots of fighting and rolling in the long grass of the meadows. The lamb was a great mascot, and there were, at all times, a few kids near the big cottonwood tree hugging and petting the lamb, bringing it treats, and generally doting on it. On Saturday evening the pioneers were all invited to the Indian camp to watch war dances—in full costume, including war paint—around a large bonfire.

We had great fun all weekend, and it all culminated with a peace agreement on Sunday afternoon. The pioneers were then invited to the Indian encampment, and they gathered shortly after noon to prepare and share a great feast. The main course for this elaborate feast was—you guessed it—roast lamb. Under a hot July sun the lamb was slaughtered (I'll leave out the details) and the entrails removed. A cooking fire was prepared under a rotisserie spit constructed of iron pipe with a large crank fashioned on each end. During the butchery, the mood of the campers became quiet and somber, there was audible sobbing from some, and some awful wailing from a couple of the most distraught. Brother Richard was the main butcher for this operation. He did not look at all happy with this responsibility. He was sweating profusely under the hot sun by the time his task was completed. Once the bloody operation was over and the carcass was splayed on the spit, attached by wires, everyone settled down and seemed to adjust to the idea of eating our pet lamb for dinner. Each of us had to take a turn at the cranks on the spit, and we all watched the meat slowly brown as the carcass rotated above the hot fire over the next few hours. The lamb was sliced, a commissary truck arrived with large metal trays of side dishes to accompany the meat, and we all lined up to serve up our plates. Everyone agreed afterwards that it had been a great meal. Just about all of the campers had some part in the preparation including gathering firewood, building the campfire, tying the carcass onto the spit, turning the spit, and helping with the carving. Several campers had helped, earlier in the day, to dig a deep hole for burial of the head and entrails as well. There remained some sadness about the sacrifice of our fluffy friend, but it certainly gave us all a good hands-on lesson of where our meat comes from.

In the late afternoon, after all the little pioneers and Indians had filled their bellies, both camps were packed up, and the campers began the hike along country roads back to the main campus. The Golden Thunderbirds and two counselors, Brother Bruce and Brother Herbert, stayed at the site with the horses which were still corralled in their makeshift pen. As twilight and then darkness fell upon us in the picturesque little meadow next to the grove of trees, we gathered more wood to stoke the campfire. We sat in a circle around the fire as we roasted marshmallows and talked quietly about the adventures and conquests of the weekend. I enjoyed the intoxicating scent of nearby honeysuckle nectar mixed with the smoke from the fire and the aroma of the roasting marshmallows. As the fire cast its eerie, flickering light on the circle of faces, the meadows and trees beyond faded, and finally disappeared altogether into the darkness.

Brother Bruce decided it was dark enough at that point to begin telling ghost stories. We all got a turn, but we knew Brother Herbert had some good ones and begged him to start with one of his Minerva stories. Anyone who had been at camp long enough to be a member of the Golden Thunderbirds had heard the stories about old Minerva. So we were all familiar with the tales about her and were dying to have the bejesus scared out of us one more time. Brother Herbert's eyes seemed to get larger as he started speaking slowly with a scary, evil smile on his face. Minerva supposedly lived in an old, dilapidated farm house which was just down the country road, a short distance from our camp. The paint on the old house had weathered away long ago, the wood siding was a faded gray, the front door stood ajar, the windows were broken out, and the shutters hung at awkward angles and banged against the house when the wind blew. It truly looked like a haunted house from a horror movie, and we always hurried along when we hiked by. A few brave campers might yell some taunting insults at Minerva as they passed, but I never saw anyone brave enough to push the gate open and approach the house.

As Brother Herbert wove his tale, it became deathly quiet around the fire. I could feel the hair on the back of my neck standing up, and as I glanced at my buddies around the fire, I saw the eyes of a couple darting nervously out into the darkness surrounding us. I don't recall the gist of the first Minerva story that night, but I do remember him telling about the awful wailing screams often heard from the old house in the middle of the night. Brother Herbert suggested we all walk in the dark down to the old house, sneak up on it, and listen for the screams. We all decided we didn't really want to do that just then, and instead, listened to more Minerva stories as we each told one in turn. We all agreed in the end that Brother Herbert's stories were the best.

A full moon rose out of the east later that evening, and I will never forget the midnight ride the band of Golden Thunderbirds took through the farm fields to take the horses back to the main campus. We rode through rolling meadows at a full gallop. The night was so clear and the moon was so bright we could see our shadows in the grass. We had to stop and open a couple of gates along our route, but we were able to ride through fields all the way back except for a short distance on the road as we approached camp. At that time in my life, age 11, I felt like I was on top of the world. I didn't think I had ever before been given that much responsibility and, at the same time, I felt so free. As an adult, I have thought about our pledge of secrecy, and I suspect a major reason for this was so our parents would never find out their little darlings were, among other things, out gallivanting through fields at breakneck speed on horseback at midnight. They had, after all, been assured that all activities at the camp were totally safe and carefully controlled by highly responsible and mature Benedictine monks. Our parents had no idea........and I loved it.

By my fourth summer at Camp St. Maur, I was 12 years old and was considered an old veteran who knew just about everything. I must have appeared that way to many of the first and second year campers anyway. My T-shirts had the "Chief" insignia on them as well as the Golden Thunderbird logo. I wore the yellow lanyard of the Golden Thunderbird around my neck, and I was squad leader. As squad leader I assisted our squad counselor in all his duties. I helped with the orientation of new campers and assisted some of the younger kids with the requirements for "Brave." I led the squad in the recitation of the rosary in the evenings as we walked around the grounds before taps and bed. I remembered then how I had looked up to the older, experienced campers when I had been one of the new guys, and I enjoyed my position of respect. I didn't want to appear cocky, despite my venerable status, and hoped I was emulating the wonderful example set by our Benedictine counselors. I tried to imitate their confident, serene and humble manner at all times.

During my last two weeks in that fourth and final year of camp, there was a new camper who had arrived for the first time and joined our squad. He was a year or two younger than I and was somewhat small for his age, but he didn't have any of the hesitancy or lack of self-confidence I had when I had arrived at Camp St. Maur for the first time. As a matter of fact, he quickly became a major thorn in my side as the squad leader. Despite his young age and small stature, he had a great big mouth and never seemed to know when to keep his trap shut. He quickly zeroed in on me and started challenging my authority. One of my main jobs as squad leader was to "muster the troops" around the flag pole before each meal and then lead the march to the refectory. That kid constantly argued with me about every instruction I gave. He often concluded an argument by slugging me as hard as he could on the upper arm with his fist and then laughing. As the end of his first week approached, he started talking about the Friday Night Fights. Every Friday night, we had boxing matches in the gymnasium for any campers who wanted to sign up. It was an official-size boxing ring, the boxers wore regulation boxing gloves, and there were two timed rounds of two minutes for each fight. My little obnoxious friend started saying he wanted to fight me on Friday night. I had watched many of these boxing matches at camp over the years but had never been a participant. I had absolutely no interest in it. I told him I wouldn't do it. I just didn't want to do it, but I also thought it would look bad for me, as squad leader, to be beating up on a smaller and younger member of my squad. The little squirt wouldn't let it go. He kept at me all week with such remarks as, "What's the matter? Are you chicken, Crawley?" By the time Friday arrived, I'd totally had it with him. I was so sick of this little jerk that I was starting to want to get into the boxing ring with him and really pound him. On Friday afternoon he taunted me one more time with his request. I felt an evil grin coming across my face and said, "Okay, I'll fight you."

As I sat in my corner of the ring that night under the bright overhead lights, I glanced out into the bleachers at the raucous crowd and felt like I was in Madison Square Garden. The roar of the crowd was deafening. I could only hear encouraging cheers for me, though. It appeared this kid didn't have a single friend and had become notorious way beyond our squad. I think everyone wanted to see him get creamed. "Get him, Crawley." "Kill him, David." "Knock his teeth out, Crawley." The bell sounded, and I was shoved from the corner toward my adversary. I had a partial leather helmet on my head, a mouth guard to protect my teeth, and two boxing gloves on that felt like they weighed 25 pounds apiece. As I approached the center of the ring and my opponent, I was wondering if I could even throw a punch. I wasn't sure I could lift my fists with these anchors on them using my skinny little toothpick arms. Before I could think too much about this, my head started snapping back and forth from a machinegun series of powerful punches. I staggered around the ring like a drunken sailor with the little Tasmanian devil relentlessly pursuing me. I had a dull awareness of the roaring crowd. They were all on their feet and screaming instructions to me. I tried to get my gloves up to protect my face, but it was as if they were just hanging from the ends of noodles. The pounding to my head was unbelievable, and I had to do something. I found that by sort of rotating my upper body quickly with kind of a snap, I could get my noodle arms swinging like a pendulum on a clock, and then, when a gloved fist reached the top of its swing, give a little punching thrust outward. I couldn't really see my opponent well because everything seemed blurry after the first few hits to my head and also because he was dancing around the ring like Rocky Marciano. I worked on the pendulum swing technique and thought I might have actually connected a couple of times. By the time the bell rang, signaling the end of Round One, I felt like I was about to hit the mat. My pit crew had to come out and direct me to my corner because I couldn't find it on my own. They shoved me down onto the corner bench and started wiping me down with a cold, wet towel, held a

102

tissue to my bleeding nose, patted me on the back and shoulders, gave me a sip of water, and told me what a great job I was doing.

The break between rounds seemed like it couldn't have been more than about five seconds. The bell rang, and I was shoved back out into the ring for the second and final round. I didn't have to find my adversary. I felt my head being snapped to and fro like a punching bag as I reeled around the ring. I still couldn't lift my fists. It felt like someone had stuffed some lead weights into the gloves while I was on the bench. It felt like they weighed 50 pounds apiece now. I got my rhythm going again, though, and discovered if I got my shoulders snapping in opposite directions, I could spin both of my noodle arms around like pinwheels. When I actually struck the other kid using this somewhat unconventional technique, I had to get the rhythm going all over again. That last two-minute round seemed like at least an hour. I thought the bell must have somehow malfunctioned and the fight would go on forever. The bell finally rang though, and the match was over. I was in a complete fog and was staggering around trying to get my bearings, but I could hear the roar of the crowd with my name being shouted with cheers. The judge then came out and lifted my gloved hand into the air above my head proclaiming me the winner.

I have had a hard time believing to this day that I actually won the fight. I suspected it was fixed and I really didn't win. I asked a counselor who was one of the judges that night how they had determined I had won, and he told me they counted each punch that connected and reassured me I was indeed the champion. Even though I have never felt so beaten up in my life, the other kid seemed to be thoroughly convinced I had whipped him. He showed me extreme respect from that point on, and I never heard another smart-alecky remark from his mouth.

At some of the Friday Night Fights, two of the Benedictine brothers would challenge one another to a bout before the entire camp. Those matches were much different than the fights between the little kids. Those guys typically fought each other with incredible ferocity. They knocked each other almost senseless and frequently staggered from the ring with blood dripping. It was frightening to me to see these otherwise gentle souls engaged in what appeared as mortal combat. I had a terrible fear one of them would be seriously injured or killed, but they always seemed fine the next day with a band aid or two on their respective faces.

Everyone at camp could participate in the riflery program. A group of campers was transported by van once or twice a week to an indoor shooting range in town. We were carefully indoctrinated in gun safety and handling using .22 caliber bolt-action rifles. We learned how to take the gun apart and put it back together, how to load and unload, how to operate the safety, and we learned the rules of the range. Since we had no guns at home and my father was not a hunter, I had no previous training with firearms. So this was a great opportunity for me. We shot at a paper target with a bullseye in the center and concentric scoring rings surrounding it. Once we started shooting, all targets were scored and medals awarded for increasing levels of marksmanship. The Junior National Rifle Association protocol was followed. The medals were Pro-Marksman, Marksman, Marksman First Class, then nine levels of Sharpshooter (called bars), followed by Expert Rifleman, and finally Distinguished Rifleman. Each higher level required increasingly difficult shooting positions from prone (the most stable and easiest), sitting, kneeling, to finally standing—the most unstable and difficult position to shoot from. In my four years at camp, I worked my way up through Sharpshooter Eighth Bar. I hoped to achieve Expert Rifleman and Distinguished Rifleman, but I ran out of time in my last year to meet the qualifications. I did become proficient enough that I was asked to help in calibrating the sights on the rifles. This was done by shooting a closely grouped pattern and then making adjustments to "move" the pattern toward the bullseye. Even though I have never become a gun enthusiast or hunter and have never owned any guns, I am proud of my marksmanship awards. I feel I could pick up a rifle today and handle it safely, over 50 years later, because of this excellent training I received at camp.

One of the first requirements for Brave, as one would expect for any good Indian, was demonstration of basic proficiency in archery. The archery range was set up on the large open expanse of grass in front of the main administration building, near the camp's entrance drive. Brother Owen ran the archery program and was an excellent instructor. There was a metal "quiver" stuck in the ground at each shooting station with six arrows stored in each one. Each camper at the range pulled out an arrow when Brother Owen commanded, "Load em up," followed by… "Pull em back"…and then, "Shoot." The target was a large bullseye surrounded by concentric rings and was backed by stacks of hay bales. Scoring was done by adding points, with the point value of each ring diminishing as distance from the center bullseye increased.

Brother Owen Purcell, my archery instructor, was ordained to the priesthood and, years later, was selected to be the Abbot of St. Benedict's Abbey. He served the Benedictines in this position for many years. I was fortunate to visit with Abbot Owen in the early 1980s. I was a guest of Bishop Matthias at the abbey for a couple of days on one of his trips back from South America. I enjoyed sitting with the Abbot in his office and reminiscing about our days at Camp St. Maur and, specifically, his archery range.

On the last Saturday evening at the conclusion of each two-week camp session, there was a final bonfire meeting of all campers with a presentation of awards and honors. At this ceremony there was an award known as "Gentleman Camper" presented to one camper. The award consisted of a beautiful gold plaque on a walnut base. It was a highly coveted honor to receive this award since the honoree was selected by the staff of counselors, whom we all held in such high esteem.

Early one day in that last week at camp, I had a conversation in the snack bar with Brother Herbert about this award. He and I were alone there as I helped him stamp awards on camp T-shirts. He asked me who I thought deserved to get the Gentleman Camper award for the session. I mentioned a few names of campers I thought were especially deserving of it. He then asked me what year I had received the award. I could see a little half smile on his face when he asked the question and thought he was acting kind of funny. When I told him I had never received the award he said, "Really? Hmm..." The little smile was still there. This, to me, was an obvious hint I had already been selected. For the rest of the week, I was extremely busy finishing up my requirements for Chief and would be honored at the Saturday ceremony as one of only a handful of campers who had attained that level in the Indian hierarchy. But during that busy week, I had the recurring thought that I might also be honored with the coveted Gentleman Camper award. As the week wore on, I became more and more convinced Brother Herbert's little comment meant I had been selected.

Then, on Friday night, the night before the ceremony, something happened that I felt destroyed all at once any chance of me getting the award. It occurred after we went to bed that night in the

105

dormitory. After the room had become quiet and many of the campers had drifted off to sleep, I looked around carefully in the dark room. I didn't see any counselors patrolling between the lines of bunks, so I grabbed my pillow by one corner and swung it over the side of the top bunk whapping my lower bunkmate in the head as he drifted off to sleep. I immediately felt a large hand slap down on my back, pressing me against the mattress so that I could hardly breathe. I had been caught red-handed, and all I could think about was my hopes of receiving the Gentleman Camper award had been dashed in an instant by my impulsive act. I was reprimanded and told to knock off this foolishness and get to sleep.

The following day, Saturday, I moped around all day. I did look forward to being honored at the campfire as a new Chief. I had, just barely in time, completed all of the requirements. But I was also wondering who the lucky recipient of the beautiful Gentleman Camper plaque would be. I knew one thing—it wouldn't be me. That night at the campfire, I was in full Indian dress with my face painted and my newly completed Chief's war bonnet on. I was accepted by all of the other chiefs (who were all camp counselors) and allowed to smoke the Peace Pipe one last time. There was then an Indian dance performed by the Braves in my honor. The final item on the agenda of the evening, on the last night of my final year at camp, was presentation of the Gentleman Camper award. A bit of sadness came over me as I thought of the fact that I had completely blown my chance for this. Chief Herbert began the presentation by describing the various qualities of the person who would receive this award. As he spoke, there were a few things he mentioned that could have applied to me, but I discounted them immediately. But as he continued, he began to say more and more specific things, and I started to realize many of the campers were looking at me, nudging one another, and actually whispering my name. Then, to my total shock and surprise, Brother Herbert said, "David Crawley, please come forward." I felt as if I was in shock as I rose from the bench and walked toward him in the flickering light of the fire to accept this great honor. I have this beautiful plaque proudly displayed today, over 50 years later, on the wall of my study. I know no one else in the world can appreciate its significance as I do.

Returning home from camp each summer was always a bit of a culture shock for me. It took a few days to get back into the routine at

106

home and to accept my share of responsibilities. I didn't like my overnight loss of independence. Also, my good friends had gotten used to me being gone and, by the time I returned, they were hanging around with other kids; I had dropped off of their radar screens. So I had to sort of re-establish myself and worm my way back into their activities. I eventually got back into the usual routine of summer vacation, though, with the Wednesday Morning Movies, swimming at the public pool, riding bikes, roller skating, building forts, exploring up and down Brush Creek, and playing "cowboys and Indians" as well as "cops and robbers." Even after resuming my expected chores around the house, there was still plenty of time for all of these fun activities.

1955 – Disneyland opens in Anaheim, California – James Dean dies in a car accident – McDonald's Corporation founded – Rosa Parks refuses to give up her seat on a bus –

Chapter 20

When I entered sixth grade, I joined the Boy Scouts. By then I was 11 years old and had earned all of my Cub Scout badges over the previous three years. The St. Agnes troop was number 195. Boy Scouts, like Cub Scouts, has a series of badges you are expected to earn. It starts with Tenderfoot and culminates with the prestigious Eagle Scout award. Every scout was required to possess a Boy Scout Manual. This manual was a thick paperback book which opened with the Scout Motto—"Be Prepared"—and the Scout Oath, both of which had to be committed to memory. The manual, besides outlining the requirements for each badge, was packed with all kinds of practical information. Our troop had regular monthly meetings, usually in the evening. They were either in the school gymnasium or the basement of the church. We attended these meetings in uniform and started by standing at attention in formation and reciting the Pledge of Allegiance to the Flag. Announcements were made, and then we divided into groups for training and testing. The skills we were required to learn and demonstrate proficiency encompassed many practical things including first-aid, basic survival skills, knots, home repairs, swimming, camping, canoeing, cooking, and more. Many of the skills I learned in Boy Scouts, I still use today. At the end of each these meetings, we mustered into formation again to conclude each meeting with an evening prayer.

Besides our regular monthly troop meetings, we went, several times during the school year, on overnight campouts and on educational field trips. All these activities were organized and supervised by the volunteer scout leaders and their assistants. These dedicated dads were wonderful. I am sure I didn't appreciate them as much at the time as I do now. Most of these leaders, if not all, had sons who were in the troop, and they were probably volunteering their time in order to be able to spend more time with their offspring. No matter what their individual motives might have been, they all gave unselfishly of themselves to all of the scouts. I am sure I learned something of value from each of them.

I loved going on the organized overnight campouts. We usually met on Saturday morning in the school parking lot for these events. Each scout brought his camping gear in a wooden army footlocker.

These boxes held a lot of gear including a sleeping bag, a hatchet, a canteen, extra clothes, food, and cooking gear. A few of us usually shared an ice chest for any food which required refrigeration, such as meat. Tents, cots, shovels, and other larger miscellaneous pieces of equipment were owned by the troop. This gear was stored and transported to the camping areas in an old, Army-green laundry truck, usually driven by one of the older Explorer Scouts. Tall double doors in the rear opened into the cargo area. There were shelves from floor to ceiling on each side for all of the gear, with an aisle down the center. Volunteer drivers took the scouts and our supplies by car to the location of the campout, which was usually either in a big farm field on private land or in a public park outside of town. The drivers drove us right into the field where we unloaded our gear. It was always "car camping" since we never hiked any significant distance into a campsite. Boy Scouts in the Pacific Northwest, where I now live, would probably laugh at this and wouldn't even consider it real camping. I suspect when the troops in this area go out on an event like this, they backpack into the mountain backcountry which surrounds us here. Our campouts were in the flatlands of Kansas, and we had none of the lightweight, high-tech gear available today. There were no trails to hike in on, and, even if there had been, we wouldn't have been able to hike in since we always took a ton of stuff, including just about everything but the kitchen sink. Many of our troop leaders were military veterans of World War II or the Korean War, so our typical overnight camp was probably modeled after an Advanced Army Field Headquarters.

We all learned how to set up a camp, and much of the first day was spent doing this. The tents were big army surplus "wall" tents which were made of olive-green canvas. The four corners were staked down first, and then four stakes pounded in on each side a few feet away from the edge. The guy ropes from the top of each "wall" were looped around these stakes, and a "tautline hitch" tied to allow them to be cinched tight. The supporting poles were then taken inside, and one was placed at each end with an interconnecting ridge pole between them. This was a two-man job. Once the poles were up, a rope from the top of each pole was attached front and back, staked out, and tightened. The last step in constructing our temporary shelter for the weekend was to "ditch" it. This involved digging a trench around the outside of the tent at the foot of the canvas and channeling it

110

downslope, away from the tent. These tents did not have floors, so this served the same function as a rain gutter to direct any rain water away from the tent and keep the dirt floor from becoming wet and muddy. After all of the guy ropes were evenly tightened, we moved our cots, sleeping bags, and footlockers in. One of the footlockers was usually placed at one end to serve as a bedside table and a kerosene lantern placed on it for use after dark. Most of the scouts had their own lanterns, so there were usually enough of them around to have at least one in each tent. The scout leaders warned us repeatedly of the danger of fire if one of these lanterns were to tip over and the kerosene spill out. We seemed to heed these warnings pretty religiously, and none of the kids or tents got burned up.

After the tent was set up, we busied ourselves with trying to make our campsite fancier than anyone else's. We built a fire ring out of rocks, made potholders out of sticks, built chairs and benches out of dead timbers and logs, strung up clothes lines, and came up with a few other innovations. Spying on what was going on in some of our neighbors' camps often gave us new ideas.

We became fairly proficient at outdoor cooking over an open wood fire on these weekend campouts. I put together some tasty breakfasts of scrambled eggs, bacon, and potatoes—all fried up in a heavy iron skillet. Toasting bread was a little tricky on a fire grate, but with a little practice, it turned out pretty well. Lunches were often cold cuts or sandwiches. Evening meals ranged from hot dogs and hamburgers to steaks and baked potatoes. We baked potatoes and cooked carrots by wrapping them in aluminum foil and burying the packets in hot coals for 45 minutes to an hour. Baked beans, pork and beans, and other canned goods were favorites since they were easily prepared by piercing a hole in the top of the can and placing the can in the coals to heat its contents. Our brave leaders cautiously sampled the cuisine, and, if it was considered edible, signed us off on the various cooking requirements. I was initially horrified when embers from the fire popped into a pan of food or another scout accidently flipped some dirt into the pot. The leaders always assured us that this improved the flavors and gave our dishes a true outdoor seasoning. I believed them and watched them eat our dishes without hesitation.

We learned the practical use of a compass on some of these weekends by navigating a course which was set up as a treasure hunt with a prize at the end. This involved learning dead reckoning techniques by walking a compass course and counting paces to calculate distance. These are valuable life skills to have for anyone spending much time in the outdoors as I do, and are potentially lifesaving. The same type of activity is done as a sport by hundreds of people today. It is called "orienteering," but now it is often done with portable GPS navigation units. This seems like cheating to me since it does not require much in the way of basic dead reckoning skills. These electronic marvels, nevertheless, have probably already saved countless lives in the back country and are often accurate to within three feet or better. I hope Boy Scouts today are still taught the basics of using a compass and map.

We almost always got a chance on these camping weekends to practice tying the various knots we had learned. Rope is used in pitching tents, rigging a clothes line, getting deadwood down out of trees for firewood, suspending cooking pots over the fire, building a rope swing, etc. For every task requiring a rope, there is an appropriate knot. I still remember how to tie quite a number of the knots I learned over 50 years ago and have occasion to use a few of them every so often. I probably utilize the "square knot" most often since it is used to tie two ropes of equal diameter together, end to end. For tying two ropes together which are not the same diameters, a "sheetbend" is the appropriate knot. A "bowline" is used to make a loop that won't slip and change size. "Two half hitches" is for securing a rope around something, such as a pole, and this knot is often used to suspend something from a horizontal bar. A "clove hitch" is also used to tie a rope to a pole, but this knot prevents the loop from sliding along the pole if tension is applied at an angle   A "tautline hitch" is for making an adjustable loop that won't slip when it is under tension and is most frequently used for securing tent guy ropes to the tent stakes. A "sheepshank" is used for shortening a length of rope temporarily without cutting it. A "figure-eight" is used as a stop knot. I learned to tie a few other knots in Boy Scouts, but these are the ones I use on occasion and still remember well. Besides camping, I have found this knowledge of knots is essential in boating, fishing, and sailing. Knots are useful for many other things, from day to day chores around the house to horsemanship.

Most of our weekend campouts were planned for early autumn or spring. I particularly remember one campout that was a planned winter adventure. This activity was to be held at Camp Theodore

Nash, which was located near Bonner Springs, Kansas, approximately 20 miles from our school parking lot. As the weekend approached, the weather forecast did not look good with a major winter storm approaching the area indicating subfreezing temperatures and snow. There was some concern among the parents, but our scout leaders were undeterred, and we all met in the school parking lot as usual and headed off in carpools for Camp Nash. The camp is located in a remote area on a heavily forested hillside. We arrived late morning and got our camp set up. All went well until sometime after dark when a wild winter storm arrived in full force. The temperature dropped dramatically, heavy snow began falling, and strong, gusty winds blasted our camp.

My tent mate was Robert Beverlin. Robert and I had apparently done a good job of erecting the tent as it held up in the gale-force winds all night. I twisted the wick down on my kerosene lantern to extinguish the flame and hunkered into my sleeping bag for the night. Sleeping bags in those days were not the high-tech, polar-fleece-filled nylon bags available today. I had a single-layer, wool army-surplus bag with old blankets from home lining it for extra warmth. There was no floor in the tent, so each of us had an oilcloth ground cover between our bags and the bare ground. We hadn't been in there long when Robert started complaining of feeling sick. I at first thought he was fabricating this as a way of teasing me for the camp meal I had cooked and served earlier to him. Then he sat up suddenly and threw up the entire meal on the dirt floor of the tent. At this point I crawled out of my sleeping bag, put on my army-green parka, pulled the fur-lined hood around my head, tightened up the draw strings of the hood under my chin, and laced my combat boots. I then grabbed my flashlight and ventured out into the teeth of the storm. I made it to the leaders' tent and told them what had happened. I supposed one of them would have to try to get Robert to a hospital or drive him home.

Mr. Fortin dragged himself out of the tent and followed me to our tent. He stuck his head in the door and made a quick visual assessment of Robert. Robert told Mr. Fortin he was feeling very sick. Mr. Fortin didn't keep his head in the tent long. He told Robert he would try to see if he could get into Bonner Springs and get Robert some medicine to calm his upset stomach. We heard a car start, some tire spinning, and then the sound of its engine faded as Mr. Fortin ventured bravely down the steep road to the highway below. I went back into the tent and piled dirt over the disgusting mixture on the floor of the tent and held my breath until I was back inside my cocoon.

It seemed like several hours had gone by before Mr. Fortin arrived back at our tent with a bottle of pink Pepto-Bismol in hand. He had to wake us both up from a sound sleep. When he stuck his head through the door of the tent, his eyebrows were caked with snow and his teeth were chattering. Mr. Fortin had roused a pharmacist from his home in Bonner Springs by calling an emergency number he found on the door of a drug store. We asked him what time it was, and he told us it was a little after midnight. Robert thanked Mr. Fortin for making the trip for him, but he said he was feeling fine now and didn't want to take any of the medicine.

Mr. Fortin trudged off to the leaders' tent and we settled back down. The storm raged on throughout the night. There were a lot of campfires going at the first crack of dawn that morning. When we all arrived back at the snow-covered school parking lot Sunday afternoon, there was a mob of concerned and angry parents waiting for us. I don't think any of our folks put much trust in our scout leaders after that, but we scouts simply took it in stride. It was a memorable experience for us, and we all had a great time. For me, it was the one scout camping trip I remember in detail over 50 years later. I doubt if our troop leaders, and especially Mr. Fortin, shared the enthusiasm we all had for this great weekend outing.

Once each year, a three-day campout was scheduled for all of the scout troops in the area. This was a major event and was known as a Camporee. There was also a similar national event known as a Jamboree. The Jamboree was always held at Philmont Scout Ranch in New Mexico. I never got to go to the national Jamboree, but I did attend at least one Camporee. The size and scope of this camping event was enormous and reminded me of pictures I had seen of military encampments during the U.S. Civil War. The long weekend was a chance for scouts to have their skills tested, with contests pitting scout against scout, patrol against patrol, and troop against troop. Looking back on this, I am amazed at the courage and dedication of our volunteer scout leaders to undertake the organization of such an event. All of the kids seemed to have a great time and came away with positive experiences.

As I mentioned, there was a Boy Scout summer camp a few miles outside of Kansas City known as Camp Theodore Nash. This

114

was the same Camp Nash of our legendary winter campout adventure. I never attended summer camp there until I was too old to go to Camp St. Maur. So during the summer of 1959, I attended a one-week session at Camp Nash. It was completely different than Camp St. Maur, and I probably would have enjoyed it much more if I hadn't been comparing the two. The camp was located in a densely forested area. We lived in tents, with three to four scouts to a tent. They were semi-permanent structures erected on wooden platforms. All of the daily activities were oriented to completing requirements for ranks and merit badges. My rank that summer was Star scout, and I was working toward my next rank of Life. I concentrated on merit badges that would be difficult to get other than at camp because of the facilities, equipment, and instructors available there—like Swimming, Life Saving, Basketry, and Archery. I earned three more merit badges that week toward the rank of Life, but I didn't really have much fun and didn't return again. Some of my friends just loved their time at Camp Nash and returned year after year....but they hadn't been fortunate enough to experience life at Camp St. Maur.

I ended up quitting Boy Scouts the following year when I was in eighth grade. A lot of kids started feeling a little "nerdy" at that age if they were still in scouts. I was becoming aware of the existence of the female gender at about that point in my life, and this may have influenced this decision. I certainly didn't want to appear "geeky" or "nerdy," so I resigned. There were a lot of drop outs from scouting at that age. Many of my good friends did the same thing. I think this is one of the reasons there are so few Boy Scouts who attain the rank of Eagle—in addition to the fact the requirements are quite rigorous. I had earned all of the required merit badges for the rank of Life, but I quit before I received the badge. I have always had some twinges of regret that I didn't stick it out and complete the requirements for Eagle Scout because I have never liked the feeling which results from starting something and not finishing it. The ultimate goal in Boy Scouts is attainment of the rank of Eagle. I was fairly close to attaining that goal, and it is one segment of my life I left unfinished.

Scouts who have attained the age of 14 do have the option of continuing as Explorer Scouts and becoming members of a separate Explorer Post. They may choose to join the Sea Explorer Scouts or the Air Explorer scouts. The Explorers wear a different uniform, and the activities cater to interests of older boys. At the time I made my decision, only a few scouts were choosing that option, so I just separated myself completely from scouting. Although I will never be able to say I was an Eagle Scout, the skills and moral standards I learned from Boy Scouts have proved invaluable and have served me well throughout my life.

Chapter 21

When I was about nine or 10 years old, my dad's brother, Uncle Kenneth, gave me a gift subscription to a magazine called *Boys Life*. I had a subscription to it for the next several years. I enjoyed that magazine so much I read every word of it and couldn't wait for the next issue to arrive. The magazine was inspired by the Boy Scouts, and there was a lot of overlap between the articles in the magazine and the training I was receiving through scouting. I especially liked articles about backyard projects you could build with cardboard boxes and scrap lumber. It had wonderful illustrations and plans for everything you could imagine from building a "crystal" radio to constructing a treehouse.

One of my favorite articles in the magazine was entitled *A True Story of Scouts in Action*. It was an illustrated comic-book feature, describing some heroic feat, often lifesaving, performed by a boy scout. I envied the scouts in these stories and hoped someday I would be in the right place at the right time to demonstrate my superb skills and become a hero too. I imagined myself diving bravely into a freezing pond in the middle of winter to save a kid who had fallen through thin ice. I wanted to be the scout in one of those stories someday. That lucky moment never materialized for me, but I never stopped hoping.

When we first moved to the house in Fairway, Kansas, there was a public golf course located at the top of our block, just across West 53rd Street. We hadn't lived there for more than a couple of years when the golf course was sold to a developer, and a new residential development was planned and named *Fairway Manor*. When the builders started construction, my friends and I had a wonderful new source of building supplies from the scrap piles at each site. We filled our little red wagon with lumber cut-offs several times every weekend and were able to put together projects we had only previously dreamed of.

During the long summers, when I was not away at summer camp, I often had some kind of project I was working on. Some of these projects were inspired by Boys' Life magazine—such as a submarine I built in the backyard that had a periscope. The deck was enclosed by scraps of lumber panels we attached to one another and then staked into the ground to form a vertical wall. It was fashioned so it came to a point at the bow, just like a real vessel, and was square at the stern. Inside this deck enclosure was an assembly of large cardboard boxes tied together, and all connected with interior "hatches." It didn't really look like a submarine at all, but our imaginations compensated completely for that. A toy periscope extended through the top of the main compartment to scan for enemy ships. We played submarine for a few days, and when we got tired of it, we tore the project apart and designed something completely different. We had the most fun designing and building. The next project might be a fort—with walls to keep out Indians and a lookout tower made from a stepladder with a plywood platform attached to the top.

Mohawk Lane continued north across 53rd street now and into the new housing development where the golf course had been. One of the first new houses to be occupied along that new extension of our street was the Davis home. Nick Davis transferred into our school and was in my fifth grade class. Nick was quite a gregarious little fellow. He and I made acquaintance and started hanging out together at school and at home. His house was a quick bike ride up the street and, for the rest of our grade school days, we were pals and could usually be found together at either his house or at our house. Nick quickly developed the reputation in school of being a total genius. I don't know what the exact definition of a genius is, but of all the people I have known, Nick is probably at the top in innate intelligence. Nick not only got straight "A"s in school, but he had an amazing mechanical aptitude. Nick's father had a mechanical mind as well and always encouraged us and assisted with our projects.

One of the first projects Nick and I worked on together was a mechanical robot we built for the Kansas City Science Fair. If we won, we would get to take our entry to the National Science Fair. The robot stood about five feet tall on wooden legs below a silver oil-drum body. It moved its arms rhythmically up and down, thanks to Mr. Davis's barbecue spit motor which was bolted into the inside of the steel thorax. The robot's arms had clothespins for fingers so he could hold things in his "hands." Rex, as we had named our new mechanical friend, had a tin can for a head with eyes that were light bulbs. He had a speaker mounted behind slits which served as his mouth, so he talked when one of us surreptitiously spoke into a remote microphone with a deep metallic voice. He was also equipped to play music through the same speaker by connection with a record turntable. One of the hit 45 RPM tunes of the day that Rex, to our delight, spouted out over and over again was *My Friend the Witch Doctor.*

The amplifier we used for Rex's sound system was built from a Heath Kit. I had found the kit at Burstein-Applebee and Company's electronic store in Kansas City and meticulously assembled it. This involved deciphering rather complex electrical schematics and soldering hundreds of electrical connections together. If you looked beneath the case of this little unit, you would see a spaghetti-network tangle of multicolored wires connected to resistors, capacitors, and sockets for cathode-ray tubes. I had no idea what I was doing, and when I finished, I was shocked it actually worked and provided a loud booming voice for Rex. When my little amplifier was turned on, it always reached an impressive operating temperature. In fact, it probably could have been used to heat our entire classroom at school.

Rex also had a heart. We cut a heart-shaped opening on the left side of the tin thorax and installed a light socket with a blinking red bulb inside the opening. The kids in our class were amazed and ecstatic over Nick's and my creation. I think I might have even been getting some credit for possibly being a previously unrecognized genius just because of my association with Nick and the robot project. I don't think our teacher was nearly as impressed with Rex as the kids were, and the judges at the science fair were even less impressed. It wasn't really an original idea, an important factor in judging a science project. I had gotten the idea and actual plans for it from an article I had seen in Boys Life magazine. It also didn't really demonstrate any scientific principal, another important quality for a good entry.

No school today would even allow this project to come through the doors. It had 110 volt electrical wires running through a highly conductive steel oil drum to open screw terminals for light bulbs. It amazes me now to think that no one at the time voiced the slightest concern about the safety of the children surrounding this hazardous contraption. I'm now surprised no one got fried. Nick and I were probably the most likely to be electrocuted, but it could have been any of the kids who came to the Science Fair. Even though we didn't impress any judges or win a prize, we impressed the heck out of our classmates, and Nick and I got something out of the whole thing. With the patient help from Nick's dad, we had honed our nuts and bolts mechanical skills a little with this project. We didn't realize it at the time, but that was just the beginning.

I always wanted to build a great treehouse, and Boys Life magazine had some wonderful designs from time to time. We had lot of trees in our yard, but none of them was quite right for a good treehouse. But the Hokinson boys—Eddie, Ricky, David, and Steven—lived on Pawnee, the next block over, and had a treehouse rivaling the one in the movie *Swiss Family Robinson*. It was like a little vacation cabin perched way up in a big cottonwood tree. It even had a covered front porch with a trap door in it for the rope ladder. The ladder could be pulled up when everyone was up there. It even had an electrical wire running from the house for lights.

I had always heard that no one was ever allowed to go up into the Hokinson treehouse except for the Hokinson boys themselves. I'm sure that was their father's rule for safety. I occasionally went over to the Hokinson's house to play. David was just a little younger than I and Rick just a little older. We were all in Boy Scouts together, and the troop's equipment truck—the old green laundry truck—was always at their house. Whenever I was there, I just ached to go up in the treehouse.

One day when I was at the Hokinson's, they were all going up and down the rope ladder to the treehouse, and I got up the nerve to ask Eddie, the oldest boy, if I could go up. I figured he was the only one who could give me permission since he was like the boss of all of them when his parents weren't around. I had never heard of anyone else ever being allowed to go up, but I thought I'd give it a shot. To my utter shock and disbelief, he approved it. Eddie and Ricky were both up in the treehouse, and David was at the bottom to help me start up the rope ladder. Well, I was totally embarrassed by the fact that I couldn't, despite lots of coaching, climb the rope ladder. I got on the first rope rung, but every time I tried to advance to the second step my legs and the rope went completely horizontal. I couldn't keep my body and the ladder in a vertical position and couldn't figure out how to climb it. I was about to give up when I heard Eddie say from way up above me, "just hold on tight." I looked up to see him squatting astraddle the trap door and pulling the 20-foot ladder up hand over hand with me dangling from the bottom rung. When I got within an arm's length of the opening, Ricky grabbed the ropes and Eddie let go of them. Eddie bent over the opening and extended his hands toward me. He told me to let go of the rope and grab his wrists. I grabbed his wrists, and his hands grabbed my wrists in a kind of interlock. He then simply straightened up from crouched position and plopped me into the treehouse. I never looked down until I was safely aboard, but when I did, it caused a little chill to go up and down my spine. It was a long way to the ground. They dropped the ladder for David, he scampered up, and they all stood there grinning at me. I looked at Eddie Hokinson and noticed his bulging biceps for the first time. He was one strong kid.

They then gave me the treehouse tour. It was basically one large room. The main trunk of the tree came up through the floor and out through the shingled pitched roof. The room had windows on all sides with no glass, but they had shutters that hinged down from the top inside to shut out the weather. There was an open front porch with the trap door in the floor from which the rope ladder was extended for entry and exit.

There was another separate platform located 10 or 15 feet above the main structure with 2" x 4" lumber strips nailed to a hefty branch as steps to it. They called it the "crow's nest." I watched Ricky scamper out the window and up the precarious steps to the crow's nest. He said this was where they positioned their lookouts and welcomed me to climb up and join him. I declined his invitation; it was a little too scary for me!

When I left the treehouse, I had no problem getting down. I just shinnied down the rope ladder without trying to use the rungs. That was the one and only time I was ever in the Hokinson treehouse, and I don't know to this day whether any other non-Hokinson was bestowed with such an honor. I have always cherished the memory of that day.

When Ricky Hokinson was in high school, he started working during the summer in the lumber mill his dad owned. One day he got his right hand and forearm caught in one of the milling machines. His hand and forearm were amputated just below the elbow. The first time I saw him after the accident, he had a stainless steel hook for a hand. It had spring pincers on it he used to grasp and hold things. I felt sorry for Ricky because of the loss of his hand, but he didn't seem to let it bother him at all. All of those Hokinson boys were great kids.

1956 – Elvis Presley makes his debut on the Ed Sullivan Show – The Hungarian Revolution puts the world on edge – The TV Remote Control is invented (attached by a wire to the TV) – Velcro is introduced – Eisenhower and Nixon are re-elected for a second term – A new Chevy Bel Air (with a padded dash for safety) cost $2025 –

Chapter 22

I will never forget a day, when I was 12 years old, on which I decided I was about as happy and content as anyone could possibly be. It was a crisp fall day, and the leaves in Kansas City had started to turn golden. I had ridden my bike to the grounds of the old Shawnee Indian Mission, which was located three blocks from our house. There are three brick buildings on the grounds that had been built as a school for the Shawnee Indian children in 1839. The buildings had been turned into a museum that was, and still is, open to the public. Most of the surrounding grounds consisted of rolling lawn, maintained by a caretaker who lived with his wife in one of the buildings. There was a small wooded area back in one corner of the property that was my destination on that particular fall day. The Hokinson boys and I had built a fort in the center of the copse of trees. We constructed the fort by digging a fairly large hole in the ground and then covering it with tree branches and leaves which served as a roof and camouflage. We had even carved out some steps at the entry which led down into our subterranean den.

When I arrived at the mission, I looked around carefully for the caretaker. He was a lanky older gentleman with white hair, who didn't seem to care too much for kids. He was quite sour, and he always chased us off when he saw us heading for the woods. We usually saw him on a big Allis-Chalmers tractor pulling an extensive array of reel-type mowers as he mowed the grass on the mission grounds. I was feeling pretty brave that day to be sneaking into the woods by myself, but the old codger was nowhere in sight, and I made it safely into the shelter of the trees without a problem. When I got to the fort, I found that the old guy had discovered our hideout and cleared all the branches of the fort's roof and partially filled in the hole we had dug.

I was, at first, crestfallen with this discovery. It didn't take me long to recover though, and I set about rebuilding the fort almost immediately. I found a Boy Scout folding camp shovel we had left there, partially buried in the rubble. I spent the entire afternoon digging the hole back out, cutting new branches for the roof, and totally restoring the fort to its original grandeur. As I worked, I stopped a few times to smell the wonderful fall air and to take in my surroundings. It is hard to describe the feeling I experienced that day.

It was a mixture of self-confidence, independence, and the sense I was capable of almost anything. I thought about the fact that I was no longer a child and, with my bike, could go anywhere I wanted. No one seemed to be keeping close track of me, and that independent feeling, even if somewhat of a fantasy, was wonderful. I consciously thought about the fact that I didn't yet have the worries and responsibilities of an adult. I knew that in a short time I would have to deal with the whole thing about girls, dating, and all kinds of other issues which would complicate my life. But on that afternoon, I had an overall euphoric feeling about myself and my life and decided that 12 years old was the best age a person could ever be. I wished that day I could stay 12 forever.

Chapter 23

I was 12 years old and in seventh grade when I heard about Doug Rollert's homemade car. I wanted to see it. Having a little car with a motor on it at that age was pretty cool. I liked my bike, but it seemed like this would be the next logical step up in transportation. So one warm spring afternoon, Doug and I rode our bikes from school over to his house. Doug lived in an area of modest older homes to the north of the new Fairway Manor development, probably a couple of miles from our house.

When we got to Doug's house, no one was home since both of his parents worked. We went into the kitchen for a snack, and Doug quickly drank a quart of milk directly from the bottle. I was shocked when he opened the door of the refrigerator and I saw that it held more bottles of milk than I had ever seen in one place except for the milkman's truck. I asked him why they had so much milk, and he just laughed and said he and his older brother, Garrick, drank a lot of milk. Both he and his brother were big tall kids and later, in high school, both of them played center on the basketball team. His brother Garrick's nickname was, in fact, "Bones." Their mother was a small woman, and their father was average size. Since that day, I have always thought those guys grew to be so tall because of the protein, calcium, and vitamin D in all that milk they drank.

Doug's car was inside the single-car garage next to the house. We opened the overhead door and pulled it out into the driveway. It was painted white with red flames artistically added, starting at the pointed front end and extending toward the rear so as to surround the driver's seat. It was basically a plywood platform that tapered to a point at the front.

There was a large, vertical steel bolt through the point at the front which served as the pivot for the front axle. The axle itself was a two-by-four piece of lumber with a groove in the underside for a steel rod which connected the front wheels. There was a six-foot loop of heavy, hemp rope with its ends stapled to the ends of the two-by-four axle. This rope served as the steering control, like the reins on a horse-drawn wagon. There was a small rectangular piece of plywood mounted vertically for a seatback behind the driver's position.

Behind the seatback, there was a gasoline washing machine motor mounted on the left side. It had a fan belt linking a centrifugal clutch on the end of the engine crankshaft to a large pulley bolted to the left rear wheel. A wire cable was attached to the throttle control arm on the engine and was routed to a foot pedal so the driver could control acceleration. There was a two-by-four mounted above the right rear wheel with an old gate hinge. It extended forward so the end of it was just under Doug's right elbow when he was in position. It had a screen-door spring attached to the top of it and to the seat back to keep it from riding on the tire until it was needed as a brake. When Doug pressed his elbow down on the end of this piece of lumber, the spring stretched and allowed it to come in contact with the rubber on the rear wheel providing a braking mechanism.

I was so impressed. What a machine! I was already starting to think about how I might go about finding a washing machine motor.

Doug and I topped off the gas tank from a red metal gas can and checked the oil. Doug grabbed the starter rope and stuffed it in a pocket. We pulled the car by the steering ropes across the street to the paved playground of the old red-brick Roseland Public Grade School. School was over for the day, and it appeared everyone was gone. We had the whole place to ourselves. The school was surrounded by a great big parking lot surrounded by a six-foot chain-link fence.

Doug wrapped the starting rope around the starting spool and gave it a pull. After fooling around with the choke a bit, and after three or four pulls on the rope, the little engine fired up. I asked Doug how fast his car would go. He said he thought it would get up to 35 or 40 miles per hour, but he wasn't really sure. He jumped into position and told me to hop on behind the seat, on the right side—between the engine and the brake board. I got on and positioned myself in a kneeling position in this little space which was about 18 inches square. I grabbed the back of the seat, and Doug tromped on the accelerator pedal. We took off careening at a breath-taking speed around the playground. I couldn't believe how fast we were going, and I had a hard time staying on in the turns. I was also concerned about being thrown against the hot motor, which was just inches from my left arm and leg.

We had done several laps when Doug got a little wide on one of his turns, hit a patch of sand, skidded out of control, and crashed into the chain-link fence. When the car hit the fence, it pushed the bottom of the fence up and outward. The car went under it along with Doug's legs. The pointed prongs on the bottom of the fence scraped all the way up Doug's legs to above his knees, trapping him under the fence. I crashed against the seatback, but was unscathed. Doug started screaming for me to get him out. I had to run down to a gate so I could get on the other side of the fence and lift it off of his legs. I ran back along the outside of the fence, listening to Doug's anguished screams as I ran. I got back to the scene of the wreck and leaned down and pulled as hard as I could to lift the fence upward and outward off of Doug's bloody legs. It was just enough room for him to wriggle out.

We got the car out too and pulled it back to his house. Doug called his mother at work, and she came tearing home. In the meantime, we pulled off his pants and cleaned up his bloody wounds as best as we could until his mother got there. By the time she got home, he had stopped crying. Doug's injuries looked much worse than they were. All of the cuts were fairly superficial, and none of them required sutures. He was in a little trouble with his folks at that point though, and he wasn't supposed to operate his car after that without an adult around. It's a good thing his mom and dad didn't know that Doug occasionally drove the car on the street after that—even driving all the way over to my house on occasion—probably passing cars and trucks on the way as if they were standing still!

It didn't take me long to relate this story to Nick. He was immediately interested. We had a number of hurdles right away. The biggest of these was finding an engine. We thought a washing machine motor would be perfect, so we started looking for one. If we had lived out in the country somewhere without electrical service we probably could have found one. But it seemed no one in our area had seen a gasoline washing machine motor for years. A lawnmower engine might work too. The problem was most lawnmowers were the rotary style with a vertical shaft. This meant we had to figure out a way to couple a vertical drive shaft to the horizontal shaft the wheels were mounted on. The only type of lawnmower that would solve this problem was a reel-type mower which did have a horizontal crankshaft. A reel-type mower engine would work.

Well, it just so happened my father had purchased the exact type of lawnmower we were looking for a few months before. It was a reel-type, self-propelled mower manufactured by a company called "Pincor." My dad bought this odd-ball mower because he thought it

127

was safer to operate than a more modern rotary type. My Uncle Gus had bought a rotary mower and promptly cut off one of his toes with it the first time he used it. This mishap convinced my father that rotary lawn mowers were extremely dangerous. Since his Pincor operated similarly to his old mechanical push mower, he assumed it was a safer choice. It didn't take him long to discover that the reason most people bought rotary mowers was the fact that they cut the grass much better. But at the time Nick and I were trying to figure out a way to commandeer the Pincor and use its power plant to propel our car, we were afraid the mower was a little too new and my father had not yet lost his enthusiasm for the new machine.

My dad had no idea there were any plans for his new lawnmower other than to mow the lawn with it on weekends. Dad really knew little about any of my projects or activities, but Nick's dad, Mr. Davis, was involved in almost all of our engineering experiments. He agreed with us that we needed that Pincor for our car. Mr. Davis seemed at times to be vicariously re-living his childhood through Nick and me. He went on a lot of our Boy Scout outings as an additional volunteer leader, attended all of our school functions, and spent most weekends with us. Mr. Davis made the suggestion that maybe the Pincor could serve a dual purpose as a lawn mower and power plant for our car. Nick and I were quite puzzled, but he then explained a design feature that would allow the lawn mower frame to slide into a sandwich-like affair at the rear of the car. His idea allowed the lawnmower frame to slide out after removal of four carriage bolts. It was then just a matter of re-mounting the handle and controls, and the Pincor was transformed back into a lawnmower—voila!

Nick and I decided it might be best to approach my mother with Mr. Davis's idea and see if we could talk her into being our negotiator. She was generally supportive of anything that kept us busy and wasn't likely to burn the house to the ground (and it is a miracle that never happened). She brought our case to my father who, putting it mildly, did not initially share our enthusiasm for the project. After several days of negotiations, she was able to broker a deal in which Nick and I would have to make the lawnmower conversion whenever the lawn needed mowing and would moreover be required to mow the lawn on a regular basis throughout the mowing season. My father absolutely hated any kind of yard work, especially mowing, since he also had little patience or understanding for any kind of mechanical apparatus. So when he finally put his stamp of approval on our project, he remained skeptical, but the thought of no more yard work clouded his better judgment.

We immediately started scrounging together the other parts we needed to build our car. We got a sheet of plywood, some two-by-fours, a steel rod for the front axle, and took two wheels off of our little red wagon to use for the front wheels. The car came together nicely. Mr. Davis stopped down at our house and supervised when he could on weekends. We used two lengthwise two-by-fours underneath the plywood platform to strengthen it and to attach to the underside of the lawnmower frame. The plywood slid over the frame to form the top of the sandwich. In order to accommodate the two-by-fours, we had to cut two slots in the front of the lawnmower where it had a downward flare. We also had to drill four holes through the metal frame for carriage bolts that effectively clamped the sandwich-affair together. We thought it best not to mention these modifications of the lawnmower to my father. When we got it all together, we rigged up a gear shift mechanism using a stiff wire through the seat-back to a lever next to the driver's position. We rigged another wire through the seat-back for a throttle control and fashioned a little handle on the end of it.

As we approached the final stages of construction, the anticipation of the first test drive had reached a fever pitch. It was finally ready to go. Even before the first test drive, we were a little disappointed in a few of our car's features, especially compared to Doug's "rocket car." The front end of our car was squared off rather than coming to a sleek point like Doug's. And our car was quite a bit wider than Doug's because we built it for two people, driver and passenger, sitting side by side. There was an awkward-looking two by four sticking a couple of feet out in front for mounting of the steerable front axle. We consoled ourselves that this actually made it look a little bit like a dragster. But whatever "coolness" our little car had was lost if you looked at it from behind. It had lawnmower blades and a grass roller between the rear wheels. We had removed the drive chain for the blades so they wouldn't operate when we drove the car. If we hadn't done that, we could have actually driven the car around the yard and mowed the grass at the same time. These minor deficiencies were overshadowed by our excitement to take the first test drive.

All of the construction on the car had been accomplished at our house. The day finally came when we pulled it out of the garage and

Nick and I posed on it for pictures. When my mother felt she had enough pictures, we set the choke and the throttle for start, I wrapped the starter rope around the start spool, and then gave it a smooth pull. The little engine fired right up. I agreed to let Nick steer, and I sat on his right and managed the gear shift and throttle. When I pushed the shifter forward and engaged the chain drive to the wheels, we immediately took off at the speed a person normally walks. Somewhere along the line, we had forgotten the fact that this machine was geared to propel itself at a speed no greater than a person could walk since it was, after all, a lawnmower. It did have a two-speed transmission though, and within a few seconds I had already moved the shift lever to the high-gear position. This was a little better. We now were going along at the speed of a brisk walk. Our driveway was fairly level near the garage, but about half-way to the street it sloped steeply downhill. When we started down the slope, we thought we would gain some speed, but we found the engine compression was enough to keep us from gaining much speed even on the down slope. We quickly forgot worries we had about having no brakes installed. We turned left onto the street at the bottom of the driveway and drove it up to the top of the block and back. This took at least 10 minutes, just as it would if we had walked up and back. My sisters stood in the driveway watching all this with great excitement. For Nick and me though, it was a bit of a letdown. We were happy we hadn't invited Doug Rollert over to watch this trial run.

Despite the fact our little car probably didn't go as fast as Sister Lucille's electric wheel chair, we had fun building it. And over the next few days, we had fun playing with it. I would drive it the two blocks up to Nick's house; he'd keep it for a couple of days and then drive it back down to our house.

One day we were tinkering with the car when Nick told me he had an idea that would at least triple the car's speed. He had been thinking about this quite a bit, and after he got through explaining it to me, it just confirmed in my mind what a genius he was. Nick had noticed the blades on the lawnmower turned much faster than the wheels. This was due to the fact that the blades were driven by a separate chain-drive sprocket which was larger, and had more teeth, than the sprocket which drove the wheels. He actually had counted the teeth on both sprockets and calculated how much our cruising speed would be multiplied if we were to switch the two sprocket positions on the drive shaft and use the blade drive sprocket to drive the wheels. The actual switching of the two sprockets required driving pins out of them, reversing their positions on the shaft, and then adding some chain links to the drive chain so it would reach around the larger sprocket. It took us a few hours to make the conversion. The resulting change in performance was dramatic. When we shifted into gear, the front wheels almost lifted off the ground and both of our heads snapped back. When we shifted into high gear, we were probably hitting 15 miles per hour. Although Doug's car, with its washing machine motor, could probably still run circles around us, we both felt this was respectable performance. Since the car could go almost as fast as we cruised on our bikes, we started using it for transportation. I drove it up to the hardware store, a distance of about six blocks, a couple of times. I even drove it over to Steve Hudson's house once or twice which was probably a couple of miles and involved driving on some fairly busy streets. This was, of course, completely illegal, and I'm not sure my parents or Nick's parents knew this was going on.

At some point that summer, Nick and I noticed the grass was getting long and needed mowing. We both realized that converting the guts of our little car back into a Pincor lawnmower would not be the simple task we had alleged during our negotiations with my father. We had made so many modifications to the original lawnmower by then that the conversion would involve much more than the removal of four

131

bolts and replacing the handle. Nick and I worried about this, but before we had started tearing our car apart to make the conversion, a brand new rotary lawn mower showed up in the garage. I suspect my mother had something to do with my dad's decision to purchase a new mower. I think she saw what a good time we were having and couldn't bear to see us disassemble it. Nick and I weren't allowed to operate the new mower. It was, after all, the same type Uncle Gus had cut his toe off with. So for the rest of the summer, it wasn't unusual to see my father mowing the lawn with his new mower while Nick and I tinkered with the Pincor in the driveway. The new rotary mower did a much better job on the lawn, but, despite this improvement, Dad seemed a little grumpy for the rest of that summer.

Once my father had completely relinquished ownership of the Pincor, Nick and I were free to make other badly-needed modifications which would permanently prevent the machine from ever mowing another blade of grass. We took the blades out first since having a car with lawnmower blades had been somewhat of an embarrassment. We then removed the grass roller at the back of the mower housing. This created a new problem since there was now minimal clearance between the rear corners of the mower housing and the pavement. The roller had prevented these corners from scraping the concrete. We solved that problem by renting a cutting torch and removing those sections of the housing on both sides. Mr. Davis supervised this operation closely to keep us from burning the house down, my mother's greatest fear. After this last modification, the Pincor's days as a lawnmower were officially over.

One day, not long after we had changed the drive sprockets and increased the speed of the car, I was driving home from the hardware with Steve Hudson as my passenger and had a catastrophic engine failure. Apparently the new gear ratio was more than the little engine could withstand and the connecting rod, which links the piston to the crankshaft, snapped and actually came through the side of the crankcase. While Steve and I were stopped in the street assessing the damage, a Fairway Police car pulled up behind us and turned on his flashing red lights. The patrolman was quite serious and informed us that we were in big trouble. Steve and I were shaking in our boots and were hoping we wouldn't have to call our folks to bail us out of the Fairway jail. He finally agreed to let us off with a warning if we agreed to refrain from driving our car on the street in the future. By the time we had pulled the car back to our house, Steve and I were feeling pretty dejected.

The next weekend, Nick brought his dad down to assess the damage. Under his guidance, we took the engine completely apart. We found what Mr. Davis suspected—a broken connecting rod. We ordered the parts we needed from Pincor and, when they arrived, rebuilt the engine. We screwed a little copper plate over the hole in the side of the crankcase, and it always leaked a little oil after that. The engine ran great after we got it back together, though, and we were euphoric. The euphoria didn't last long. After a few more trips, the engine threw another rod, and we were again out of business.

Not long after our final engine failure, Nick's dad bought him a real, commercially-made Go-Kart powered by a McCullough chainsaw engine. Mr. Davis put it in the back of the car and took us up to the school playground on weekends to drive it. Nick and I took turns racing it around the asphalt. The Go-Kart was built on a tubular steel frame, had a good steering system, and had four-wheel disk brakes. It was well-built, went incredibly fast, and was very fun to drive. Despite all this, I don't think Nick and I ever had as much fun with his new, factory-built Go-Kart as we did with the one we built ourselves. Our little car taught us, among other things, how an internal combustion engine works. We learned this by taking the engine completely apart and putting it back together. Nick and I both became life-long tinkerers and do-it-yourselfers. I have never been afraid to take something apart to try to figure out why it is not operating properly. There have been a few times when I regretted tackling one job or another and should have left it up to a professional. But as I have gotten older, I have gotten wiser and more selective whenever I think about popping the back off of an appliance, for example. Still, the lure of the mechanical still tantalizes me, and the satisfaction I get out of fixing a problem myself sometimes pushes me to test the limits of my abilities one more time.

Nick's dad, Mr. Davis, used to advise us both, "If it ain't broke – don't fix it." Nick and I joked that our motto was, "If it ain't broke – fix it 'til it is."

1957 – The Soviet satellite "Sputnik" is launched and the space age begins – The governor of Arkansas uses the National Guard to prevent de-segregation of Little Rock High -

Chapter 24

At some point during the same year we built the car, I began thinking about getting a job. I was 13 years old and thought my independence might be enhanced by increasing the balance in my savings account. What I really had in mind was buying some tools of my own. Whenever Nick and I had a project, like the car, we always used his dad's tools. My dad did have a hammer, a pair of pliers, a monkey wrench, and a couple of screwdrivers; that was about it. I had seen a Craftsman socket wrench set at the Sears Roebuck store on the Plaza. It had a really cool reversible ratchet handle, came in a gray sheet-metal tool box with a handle on top, and was similar to Mr. Davis's set. It was expensive, though, and I knew I needed a lot of other tools too. I didn't just need mechanic tools. I wanted to get some woodworking tools as well, and I didn't even have enough money for the socket set.

One evening late in the summer while we were all sitting around the table after dinner, I started quizzing my parents about how I might find a job—not a full-time job, of course, but one I could do during the summer, after school, and on weekends. My dad sort of scoffed at the idea. He couldn't understand why I wanted a job, and besides, I wouldn't even be legal to have a job until I was 14. That really deflated me. I didn't know anything about child labor laws, but my mother got into it with him and pointed out that she knew lots of exceptions. It was not surprising to me that my mother jumped in on my side. She had always encouraged me to do extra chores around the house, and she occasionally paid me for the work if it was anything significant. She also hired me out a few times to do odd jobs for neighbors and friends, and I liked those opportunities to earn some money. Anyway, my mom kept the conversation going in the right direction that night, and one of several suggestions she had was that I try to get a paper route. My dad then spouted out a bunch of mumbo-jumbo about newspaper distributors paying large sums of money to purchase the routes they owned and said they rarely changed hands. He pointed out that I certainly didn't have money to do that and then added that I wasn't even old enough to drive. The girls drifted off, one by one, until it was just the three of us at the table. The subject of my employment gradually heated up into a fairly lively argument which I watched from the sidelines. I finally got up and slipped out of the room as well.

My mother and I talked about this issue, now just between the two of us, over the next few days. We both did some checking, and it appeared my dad's assertion about paper routes was probably true for the main newspapers in town—the morning *Kansas City Times* and the evening *Kansas City Star*—but there was a much smaller newspaper on our side of the state line called the *Kansas City Kansan*. This paper actually contracted with an army of paper boys to distribute it on their bicycles. My mother did a little snooping and found out the son of a friend of hers had the contract for a large area that included our neighborhood. It just so happened the kid had done it for a couple of years, was tired of it, and was ready for someone else to take it over. And, just like that, I had my first real job!

I had a great bike for a paper route. It was what we called an "English" bike. My first bike had been one of the old fat-tire, one-speed bikes. It was a real tank, but had served as my transportation for several years, and I hadn't known anything better. When I turned 12 years old, my Uncle Kenneth, for my birthday, gave me a brand new, bright red, light-weight Schwinn bike with a three speed gear system and caliper hand brakes. It was quite expensive and was state-of-the art at the time. Bikes were measured by the size of their wheels in those days and mine was a 26-incher. It fit me well. That bike was light-years ahead of my old bike, and I loved it. With its sleek design, skinny tires, and light-weight frame, it was just like racing bikes I had seen. One of the accessories Uncle Kenneth bought for me was a speedometer, and I had fun seeing how high I could get the needle. The speedometer also had an odometer mileage window that tracked total mileage, just like a car odometer. I had wire baskets mounted on either side of the rear wheel for my school books and, with my new job, for the rolled-up newspapers for delivery.

The kid whom I was replacing on the paper route went with me every day for the first week to teach me the ropes. He told me which houses had loose dogs to watch out for, which customers were hard to collect from, which ones wanted the paper placed on the front porch, which ones were nice, and which ones were just plain ornery to deal with. On these check-out rides, it seemed like my mentor was extremely competent and knew just about everything there was to know about the newspaper business. It turned out that he had very few customers over a long route. Later, after I got to know some of the customers, I found out why. Quite a few of his customers had stopped the paper because he had been a somewhat unreliable paper boy. Also, he apparently hadn't put much effort into signing up new customers, and this was expected of all carriers. As a result, the number of customers had decreased significantly during his tenure, and when I took over the route, I started with a total of 18 customers. These customers were spread over a large geographical area, and I probably pedaled my bike 10 miles every day to deliver those 18 papers. The paper was an evening edition six days per week, with a morning edition on Sundays. The cost of a subscription was 25 cents per week, collected by me every Wednesday.

Not long after I nailed down this first job, my friend Steve Hudson found a similar deal. He got the contract for another *Kansas City Kansan* paper route as well. His area was about the same geographical size as mine, but he started out with about 80 customers. He actually had several customers on every block on his route. It was a much better deal.

I was excited to have this job and the responsibility that went with it. The compensation was not great, and here is the way it worked. Every day when Steve and I came out of school, there was a greasy, sleazy-looking guy waiting for us with a stack of papers for each of us. He drove an old junk-heap Nash Rambler, and the back seat was always stacked to the ceiling every day with the latest edition of the paper, hot off the press. This guy always had a cigarette hanging out of his mouth, and he looked and talked like a mobster. We had to make a payment to him every week for our papers. We did this from the proceeds of our Wednesday collections. He also sold big boxes of rubber bands to us which we placed around the papers after we rolled them. On rainy days, he had a supply of brown waxed paper to wrap around each newspaper. We had to buy the waxed paper too. These items were added to our weekly bills. My net profit worked out to about three dollars per week after I had signed up a bunch of new customers and was throwing about 30 papers each day. Until then, I had barely been breaking even.

Steve and I sat on the concrete steps at the corner of St. Agnes School and rolled our papers and placed them in our bike baskets. Sometimes the mobster guy hung around while we prepared our papers and berated us for not signing up more new customers. Steve and I hated it when he did that because, otherwise, we enjoyed that time we had to talk to each other before heading out in different directions on our routes.

Neither snow nor rain nor heat nor gloom of night stays these couriers from the swift completion of their appointed rounds.

Steve and I didn't realize it, but we had it easy as far as the weather went during those first few weeks at our new jobs. Even the occasional rainy days weren't too bad while the fall temperatures were still moderate. Rain in Kansas City usually manifests itself as intermittent showers. Sudden downpours are more common than continuous, steady, soaking rain. We couldn't ride our bikes well in our yellow rain slickers, and so we didn't wear them. As far as rain gear goes, waterproof coated nylon jackets had not been invented yet. Breathable Gortex fabric appeared decades later. So when I was on my route and got caught in a downpour, I got soaked unless I was able to find shelter under a leafy shade tree, a customer's front porch, or beneath a bridge.

As fall transitioned to winter, the days got shorter and the mercury dropped. The weather became more of an impediment to the "swift completion of our appointed rounds." I got a "generator light" for my bike since it was starting to get dark by the time I reached home, and always on collection day. The generator light worked off of a little wheel against the front tire and was nice since it didn't require any batteries, but it went out whenever I stopped my bike, and I was in the dark until I started pedaling again. So I had to be careful to be well off to the side when I stopped so I wouldn't get whacked by a driver who couldn't see me.

Steve was a little tougher than I was with regard to the weather. When the temperatures dropped into the twenties and teens, or if snow was falling, I sometimes rode home with my papers and asked my mother to drive me along the route. If she was home, I never seemed to have much trouble talking her into being my chauffer. If it was a really nasty day, I could sometimes coerce her into driving Steve on his route too. Our family car was a 1958 model brown and white Dodge station wagon with big dramatic tail fins—the latest style. I sat in the third seat, which faced the rear, and threw the papers out the rear tailgate window. This was ideal since it allowed me to throw papers to both sides of the street. I never once thought of what it would do to my profit margin if I had to reimburse my mother for the fuel she burned on these excursions, but I don't believe she ever brought up the point. By the time spring weather arrived, my mother had driven our routes enough that she knew where every customer lived. That was good because I think there were a couple of days when I had the flu or some other illness, and she had to go solo.

Loose dogs on my route frequently added a little excitement to my day. There were probably leash laws in our area, even in the 1950s, but there was no enforcement. Everyone just let their dogs run loose. I wasn't too afraid of most of the dogs on my route, and, if a serious chase started, I pedaled really fast and was usually able to outrun them. If I saw a dog coming after me too late, or if it managed to get a good intercept angle on me, I would grab one of my rolled papers out of the basket and use it as a sort of soft club. They always went for my feet. There was something attractive to all of them about my feet whirling around on the pedals. I'd lean down and try to whap the attacker on the nose. That worked sometimes. An easier tactic to avoid getting a bite on my foot or ankle was to pull my feet up and put them out in front of me on the handlebars. That only worked if I was coasting downhill or had pedaled hard enough to develop a good momentum.

There was one dog on my route that scared the daylights out of me. His name was Bruno, and he was a full-grown Saint Bernard. My predecessor on the route had warned me about this dog in particular, but Bruno wasn't always out in the yard, and we never saw him during my training runs. When I did see him for the first time, I was horrified. He was about the same size as the baby elephant I had seen at the zoo. I believe the highlight of Bruno's day, for which he waited with great anticipation, was the arrival of the paper boy. I developed some pretty gruesome mental pictures of what it would look like if he ever caught me. Fortunately, he never was successful. For one thing, his owners were not customers of mine and neither were any of the people who lived in neighboring houses. For another thing, the house where this monster lived was near the bottom of a slight hill on Belinder Road. So I was always sure to have my speedometer pegged by the time I sailed past his house with my feet up on the handlebars. Not that having my feet up on the handlebars would have done any good, since his massive jowls were about the same level as my ears. I think he slept in the yard with one eye open in hopes he would someday see me soon enough to make an intercept and have a nice afternoon snack. Once he saw me and got to his feet, he was amazingly fleet of foot, but it always took him awhile to get up when he was lying in the grass, and I guess he never had any reason to be on his feet unless he saw me coming. There were a couple of encounters that were closer than I would have liked, but otherwise it all worked out. I never even once let down my guard as I approached Bruno's yard.

I actually did get bitten by a dog one day on my paper route, but it happened when I least expected it. I was on the Hutchinson's front porch collecting for the week when it happened. The Hutchinson's were a retired couple who lived on our block, only three doors up from our house. Mrs. Hutchinson opened the storm door just a crack to hand me her quarter and Barney, their little black Scottie, charged out through the opening, took a nice chomp into my ankle, and then scurried quickly back into the house and hid behind his mommy. It all happened so fast that neither of us could believe it had actually happened. Mrs. Hutchinson was mortified and apologized profusely. I assured her there was no harm done, that I was okay, and she need not worry about it. That was the last collection of the day, so I grabbed my bike and headed on home.

When I got to our house and pulled up my jeans, I was shocked to find multiple bleeding puncture wounds through the skin of my ankle. It amazed me because it really didn't hurt much at all. Since Mom and Dad weren't home, I just got to work with a little of my Boy Scout first aid training. I cleaned up the wounds, applied some merthiolate, wrapped my ankle in a light gauze dressing, and put my sock back on. I forgot all about it until everyone was home and sitting at the dinner table that night. I announced that I had a funny story to tell and proceeded to describe Barney's sneak attack on me. Everyone laughed and enjoyed the story until Mom and Dad heard that the skin had been broken. That set off a panic over the possibility of rabies exposure.

While Mom was on the phone calling the Hutchinson's, their veterinarian, and Dr. Wolthal, my sisters were busy warning me that I would have to undergo daily rabies shots in the abdomen for days and days. They assured me those shots were extremely painful. My funny story didn't seem so funny by this time. It was all up in the air for quite a while whether I would have to get the series of shots or not. I don't know how the final decision was eventually made. All I know is that I didn't get the shots, I didn't get rabies, and my wounds all healed without getting infected.

The Wednesday collection day continued to be a real pain. It took me three or four times as long to complete my route on those days. Some people liked the once per week collection, others wanted to pay for two weeks or a month at a time. This meant I had to keep a written ledger in order to keep track of it all. This also made it harder for me to track my net profit. I soon figured out a way to put myself in a better mood for collection day. I started out collecting from the first house on my route, pocketed the first quarter, and then backtracked to the Crown Drugstore in the Fairway Shopping Center where they had a soda fountain. I parked my bike in the rack outside, went in, and took a seat on one of the round, red leather stools at the counter. There was usually a high school kid working behind the counter. He wore the typical "soda jerk" hat which was like a soldier's fore and aft cap, but white with red trim. I ordered a hamburger from him and sat there and watched hungrily as he cooked it on the open grill. After wolfing it down, I pulled the quarter from my pocket, paid my bill, and was off to happily complete the rest of my collections. The hamburgers were 25 cents, so I didn't receive any change when I paid the bill. I enjoyed this routine so much that I later modified it. I collected from my first two customers before going back to the Crown so I could get a chocolate malt with my burger. A malt was 10 cents, so I left the drugstore with 15 cents change in my pocket. The kid behind the counter got so used to me coming in that he started saying, "Oh, is today Wednesday already?" The soda fountain expense was a significant percentage of my profit, but it was worth it. I think I actually looked forward to collection day after I started that routine.

One Saturday in the spring of that year, I rode my bike over to Steve's house for the day. I took along an old kite I had built from scratch, with the help of my dad, when I was a Cub Scout. My dad had built and flown many kites when he was a boy and knew a lot about it. I had actually won a kite flying contest sponsored by the Cub Scout pack with that same kite. The trick to making it fly well was to connect the ends of the horizontal cross-piece with a piece of string and put just the right amount of bow in it. No one else in the contest seemed to know a kite simply won't fly correctly without that bow, and that is why I won. When I got over to Steve's that day with my famous kite, the wind was coming up and it looked like it was going to be a good day for flying. I had a 300-foot ball of kite string, and we had no trouble quickly getting airborne from Steve's front yard. We fed out all 300 feet and watched the kite dance around in the sky below white, billowing cumulus clouds. We decided we needed more string and that one of us would ride to a small hobby shop located just a few blocks away and buy some. I was elected, and Steve was to stay and monitor the kite. But before I left for the store, we got into a discussion about how much string to buy. We decided it would really be cool if we could fly the kite with a mile of string. It seemed like a preposterous idea at first, and I don't think we were entirely serious. I suggested getting twenty 300-foot rolls. That would be 6,000 feet of string—more than a mile. So I took off for the store while Steve monitored the kite. The owner of the hobby shop was curious about why I wanted all that kite string. When I told him, he said it would never work since that amount of string would be too heavy and the weight would bring the kite down. I couldn't imagine that, but Steve's father was out in the front yard when I got back, and he told us the same thing.

We tied the first ball of string on and started feeding it out. When we got to the end of each roll, we had to be careful not to let go of it until one of us had tied a new knot. It took a long time, but we finally got to the end of the twentieth roll and, lo and behold, the kite was still flying. We tied the end onto a stick we planned to use for the re-winding process. The kite was now high in the sky and, at times, it disappeared completely as it danced among the cumulus clouds. It rose and fell intermittently with the wind, but even when it was below the cloud layer, it was hard to see and appeared small and far away. The string itself did have a fair amount of sag from the weight of it, and at times, almost touched the ridge of the roof on the house across the street.

By the time we got all the string out, it was late in the afternoon and almost time for us to leave for St. Agnes to meet our newspaper boss and start our afternoon deliveries. We started the process of reeling the kite back in, but it didn't take long for us to realize it was going to take several hours at the rate we were going. So we decided to pound the stick with the string attached into the ground, and we jumped on our bikes, hoping the upper-level winds would keep blowing and the kite would stay airborne while we were gone.

I don't think Steve and I had ever navigated our paper routes as fast as we did that day. We arranged to meet each other on a corner,

142

where our two routes came together, after we had thrown all of our papers. Steve was there waiting as I came barreling up. From there it was a ride of a little over a mile back to his house. We both pedaled furiously, as if the fate of the world depended upon us. We had been gone over an hour and prayed the kite was still flying. As we got closer and closer to Steve's house we began scanning the section of the sky where we had last seen the kite. We didn't see it, but when we were still a few blocks from Steve's house, as I was looking upward, I saw a string resting on the power lines above our heads. We stopped and looked at it for a few moments, but then continued on, hoping it was not our string.

When we got back to Steve's house we found the kite string still attached to our stick, but its path was along the ground, then up over power lines, and it disappeared, draped loosely over the roof of the house across the street. We jumped back on our bikes and rode several blocks—actually almost exactly one mile—to the place we had seen the string above our heads. We followed the string to where it went over the roof of a house and found the kite in the backyard. My kite was unscathed and would fly another day. We yelled and cheered ecstatically as we rode back to Steve's house. It took us a long time (and several sticks) to wind up all that string, but we salvaged all 6,000 feet of string as well. It was a great day, and one I never forgot.

Steve and I saw each other every day that year. We occasionally had to cover for each other on the routes, and by the end of the school year I knew his route and he knew mine. Steve made more money than I did, but by the end of the school year, both of us realized the job wasn't worth it for the measly compensation we got. I still didn't have enough money to buy the Craftsman socket set. I would have been close if I hadn't indulged myself with Crown Drug hamburgers every Wednesday. But if I hadn't done that, I probably wouldn't have lasted through the end of the school year. As the summer vacation was quickly approaching, Steve and I both decided to quit. Our boss didn't take it well, and I think he went through a whole pack of cigarettes trying to convince us to stay with it. Steve and I remained firm, and that was the end of our careers in the newspaper business.

At some time that spring, the speedometer on my bike broke and stopped functioning completely. I must have overworked it. When the odometer numbers froze, it indicated a little over 3,000 miles, most of which had been ridden on my paper route. This was equivalent to riding my bike from Kansas City to New York City almost three times! I rode that bike many more miles over the next few years, and I suspect I may have put at least another 3,000 miles on it, but I will never know since the odometer numbers never moved again.

1958 – The National Aeronautics and Space Administration (NASA) is founded – Hula Hoops become popular – Xerox introduces us to the copying machine -

Chapter 25

That summer, 1959, Steve and I each made the decision, separately and independently, to start our own businesses. There must have been some collusion on this, however, since we both ended up in the same line of work. I don't exactly recall how Steve kicked off his venture into the lawn service business. For me, it was again my mother who primed the pump of my entrepreneurial tendencies. She had a friend who had an elderly grandmother who lived in a little house in Roeland Park, a couple of miles from our house. This little old lady lived by herself and did her own gardening, but she needed someone to mow her lawn. My mother decided I was the man for the job. By this time my father had already turned over the maintenance of our own yard to me. He had, through some type of rationalization, decided I was fully capable of safely operating the "extremely dangerous" rotary lawnmower—the exact type of mower that had claimed Uncle Gus's toe a few years before. There was one rule however: I had to wear steel-toed safety boots whenever I operated the mower. We called these my "Lil Abner" boots.

So my mom helped me load the scary machine into the back of the Dodge wagon and drove me over to my first customer's house on a weekly basis. She was a little tiny woman, in a little tiny house, with a little tiny yard. She looked to me like she must have been close to 100 years old. She introduced herself as Fanny, and that was the name she told me to call her by. I suspected it was a nickname since there was one part of the woman's anatomy which wasn't tiny. I never got up the nerve to ask her about the name though. Fanny lived by herself, and her little house was immaculate. She had flower beds along the front, sides, and back of the house which were a riot of color. Every time I went to her house to mow that summer, I found her outside, wearing a wide-brimmed sun bonnet, and tending her flowers. She was very particular about the small lawn as well and helped me develop high standards for my lawn mowing business from the first day. I always cleaned up all the clippings and trimmed carefully with hand shears around her trees, lamppost, and along the flower beds. Fanny paid me $1 for each mowing.

My mother suggested I canvas the neighborhood around our house and see if I might drum up more business a little closer to home.

It didn't take long for me to fill my schedule. I signed up Carl Standiford, next door, and the Hamilton's, who lived just up from him. The Hutchinson's were next, and then there was Corny Ashley on the corner. Midway up the block on the opposite side was Eugene Parsons. Everett Weatherly was just down the street from the Parsons. He was my best customer since he had a double-wide lot which paid a whopping six bucks per mowing. Dorothy Welsh, across the street, signed up too. I had two customers on Pawnee, the next street over from Mohawk—Mrs. Daly and Mrs. Riley. All of these folks knew me, knew my folks, knew each other, and knew all of the other kids in the neighborhood. I was aware of the fact that I needed to do high quality work from day one, or the word would spread quickly and my business would be history. I did a good job and actually added a few new customers by the end of the summer. By the time school started in the fall, I was sending out monthly invoices so my customers could pay by check at their convenience. I was making $35 to $40 each week. I was still out in the fresh air and sunshine and getting plenty of exercise every day, but this was turning out to be a much more lucrative venture than the paper route.

Steve's lawn mowing business was off to a great start that summer too. He was working much harder and earning a lot more money than I was though. Steve had a different business model than I did. He had way more customers and I suspect this was mainly due to an aggressive pricing structure. While my business philosophy was one of high quality and low volume, Steve's approach was one of low quality and high volume. He insisted this was what his customers wanted—a basic mowing job for a low price. For the one or two dollars he charged for the average lawn, he wasn't about to clean up the grass clippings or trim with hand shears. Besides, he didn't have time. He raced from lawn to lawn, from dawn until dusk, seven days per week that summer. If we had a stretch of rainy days, I always postponed my mowing jobs until the grass dried out and cut nicely. Steve couldn't wait out the rainy days or he became hopelessly behind. Even with mowing in the rain, he still got behind schedule sometimes since the rain made the grass grow faster and require more frequent mowing.

There were a couple of times that summer when Steve got so far behind on his mowing schedule he had to call me to come over and help him. I rode my bike over to his house pulling my lawnmower

146

along behind. This was always a little tricky since I carried a gasoline can in one hand, used that same hand to hold one handlebar grip and steer, and used the other hand to pull the mower along by its handle, backwards, behind me. When I arrived at his house we immediately departed on our bikes for the various jobs, each of us toting our mowers and gas cans in an identical fashion. We mowed each lawn—sometimes one of us in the backyard and the other in the front, or we worked together, crisscrossing paths with drill-team precision. The grass was so high in some cases that it didn't cut well and really needed to have a second pass. Steve wouldn't even consider that if I suggested it. I also started to trim around trees and posts with my hand shears, but he put a stop to that as well. We never spent more than a few minutes on each lawn, and when we finished, it looked like my hair does when I wake up in the morning. There were shocks of grass sticking up all over the place and big clumps of wet clippings everywhere. Steve assured me it was fine that way, and we jumped on our bikes and pedaled furiously to the next one.

One day I was helping Steve catch up after a period of particularly wet weather when his mower suddenly quit. We took it back to his house and fiddled with it for a while, but it refused to start. We knew we had to get it going again quickly if we had any hope of putting Steve back on schedule. So we hopped on our bikes and pulled his mower down to a small engine repair shop in the Mission Shopping Center. The owner of the shop placed a tag on the handle and told Steve he could pick it up in a week to 10 days. Steve had a fit. He argued with the owner, explaining that the mower was his livelihood, but the man wouldn't budge. The shop also sold new lawnmowers, and Steve then pointed toward a brand new, top-of-the-line Lawn Boy mower and asked the owner the price. The man gave a cocky little laugh and informed Steve it was $85. The next thing that happened shocked both me and the owner of the business. Steve pulled his wallet out of his hip pocket and peeled off $85 dollars in cash. I think the owner was still standing in the doorway with his mouth agape as these two 13-year-old kids rode off pulling the new Lawn Boy behind their bikes. Steve hollered over his shoulder and asked the man to call him when his old mower was ready to pick up.

Steve and I each continued our lawn mowing businesses for the next four years until we were seniors in high school. I continued to help Steve out when he got behind on his schedule, and he came over to our neighborhood and substituted for me when our family went out of town on vacation. On those occasions, I gave him a little lecture about what my customers expected as far as quality was concerned. I think this did intimidate him into doing a better job, but he simply didn't have time to be as meticulous as I was. So I expected a few complaints when I got back in town, but it was, nevertheless, nice to know I had someone I could rely on to cover for me while I was gone.

Steve and I both noticed that each of us had a few customers who had sons who were about our age. A lot of times when we were at one of the houses mowing, the kid was out playing with friends in the yard or driveway. We were always amazed someone was willing to pay us to mow their lawn when they had a kid who was perfectly capable of doing it. We were both more than happy to have the business, though, and didn't begrudge those kids their playtime in the slightest.

The lawn mowing business made me realize my earning potential was much greater than the paper route had demonstrated. It was at about this same age that I started earning money in the winter by shoveling snow from driveways and walkways. I often paired up with Steve or one of my other friends in this enterprise. Kansas City consistently got a lot of snow every winter and, to me, it was like white gold. I quickly decided my favorite snow-shoveling partner was Doug Rollert. I think Doug liked to come to our neighborhood because it paid a little better due to longer driveways and walks. Doug was a big strong kid and threw snow like a snow blower. He started at one end of a drive and I started at the other. I couldn't possibly shovel as fast as he did, and by the time we met, he had usually done ¾ of the drive and I had done the other ¼. Doug never complained about it though, and at the end of the day, we split the proceeds 50:50. For me it was a great deal. We usually charged $3 for a driveway and 50 cents for a walkway. We worked from before dawn until after dark, and we came home with a nice little wad of money every time.

The following spring I formalized my lawn business by having business cards printed. I also sent out form letters to previous customers with self-addressed postcards enclosed which were designed to renew my service for the season.

CRAWLEY'S LAWN SERVICE

5424 Mohawk   SKyline 1-2360

March 15, 1961

Dear Sir:

Last summer, I mowed eleven lawns regularly in this neighborhood, and I am planning to do yard work again this summer. I would like to find out whether or not you are interested in having me mow your lawn.

Enclosed is a self addressed post card..If you will please fill this out and drop it in the mail, I would appreciate it very much.

In addition to mowing, I am available for other yard work, such as raking leaves, removing excess grass clippings and hedge trimming.

Thank you very much - I hope to hear from you soon.

Sincerely,

David Crawley

David Crawley

P.S. Don't forget to sign your name at the bottom
      of the post card.

PLEASE CHECK ONE OF THE FOLLOWING:

✔ I Definitely Want You to Mow My Lawn This Summer.

__ I Plan to Mow My Own Lawn, But I May Want You to
Do it if I Happen to Leave Town.

__ I Have Already Lined Up Another Man to Mow My
Lawn.

Criticism of Last Year's Work:

Is the price still all right?

Mr E Parsons

Signed,_____

FOR EXCELLENT

LAWN SERVICE

OR

SNOW REMOVAL

CALL:
DAVID CRAWLEY
SK 1-2360   5424 MOHAWK

150

OLATHE, KANSAS

The Board of
County Commissioners
Johnson County, Kansas

March 26, 1961

Mr. David Crawley
President, Crawley's Lawn Service
5424 Mohawk
Shawnee Mission, Kansas

Dear Mr. Crawley:

I was most happy to receive your letter of March 15, explaining the services your company performs.

David, as you know, at my house I have been relegated to the
office of Chairman of the Board. Mrs. Standiford, of course,
is the Executive Vice President in charge of all activities,
including mine.

All winter long the argument has gone on as to whether I am to
take care of the lawn, or someone else. The Vice President con-
tends strongly that I am big enough to do the job, and I counter
with the statement that while this may be true I do not have the
ability. I offer further proof that to do this type of work it
takes more than size.

Now, David, here is where you can help me out. You call on Mrs.
Standiford with your proposition and be prepared for some sharp
trading. If you can sell the deal on your own, I will enter
into the picture sufficiently to close it up.

Frankly, I am horrified at the prospects of having to rake the
yard. You go after this now, and I will be on your side.

Very truly yours,

C. M. Standiford

C. M. Standiford
Chairman of the Board

CMS:hw

P.S. - David, we are real happy to be neighbors to a young man
as ambitious as you are. Good Luck!

My lawn service and snow removal company involved hard work but was quite lucrative. I had not been in business long when I was finally able to purchase the Craftsman socket wrench set I had dreamed about for so long. After that, every few weeks, I stuffed some money into my pockets and rode my bike to the Fairway Hardware to buy a new tool of some sort. I set up a workshop in a room in the basement of our house that had originally been designed as maid's quarters. The room was separated from the unfinished portion of the basement, had knotty-pine paneled walls, and a window set in a deep window well. It even had a closet and a small adjacent bathroom. Our deep-freeze was against one wall, but that was the only thing the room was used for. I bought some lumber and built a sturdy work bench. The legs were four-by-fours which were braced with two-by-fours, and the top was two-by-tens. When finished, it was all bolted together with carriage bolts and was almost indestructible. I mounted a machinist's vice on one corner of the table. I suspect the workbench is still in that room today. I know, though, that the vice is no longer there since it is mounted on the workbench in my Montana shop.

I put a peg board up on the wall behind the work bench and began hanging each of my tools on it, one by one, as I slowly expanded my collection. Many of the hand tools I still use were bought with lawn-mowing and snow-shoveling money.

I kept busy with my lawn care business each summer while I was in high school, but I also did some farm work. One of my lawn customers, Dr. Eugene Parsons, owned a small farm just outside of the city to the south, on the Kansas side of the state line. The doctor and his wife, Tiny, lived on our block—just up the street. They spent several days or weeks living on the farm during the summer, and Dr. Parsons commuted to work from there. When they had work for me, they took me along and I stayed out there, sometimes for a week or two at a time. I kept track of all the time I was actually working, and they paid me $1 per hour.

The farm encompassed about 250 acres of pastureland, and they had a few horses and several cows on it. They had a model 8N Ford tractor, and I learned how to operate it and do the routine tractor maintenance. I was 13 years old when I started working on the farm and wasn't old enough to drive a car yet, so driving a tractor was a real kick for me. The tractor had a 60-inch rotary mower behind it on a three-point hitch, and I spent a lot of my time mowing pastures that weren't in use. Dr. Parsons explained that the mowing had to be done to keep the pastures from being overgrown with brush. The doctor taught me how to install fence, and I learned how to dig post holes, tamp a new post in so it was solid, how to string barbed wire, and how to brace a fence corner. I had gotten pretty handy with tools by this time and knew how to fix things, so Tiny also kept me busy with some of the general maintenance of the farm and basic home repairs.

Dr. Parsons was a general surgeon. His surgical practice was in Kansas City on the Missouri side of the state line. He was probably in his late fifties then. The doctor was a little tiny fellow with a great big personality. Despite his small stature, he always appeared strong and fit. He peered through wire-rimmed bifocal glasses, he was almost always dressed in a three-piece suit when I saw him at their house, and no one could look more like an old-time country doctor than he did. He was always extremely cheerful, had a big smile on his face, and loved to kid around. His wife, Tiny, was almost a carbon copy of him. She was a little tiny woman who also wore wire-rimmed bifocal glasses and had an extremely cheerful personality. They had two adult children who were already gone from home by that time. I only met them once or twice; they were fraternal twins, a boy and a girl. They introduced them to me as Tippy and Toppy. I couldn't imagine those were their real names, but I never heard them referred to by any other names. So the Parsons family consisted of Tippy, Toppy, Tiny and Eugene.

When I stayed out on the farm, all three of us were up before sunrise and had finished a big country breakfast by first light. We worked until sunset. Tiny was a good cook, and there was always plenty of food at every meal—even enough to satisfy a hungry teenage boy. I thought I could eat almost any amount of food placed before me, but soon I found I couldn't begin to put away the amount the old doctor did. All of our meals were served family style in the kitchen at a big farm table. One night we had enormous T-bone steaks with mashed potatoes and gravy. The steaks actually lopped off the sides of our plates. I somehow ate every bite, but I felt like a stuffed hog when I was finished. Dr. Parson's looked over at me and said, "Are you going to have another steak, Dave?" I started laughing, thinking he was surely kidding, when Tiny got up and brought a huge platter out of the oven with two more giant T-bones on it. She didn't even ask the old doctor if he wanted another one. She just dropped it on his plate.

She held the platter toward me and said, "David?" I didn't want to be rude, but there was no way I could eat one more bite, so I just said, "No thank you, Ma'am." They both looked a little hurt as she slowly put the platter down on the table. Then Dr. Parsons said, "What is the matter with you boy? Don't you like steak? Maybe I didn't work you hard enough today." Tiny then spoke up and said, "Gene, leave him alone. No one can eat as much as you do." And it didn't take the little man long to devour a second enormous T-bone steak. I related the whole scene to my mom and dad when I got home, and they had me tell the story over and over for many years. We all marveled that the old doctor, who probably didn't weigh 120 pounds, could eat the way he did and stay so petite.

I worked on three other farms, all belonging to Warren Newcomer, who owned Newcomer Funeral Homes in Kansas City. These were all "gentleman farms." Each one had a nice house on it and they were all beautiful pieces of property. There were rolling green fields, split-rail fences, ponds, and gorgeous stone walls. I got this job through a high school classmate, Jack Hove, who was dating

Warren's daughter, Mary Lynn. I met Mary Lynn only once when she came out and visited us one day while we were working. She was a beautiful girl, and I was a little envious of Jack that day.

Jack and I usually worked together for Warren and most of our work was installing and repairing fence. Warren worked with us sometimes, but other times it was just Jack and I. We put in some wire fencing, but most of the fence was beautiful, decorative wood fence. We sometimes hauled our post-hole diggers and other supplies around between farms in one of Warren's big black hearses. One afternoon we pulled into Allen's Drive-in Restaurant and ordered hamburgers and ate them in the hearse. The car hop said that was a first for her, and we got a lot of stares from the other patrons. They might have wondered why a couple of teenaged boys with dirty faces and filthy work clothes were eating lunch at Allen's in a Cadillac hearse.

One night Jack's girlfriend, Mary Lynn, was out on a date with some other kid and they had a terrible wreck. Mary Lynn was killed. Jack was a quiet, humble fellow, so it was a little hard to tell how much he was hurting from the death of Mary Lynn. He was a competitive swimmer and was rated as the number six freestyle swimmer in the nation for his age group. He went on swimming, though, and seemed to recover as much as could be expected from this awful tragedy.

1959 – Fidel Castro becomes the dictator of Cuba – Alaska and Hawaii become states – "The Sound of Music" opens on Broadway –

Chapter 26

Practically everyone in our neighborhood employed a maid, and our home was no exception. We had a maid every day to clean house, do the washing and ironing, and babysit for us when we got home from school. The maids all arrived in the neighborhood at about the same time every morning on a city bus that stopped at the end of our street. They all walked up the street together and then split off at the various homes where they worked. The maids were all African-American women, but in those days they were referred to as Negros or "colored people." I think they all worked for fairly low wages since it seemed almost every middleclass family could afford to employ a maid. We had several different maids over the years, and we kids got to know them well since they took care of us whenever we were home and both of our parents were working. There was Geneva, Cora, Clara, Beatrice, Billy, and Bertha.

I remember Bertha more than the others because she worked for our family the longest. Bertha spent a lot of time with us when we got home from school. My mother was often upset to find Bertha sitting in the den watching television or playing a board game with us when she arrived home from work. She expected her to be constantly cleaning, washing, or cooking to earn her pay. She wanted her to babysit with us while she did those things. The "problem" was that Bertha was such a fast and efficient worker that she had all of her household duties done to perfection by the time we got home from school. She pointed out to my mother that everything was done, and my mother, after doing a little inspection, softened a bit. But paying Bertha an hourly wage to watch television never quite sat right with her.

Bertha was a stern disciplinarian and came down hard on us if we misbehaved. It is interesting for me to think about how humble and respectful Bertha was when she talked to my mother or father, but how there was no mincing of words when it came to disciplining the bad little Crawley kids. I don't recall her ever spanking us, although she may have gotten in my face and shaken my shoulders a few times. Her stern verbal reprimands were usually sufficient to bring us to attention. She had a deep furrow between her eyebrows which became deeper when she frowned at us. In fact, her face seemed to always exhibit a look of worry. I believe that she decided she had to shoulder the responsibility of raising us and that if any of us turned out badly it would be her fault.

Bertha was probably the most efficient housekeeper we ever employed. When she worked for the Crawley family, our house was spotless. My mother and Bertha had a sort of love/hate relationship though. Mom loved the way Bertha maintained our home, but their personalities did not mesh well. When my mother complained to Bertha about something she was unhappy about, Bertha respectfully held her tongue—at least as long as she could. When she reached her limit, she occasionally dished out a little sass to my mother. An episode like this occasionally resulted in Bertha being "let go" for a while or, on other occasions, Bertha would quit. We then had a new maid for a short period of time until my mother called Bertha and begged her to come back to work, which she always did.

Despite Bertha's stern discipline, my sisters and I all had a wonderful time with her most of the time. After many years of service, she was like one of the family, and we all loved her, including my mother. My parents eventually moved to Houston after my senior year in college. There was a lot of hugging and crying on Bertha's last day of service to our family. I feel badly none of us kept in touch with Bertha after that. I think she would be proud to know she did a pretty good job of teaching the five Crawley kids how to be good people.

Geneva was a large, jolly, loving woman who had diabetes and had to inject herself with daily insulin. Everyone loved Geneva.

Cora was a tall, thin woman with gray hair who was nice, but she never paid a lot of attention to what we kids were up to.

Clara had a physical appearance similar to Cora, but I don't recall much about her. I don't think she kept track of us too well either.

Beatrice probably worked for us longer than anyone other than Bertha. Beatrice was a very thin woman of medium height. Her face was young looking, but she had wisps of gray hair. She probably had the sweetest disposition of any of our maids. Her voice was so soft that you had to stand close to her and listen carefully to hear her. She had a thin little smile on her face at all times, even while she scrubbed the floors. Beatrice had 11 children of her own, and we saved our outgrown clothes for her kids. When we had accumulated a good-sized pile, we packed them into a box, put the box in the trunk of the car, and delivered them to her house in the black neighborhood of Kansas

City, Missouri. My mother always took one or all of us along, and we stayed at her house for an hour or so to visit. She kept her own house as clean and neat as she kept ours. Everything in the house was arranged in perfect order and it was spotlessly clean. She had the kids dressed up in their Sunday-best clothes for our visit, and, when we came in, they were all lined up on a long bench along one wall in the living room. Beatrice was a perfect hostess, offering beverages and cookies. Since none of us had ever been around any black children, and her children had probably never been around any white children, we all just stared at each other awkwardly in fascination. Beatrice thanked us profusely for the second-hand clothing. She was so humble and deferent that she never looked us in the eye when she talked to us. She always looked at the floor or to one side as if she wasn't worthy. This manner of hers always made me feel sad.

Of all the maids we had, the one who was the most colorful was Billy. She also probably had the shortest tenure of any maid at our house. Billy was a big woman whose personality was the exact opposite of practically all of our other maids. She didn't have an ounce of humility, talked loudly and, at times, somewhat crudely. We kids were all a little afraid of her and steered clear; we didn't want to be disciplined by Billy. One day Billy came to work with bruises all over her face and arms and with one eye almost swollen shut. She said her boyfriend had gotten drunk, beaten her up, and chased her around her apartment with a butcher knife in his hand. She thought he would kill her if she went back home, and so she asked if she could move in with us and be a "live-in" maid. Our old maid quarters in the basement were not adequate since I had turned the room into a workshop. So I moved out of my room on the third floor, and that became Billy's room. I took a room on the second floor which had been Martha's room, and Martha moved in with Betsy and Helen. All went well for a few days until Billy's boyfriend showed up at our front door one evening. Billy and her boyfriend went out for a night on the town, and they both came back drunk in the middle of the night. My father fired Billy the next morning. That was the one and only time we had a live-in maid. I was happy to have my third-floor room back, and all of us kids could then walk safely through the house without having to be afraid we'd run into Billy.

Chapter 27

When I finished eighth grade at St. Agnes, there was a grade school graduation ceremony, complete with caps and gowns and presentation of diplomas. The Catholic schools didn't have junior high like the public schools did; grade school was followed by four years of high school. Our high school, Bishop Miege High, was in its second year of operation when I entered the freshman class. My sister Judy had gone to St. Agnes High, located in the basement of the church, for her first three years of high school. Her senior year was in the new high school, and she was in the first graduating class the year before I started. The new school was located on property adjacent to St. Agnes grade school and St. Agnes church. It was a beautiful modern building. It had a cafeteria where lunch was served, a gymnasium, and, of course, a chapel. There was also a new outdoor sports field for football and track.

The students at the new high school came not only from St. Agnes Grade School, but also from several other Catholic grade schools in the diocese. So the classmates I had been with for many years were now all mixed in with several new groups of students. At first everyone seemed to hang around with their old buddies, but as the months and years went by we all loosened up and formed some new friendships.

Two of my three best friends from grade school went to Bishop Miege with me – Steve Hudson and Richard Butler. My old friend Nick Davis went to Rockhurst High School, a Jesuit school in Kansas City, Missouri. Even though Nick now went to another school, we still saw each other a lot.

Even before we went to our first day of high school, some of the mothers decided some social events were required. I think the idea was to introduce the new young teens to the world of parties attended by both girls AND boys, as well as to prepare us for upcoming school "mixers," formal dances and actual dating. I don't know what the rush was, but all of this started during the summer between eighth grade and our freshman year. I got invited to one of these events at the home of Barbara Tremble, who was probably the most popular girl in our eighth grade class. I am not sure how I got on the list for this gala since I don't believe I had ever even spoken to Barbara Tremble, and I

161

probably would have trembled in my boots if someone had forced me to actually talk to her face to face. The party was held on their patio, which was decorated with colorful hanging lanterns. There was a portable phonograph set up, and records of popular music—45 RPM singles—were played all evening: *Venus* by The Platters, *Mack the Knife* by Bobby Darin, *Heartaches By The Number* by Guy Mitchell, and *Put Your Head on My Shoulder* by Paul Anka are a few I remember. This was intended to introduce us to dancing, and I think most of us had received some introductory lessons at home on Jitter-Bugging and "slow dancing" prior to the party. My older sister Judy had given me a crash course that afternoon. I believe the whole thing was somewhat of a failure, though, since the girls stayed together on one side of the patio, and the boys stayed together on the other side all evening. I couldn't even imagine getting up the nerve to cross over to the girls' side and strike up a conversation with one of them—let alone asking one of them to dance. In fact, I was careful not to even glance in their direction for fear I might catch the eye of one of the girls and she might come over and ask ME to dance. The awkward evening seemed to last an eternity, and I didn't feel relief until one of our parents finally arrived to take us home.

It is interesting to note that prior to this time in our young lives, few of us had ever socialized with the opposite sex. All during grade school, the only girls I had ever interacted with at all had been my sisters. During our recess play time at school, the boys and girls were always kept completely apart and never played any outdoor games and sports with one another. I actually think this segregation of the sexes was a characteristic limited to the Catholic schools. I suspect this practice probably did not occur so much in the public schools. I never really gained a perspective on this though since we were continuously reminded that the church did not want us associating with non-Catholics, as they were all considered "near occasions of sin." I actually violated this rule by playing occasionally with Mike Dunn, my non-Catholic friend on the next block from our house. But Mike didn't broaden my perspective on this at all since he attended a rather elite private academy for boys only, known as Pembroke Country Day. Mike and I actually had a lot of fun together, and as far as I could tell, he didn't lead me into sin any more often than some of my Catholic friends did.

So, during all of our previous years before high school, it seemed that intermixing of girls and boys in any social situation was carefully avoided and almost forbidden. I must assume our parents and the priests and nuns felt we had not been, heretofore, ready for such integration. But now, at the start of high school, this ban had apparently been lifted. Not only was socialization with the opposite sex allowed, it was, under careful supervision, actually encouraged. This sudden apparent change in unwritten policy certainly created some anxiety and awkwardness for me and obviously had a similar effect on many of my classmates, both male and female. During our freshman year many "mixers" were scheduled, often after a football game or basketball game. At these events Rock and Roll music was played, the lights were turned down low, and the boys were expected to ask the girls to dance. I went to a lot of these, but I don't think I ever got up the nerve to ask a girl to dance. The boys usually all stood along one wall of the room, and the girls stood along the opposite wall. My friends and I stood there and chatted and watched the upperclassman dance so that maybe someday in the future we might know what to do. Some of the nun chaperones, apparently distraught by the fact that the mixer might be a total failure, occasionally tried to pair up a freshman couple and encouraged them to dance by pulling the two people onto the dance floor. My friends and I kept a close eye on the nuns, and if we saw any of them casting an eye our way, we quickly headed for an exit.

The most obvious difference between our grade school and high school daily academic lives was the fact we now moved from classroom to classroom throughout the day instead of remaining in the same room. Each time we changed classrooms for a new class, we had a different teacher who specialized in that particular subject. This was a notable transition from grade school. There were many more lay teachers and fewer teachers who were nuns.

During the period between each class when everyone was moving to a new classroom, it seemed like mass chaos with girls and boys of all sizes moving in a million different directions. Metal lockers lined the walls of the hallways, and you had to be careful not to run into a locker door as they were opened and slammed shut.

One thing I noticed almost immediately was that I had a lot more homework assignments to do than I ever had before. In grade school, it seemed the teacher adjusted the amount of homework in the various subjects so the total for a given evening wouldn't be too great. But now, each teacher seemed to dish out assignments while being apparently oblivious to the fact that the other teachers were piling on the work too. There were many afternoons in high school on which I worked on my homework from the time I got home until late in the evening.

I worked hard academically all through high school and always got good grades. I usually considered my homework to be my first priority when I got home from school and rarely considered doing anything else until my assignments were complete. I wasn't on any of the school's formal sports teams and often wondered how the athletes ever had time to complete their homework since they had long practice sessions every day after school. I eventually realized that most of these kids, with a few notable exceptions, never did as well as I did academically. The school athletes were, nevertheless, held in the highest esteem by everyone, and they were good kids.

My favorite subjects in high school were the sciences—math, physics, chemistry, and earth science. The logic was easy for me, and I remembered what I learned because it all made sense. I generally got "A"s in all of these courses. I also really liked a couple of drafting courses I took. It was the precision and neatness that agreed with me.

I had some interest in History, but I couldn't stay excited about it because of the way it was taught. We were required to memorize names and dates and were tested on them. It wasn't a good way to provide a real perspective of the past. History has since become one of my most avid interests, and I enjoy reading non-fiction books as well as historical fiction. I think most people become more interested in history as they get older. I believe part of the reason for this is that as you get older your relative perspective of time broadens, and events that seemed like ancient history when studied as a child now don't seem so long ago and have greater relevance. That's my theory on why I now like history.

English literature was usually combined into the same class as English grammar in high school. The grammar part wasn't hard for me. I just had to learn the rules that applied, as in math, and a sentence could be parsed into its component parts. We were taught to diagram sentences to demonstrate that we understood all of the parts of speech. This was easy for my logical mind, and I think this helped teach a student to write well with coherent sentence structure. But when it came to the English literature portion of the course, I had problems.

Miss Blake (not her real name) was one of my teachers. Miss Blake was a manly woman. She was built like an NFL lineman—short and sturdy-looking. Her body had no shapes or curves to it, and her legs looked like fence posts. Her arms were so muscled that they hung at an angle, out away from her body, instead of straight down. Her hair was done in a short, no-nonsense type haircut, and there was the hint of a mustache above her mouth.

Miss Blake was a strict teacher and did not tolerate any frivolity, and no one was dumb enough to cross her. She gave us reading assignments, and we then had class discussions. We were often asked to describe the literary techniques the author used to set certain tones or emphasize certain points. We were supposed to find examples of symbolism, irony, hyperbole, imagery, word play, etc. Miss Blake was dramatic in class sometimes, and she clopped back and forth in the front of the classroom with her eyes rolling back and forth in her head while she spouted out examples of each of these. I didn't get any of this and had no idea what she was talking about. I read each assignment completely literally and didn't see anything else. If Miss Blake called upon me in class to point out or explain one of these literary techniques, I was like a deer caught in the headlights.

One day in English we were given a pop quiz to demonstrate our abilities in abstract thinking. My brain works so literally that I couldn't even understand what the word "abstract" meant. The test involved interpreting the meaning of various adages, such as "A stitch in time saves nine," or "A rolling stone gathers no moss." I thought the answers to these were completely obvious: "A stitch in time saves nine" means that if a seam starts to come apart you should sew it up right away. And "A rolling stone gathers no moss" means that the friction of a stone rolling down a hill will rub the moss off of it. As soon as we finished the quiz we could leave for the day. I whipped mine out, dropped it off on the teacher's desk, and was the first one out of there.

I did manage to get a "B" in English most of the time, but it seemed like a gift. It is possible my failures to understand English literature were somewhat offset by my skills in grammar, but I still felt like my teachers had been generous to me with their grading.

165

We were introduced to term papers in high school and were told this was good preparation for college, where most courses required some type of paper or thesis to be written. A high school term paper often was assigned with a minimum number of words expected. 1,000 words was typical. Library research had to be done, and references in the form of a bibliography were always required, but copying anything word for word was always forbidden unless it was placed in quotes. This was before the days of computers, so all research was done by paging through various reference materials or even microfilm in the library. Encyclopedias were often the main source of information for most students since they contained a ton of easily accessible information in one place. Some families had their own set of encyclopedias, and I envied the kids who were lucky enough to do their research at home. These sets were sold by door-to-door encyclopedia salesmen who came back to the same houses year after year to sell the latest updated set. We had an old set that was probably at least 20 years out of date, so it wasn't very useful to me. I often went over to someone's house who had a set, or I did my research in the library. Our teachers were always trying to get us to use other sources for information besides the encyclopedia, but I never got much beyond that until I was writing papers for college classes.

One of the most difficult parts of writing a term paper was typing it. Our high school had a typing class, but it was considered a course for girls (who might later become secretaries). I didn't want to take a girl's class, so I never took typing. When I typed a term paper it was by the "hunt and peck" method. We had an old Royal mechanical typewriter at home that was made out of steel and painted bright red with black keys. We kept it on the floor of the hall closet behind the coats. After my paper was all written out by hand in pencil, I lugged the heavy typewriter out to the dining room table and started typing it.

The typing paper was fed into the roller behind the array of key arms. I often wanted a carbon copy for myself, so I would feed two sheets in with a piece of carbon paper between. When a key was depressed, the corresponding key arm would strike forward and hit the ink ribbon to imprint the letter on the page. The roller holding the paper was part of the "carriage" which then moved to the next space and was ready for the next letter. If you punched the key too softly, the letter would be imprinted lightly. If you struck the key too hard, the letter would be imprinted darkly. If you inadvertently struck two keys at the same time, the key arms would frequently jam together and have to be pulled apart.

The typewriter ribbon fed along in front of the roller from one round spool to another spool. When it got to the end, it reversed and fed back through in the opposite direction. So each time this cycle was repeated, the typewriter ribbon was a little more worn, and the words and letters appeared lighter. If you noticed this was happening, you could install a new ribbon, but then you had a sudden transition to dark letters.

The other big issue was typos. If you made a mistake, you could use a special typewriter eraser to try to remove it and then retype it. This often resulted in abrading a hole in the paper. Attempts to fix the carbon copy often ended up with a dark smear that was illegible. Toward the end of my high school days, a product known as "white-out" was invented. This made corrections much easier. It came in a bottle with a little brush attached to the inside of the lid, and you used the brush to just paint over the error. This was a little better, but the whole typing experience was still laborious. I frequently ripped the paper out of the machine and started completely over. I typed some of my term papers a half dozen times before I got a decent, legible copy.

The typewriter itself needed regular maintenance to keep it working properly. Most of the typewriter stores had repair facilities that offered service. If you did a lot of erasing like I did, the machine often just needed cleaning to fix problems. Carbon tetrachloride was the chemical used for this. The typewriter repairman also adjusted sticky or misaligned keys and always put a new ribbon in. When our typewriter came back from maintenance, it worked great....for a while.

A revolutionary improvement to the mechanical typewriter was the invention of the electric typewriter. The big advantage of this was that it required no force to strike the keys, and it was much less tiring to use. Also, the key arms all struck the ribbon with the exact same amount of force so the letters had the same degree of darkness on the page. My parents gave my older sister Judy a Smith Corona portable electric typewriter as her graduation gift from high school; unfortunately, she took it to college with her, and the rest of us were stuck with the old Royal.

The awakening of my interest in the opposite sex plodded along at a glacial pace throughout my first three years of high school, and I didn't really start dating any girls until my senior year. I never had a good time at any of the early parties and mixers, and they were actually a little stressful for me. Also, being on the football or basketball team seemed to be a prerequisite for having a girlfriend. Since I was not one of these adulated heroes, I decided there was probably not much of a future for me as a magnet for the girls. It seemed easier, and less stressful, just to revert back to socializing with my guy friends as I always had done.

There were actually some apparently precocious kids who started dating right away in high school. But since these Romeos were not old enough to drive a car, their parents had to chauffeur them on their dates. When I thought about my dad or mom driving me to pick up a girl from her house and then transporting us to and from a movie theater, it deterred me further from any thoughts of going on an occasional date.

1960 – The first televised presidential debates - John F. Kennedy elected President of the United States with his running mate, Lyndon Johnson as Vice-President – Lasers were invented – The lunch counter sit-ins in the south marked the beginning of the Civil Rights Movement – Alfred Hitchcock's movie *Pyscho* released –

Chapter 28

Even before I started high school, I had a fascination with cars. All of my buddies were the same way. The cars of the day were distinctive, and we could spout off the year, make and model of almost every vehicle on the road with only a quick glance—'40 Ford, '38 Chevy, '53 Packard, '51 Kaiser, '31 Ford, '56 Olds, '53 Hudson, '51 Plymouth—we could name them all! In the mid-1950s, the styling became dramatic with fins on the rear fenders. First the fins were just vertical, like on the '56 Chevy and '56 Ford, but in 1957, the automotive designers boldly canted the fins outward—the '57 Chevy and '57 Ford being examples.

Our family car in 1958 was a new '58 Dodge station wagon, and it had massive fins slanting out at a dramatic angle. That car also had "push-button drive." To put the automatic transmission into Park, Drive, or Reverse, you pushed a button on a square panel on the dash to the left of the steering column. It also had "torsion bar suspension" instead of springs—a new engineering innovation by the Chrysler Corporation. This suspension system worked fine until the torsion bar on one side suffered from metal fatigue from too much twisting and broke. We drove the car around with the broken torsion bar for a while until we could get it repaired. During that time, the left end of the front bumper was about four inches off the ground, while the right end of the rear bumper was about three feet off the ground. The car looked strange driving down the road, and, from the driver's perspective, it looked even stranger …. and a little scary.

Some of the other styling features during the mid to late 1950s, besides big fins, included dual headlights, tons of chrome trim strips, big hood ornaments, fender skirts, curb feelers, naugahyde (vinyl) upholstery, and continental kits for the spare tire. Major style changes occurred and were expected every year. This was the "muscle car" era, engines were getting bigger and bigger, and almost every teenage boy knew the displacement in cubic inches and horsepower of almost every engine in production. These cars, possessing gigantic engines and being extremely heavy, were horrendous gas guzzlers, but no one really worried about that in those days. A car with a 20-gallon tank could be filled up for between three and four dollars at 15 to 20 cents per gallon. The '57 Chevy 2-door sedan or convertible was considered a stylish set of wheels, but if it only had a straight-six engine in it, it wasn't considered much of a car. If the same model had a 283 cubic inch V-8, then that was a REAL machine! It wasn't until the early 1960s that General Motors came out with the 327 and then the 427 engines. These engines were enormous and incredibly powerful—designed for speed. It was an exciting time in the automotive world, and it seemed like every American was caught up in the car fever, anxiously anticipating the annual introduction of new models.

Most families only had one car. My dad bought a new family car every few years, and I always went with him for the negotiations. We went to a dealership with an idea of what we were looking for. We looked at the models in the showroom and then sat down with a salesman. Once we had nailed down a model and color, the salesman would then tell my dad the basic price, what was included, and then started down a list of available options. As he read off each option, Dad always asked, "How much is that?" for each selection and then decided whether or not he wanted to add it to the factory order. There were no option "packages" for each model as there are today when you select a vehicle. There was just the base model and a wide array of individual options. These included items like a heater, rearview mirrors on the doors (would you like one just on the driver's side or on the passenger door too?), whitewall tires, a radio (AM only—there was no FM radio yet), automatic transmission, power steering, power brakes, naugahyde upholstery, a strip of tinted glass along the top of the windshield, etc. I loved this selection of the options and always tried to talk my dad into some of the accessories I liked. When we were finished, the order was sent to the factory, and the salesman later called us and told us the expected delivery date to the dealership—usually six to eight weeks down the road. I then started counting the days, and as the date approached, my anticipation would reach a fever pitch.

In the state of Kansas, where we lived, a young teenager could start driving with a learner's permit at age 14. This permit required a driver over 21 years of age to accompany the new driver. The licensed driver, acting as chaperone, had to be in the vehicle but could even sit in the back seat to meet the requirement. Another driver did not have to be in the car if the young driver was driving to or from school or church. For a kid on a farm doing farm chores, this rule did not apply, and he or she could drive solo at age 14. Driver Education courses were in their infancy at that time, and such a course was not required to be issued a learner's permit or, later, an unrestricted license at age 16. So most kids' parents had to be the driving instructors and would then decide on their own when the new driver was ready to head off to school or church on a first solo trip.

My dad taught me to drive when I was 14 years old in his 1953 Ford sedan he owned with two other friends. These three executives carpooled to their jobs in downtown Kansas City, Missouri, in "The Green Hornet," as they called it. The car was pretty basic, and my dad wanted me to learn on it because it had a manual transmission. He didn't want me to learn on the Dodge wagon because then I would be limited to driving a vehicle which had an automatic transmission. Manual transmissions were, at that time, more common. The Ford had a three-speed transmission with the shifter on the right side of the steering column. We started out with instruction in the high school parking lot. There was a lot of jerking, lurching, and grinding at first as I got used to the clutch and figured out how to coordinate it with the throttle and gearshift. After a couple of hours in the parking lot, he let me drive on the street the few blocks from the school to our home. After a few days of lessons with my dad, I took a test and got my restricted license.

Not long after I got my permit, my cousin, Tom Roy, came to visit for the Thanksgiving holiday from St. Louis where he was in college. My mother was fond of her nephew and wanted to "fix him up" with Laney Hoy, the daughter of a good friend of hers. I think she wanted Tom to come back and visit often and thought having a girlfriend in Kansas City would entice him. Tom had also brought a friend from college with him, so my Mom lined up Laney Hoy and my sister Judy to go out with the boys for a little afternoon outing in the car to see the sights of Kansas City on the day after Thanksgiving. I had been in possession of my driving permit all of about one week at that point, and I immediately offered my services to be their chauffeur and chaperone for the afternoon. Since my cousin Tom had just turned 21 at the time, he could be the required adult in the car, and it would all be legal. It gave me a chance to hang out with the college kids, demonstrate my driving skills, and sit next to Laney Hoy; she was very cute and I had a slight crush on her myself. My mother must have had a mental lapse of some sort to agree to this plan, but she said it would

171

be fine, and we all took off in the '58 Dodge wagon with the radio blaring and a 14-year-old new driver at the wheel.

Everything was going quite well for the first hour or so as we completed a tour of the beautiful Country Club Plaza. I was on "cloud nine" at this point and showing off my skill at maneuvering the big "boat" of a car through the busy holiday traffic. I was actually feeling a little cocky. I was aware of Laney's shoulder snuggled up next to me in the middle front seat and was almost intoxicated by the smell of her perfume. I wanted to keep this tour going! I made a little loop around the Kansas City Art Institute and pointed out its beautiful buildings. Then as we approached an intersection with a four-way stop, I leaned down to change stations on the radio. The radio was located low on the center console, just above the hump in the floor, and Laney's feet were interfering with my manipulation of the dials. I stared down at the radio and manipulated the dials for at least 15 or 20 seconds as the car continued at 25 miles per hour toward the intersection ahead. I started to raise my eyes back to the windshield and the road when I heard Cousin Tom scream, "LOOKOUT!" There was a loud crash as we plowed into the back of a car stopped at the stop sign. Then there was, almost immediately, a second crash as the car in front of us shot forward and crashed into the back of a third vehicle in front of it.

The driver of the car in front of us was a woman who immediately became somewhat hysterical and started saying her young daughter in the car had a neck injury. Then the driver of the third vehicle came back and informed us he was an attorney. When the police arrived, I was issued a citation. This day had gone to Hell in a hand basket faster than could be imagined. It turned out no one was injured, but the only drivable car was our Dodge wagon. The two vehicles I hit had to be towed away. My dad showed up at the scene after about an hour and drove us all home. My dad and mom never said too much about the accident other than to advise me to keep my eyes on the road. I think they realized how humiliated and embarrassed I was and probably felt I was punishing myself enough. My dad gave me several more driving lessons over the next few days, and I was back on the road.

In the spring of 1961, I was approaching my 16th birthday, which would be celebrated in July; I looked forward to this day with great anticipation since I would be able to get an unrestricted driver's license. As I approached this milestone, I was coveting ownership of a

172

car of my own, as were all my male friends. My dad had always said I wouldn't be allowed to own a car until I was able to afford to buy one with my own money and pay for the insurance and maintenance. He didn't end up standing firm on the insurance issue and, when I did buy car, he paid the premiums for me.

I had been saving my paper route, lawn mowing, and snow shoveling money for a long time and had several hundred dollars in my own savings account at that point. I started searching the want ads in the Kansas City Star each week. I found most of the interesting ads in the paper on the weekends—Friday, Saturday, and Sunday. I narrowed my search down to the "Imported, Sports, and Antique Cars" section and, within that, honed in on the antique cars. It seemed almost every teenaged male at the time wanted an antique car because they were cheap to buy and, with a little work, could be customized and/or converted into a hotrod. For example, a kid could buy a classic like a 1930 Ford Model A Coupe or sedan for $150. He could then drop a big V-8 engine into it, add chrome headers with dual chromed lake pipes, lower the front end, raise the rear end, chop the top, change out the wheels and tires, and upholster the interior with "rolls and pleats" and "button tufting." He would then have a real conversation piece for the high school parking lot!

So I started circling ads for old cars I could afford. I begged my dad to take me out looking at these cars on Saturdays and Sundays. At first I had no luck getting him interested in doing this. It was fall (1961) when he got tired of my haranguing, and one Saturday we set out to look at some of these advertised vehicles. It was a crisp and breezy autumn Saturday with brilliant yellow, orange, and red leaves blowing from the trees in swirls. The first car we looked at was a 1940 Ford Coupe. I thought at the time, and still do, that it was one of the classiest cars in existence. When we pulled up to the house of the owner, we found both garage doors open with the car inside, the hood open, and several greasy teenaged "mechanics" bent over the engine compartment. The floor of the garage was strewn with various mechanical parts, and the concrete was stained with oil and grease spots. The front end of the car had been lowered, and the back end had been raised. It had a big V-8 engine block which was painted red. The body needed a little work, but a couple of the fenders had gray primer on them and looked like they were ready for paint. The owner was asking $200 for it. It seemed like the perfect car for me, but when I looked at my dad's face, it appeared he had more than a little skepticism. He started asking the boys picky questions like: "Does it run?" and "Do the brakes work?" I had $200 and I was ready to buy, but after hearing the answers to these questions and few more, my dad said, "I think we need to go home and think about this."

I had a few more ads circled that day, and my dad patiently drove me around to look at several more jalopies. At each of these homes, without exception, there was a garage full of greasy kids working on a partially disassembled hotrod. We didn't see a single car that day that was actually ready for a test drive. I was undeterred.

After that weekend of driving all over Kansas City to inspect old cars, I continued to circle ads and to beg my father to take me out to look at the cars described. I think, after the first weekend of doing this, he felt this was a total waste of his time and my time. He begged off with new excuses each weekend. I think Dad realized it would only be a matter of time until I wore him down and he allowed me to buy a car, but he had a different idea of a proper car for me. He wanted me to have a whole car that I could drive right out of the former owner's driveway. Dad thought the car I envisioned would be one we would cart home on a utility trailer to spread out on our garage floor with the hope I would someday have it operating.

Fall turned to winter and winter to spring. The fragrant air of spring arrived and the trees budded with new growth. Then one beautiful, warm Saturday afternoon, my friend Nick Davis raised the pressure my dad was already feeling when he and his father pulled up our driveway in Nick's "new" hotrod with the top down—a 1931 Ford Model A roadster. And it was a real hotrod! It had a flathead V-8 engine, a truck transmission, and fancy chromed wheels and hubcaps. It was very cool and very fast, and one of the most fun features was its rumble seat. I am sure Nick was allowed to get the car because HIS DAD wanted a hotrod. His dad was not like my dad. He was a real car guy. He loved cars and actually sold Oldsmobiles for a living. Whenever Nick and I tinkered with Nick's car over the next couple of years, his dad was right there with us, wrench in hand.

At this point, I think my dad decided he was going to have to take control of the whole car situation and do something to avoid ending up with a pile of car parts in our garage. So one evening he announced at the dinner table he had found a car he thought would be just perfect for me. He had gotten a haircut that day at his downtown

174

barbershop, and apparently he had been unloading his troubles on his barber. Well, the barber said he would be happy to sell me his own car. It was a 1938 Chevy business coupe he had bought new in 1938 and had only driven it to work and back for the previous 23 years. He told my dad it ran well and only had 75,000 miles on it. He said if I wanted it, he would take $75 for it. I was pretty excited about this. The next weekend Dad and I went to look at the barber's car. It wasn't exactly pretty. The paint was a faded navy blue with lots of scratches, and all four fenders had been bashed in at various times and had never been repaired. The interior upholstery was pretty drab. It was beige mohair—the kind that used to be in all cars—and it looked dated. The car did run well though, and I loved the coupe body style with no rear seat and a huge trunk extending way back. Its lines were similar in style to the classy 1940 Ford I thought was so cool. Although it wasn't a hotrod (yet) and only had a straight six in it, there were some pretty neat features about it, including the long straight gear shift sticking up out of the middle of the floor between the driver and passenger. The car had potential. I was sold on it and handed the barber my $75.

1961 – United States involvement in Viet Nam War escalates – The cost of a gallon of gas rises to 27¢ - Soviet Yuri Gagarin becomes first human in space – Alan Shepard becomes first American Astronaut in space – The Peace Corps is founded – The average price of a home is $2770 -

175

Chapter 29

One of my good friends in high school was a kid named Rich Butler. Rich and I hung out together quite a bit—going to football and basketball games, shooting baskets after school at his house or our house, and even working on homework together sometimes. Rich's family had taken me with them on a couple of their family vacations to the Lake of the Ozarks. They had a ski boat, and Rich and I had fun water skiing together while his dad drove the boat. I had a great time on these trips with him, his mom and dad, and his younger sister.

The same spring in which I bought my first car, my junior year of high school, I had been reading and hearing about the 1962 World's Fair in Seattle. The fair was to be the first World's Fair held in the United States since World War II, and it was expected to be fantastic. I started talking to Rich about the two of us going to it. Rich and I were both 16 years old at the time. My idea was for us to pack up my 1938 Chevy and drive out to Seattle. Rich loved the idea of going to the fair, but he had a different idea about how we could get there. After all, anyone could drive to Seattle, but how many people would get there by bicycle? Yes, Rich thought we should ride bikes over the 3,700-mile roundtrip. It sounded a little crazy at first, but then I started warming to the idea. Rich was always conscious of the way he looked and dreamed of having the physique of a weight-lifter someday. I remember him saying, "Dave, can you imagine what our calf muscles will look like when we get back? They will be the size of basketballs!"

When Rich and I approached our respective parents about the plan, it was soundly rejected by all four of them. Rich and I didn't give up the idea easily and kept working on them for several weeks. Our folks claimed their objection was not a question of trusting their two 16-year-old teenage sons. Their concern was the danger of riding bicycles along the edge of busy highways with cars and trucks whizzing by just a few feet away.

Rich and I finally realized, as summer approached, we were not getting anywhere with these negotiations and would have to take a different tack if we were going to make it to the World's Fair. So we approached them with my original idea—driving my Chevy to Seattle. My dad came back with a quick answer to our new request, and I'm sure the four parents had a good laugh over it. We lived in a big, old three-story house that was in need of a paint job. My dad told us all four parents had agreed to allow the two of us to take the Chevy to Seattle if Rich and I painted the house first. My dad would pay us for the job, and we could use the money to finance the trip. This sounded fine to me. Rich wasn't so sure. Rich had never before had a job of any kind, his parents rarely asked him to do any chores around their house, and they had always given him money for whatever he needed. I was finally able to talk him into this plan, but he complained his head off as we worked at this job during the early days of summer. This was the time he was used to sleeping until noon every day and then hanging around the local community swimming pool in the afternoons.

It didn't take us long to realize we had possibly bitten off more than we could chew. Rich did rally to the cause and worked hard alongside me, but the paint on the house was in poor shape, requiring lots of scraping, sanding, and priming. This increased the man-hours significantly, and we started to wonder if we could get the paint job finished before the snow started to fall that winter. It became clear to both of us that, at the rate we were going, our summer vacation from school would be over before we could finish painting the house, and there would be no time left for us to go to Seattle.

As I recall all of this, 50 years later, it seems obvious there was collusion among the four parents, and none of them ever expected us to finish painting the house that summer. It had been a clever way to deal with us on our plan to go to the World's Fair since we would not take "no" for an answer. I don't think Rich and I suspected this deviousness at the time though. I've always wondered if our folks had compared the danger of riding bicycles along the side of the road with the dangers of running up and down ladders to extreme heights while carrying buckets, scrapers, and brushes. There were times, working on the third story of the house, when each of us pulled the ladder over at a precarious tilt to paint a section in order to avoid climbing down and repositioning it.

By the end of June, Rich and I had finished scraping, sanding, priming, and painting the back side of the house and the attached garage. We had two more months of summer left and almost 75% of the job still remaining. We approached my dad at this point and talked to him about our predicament. To my utter shock and surprise, he agreed to release us from our unwritten contract. He said he would pay

178

us for the work we had completed and hire professional painters to finish the job. If Rich's parents agreed, we could start on our way for Seattle—but only if we took my car. He remained adamantly against the bicycle plan. To our delight, Rich's parents came around as well, and we started packing up the old car the next day.

As soon as Rich and I got the green light on our trip, we cleaned our paintbrushes and other tools, folded our tarps, stored the cans of paint in the garage, and put away the ladders. We then started packing the '38 Chevy with gear we needed for the trip. We planned on camping out each night, so we put in a canvas wall tent, two army surplus cots, sleeping bags, flashlights, a kerosene lantern, my old Boy Scout cook kit, a cooler, a big box of matches, a sheath knife, and a small hatchet. We each packed a small bag of clothes and toiletries, and also added our heavy winter coats for cold nights in the mountains. Rich and I each had about $100 in cash we planned to take, and that seemed like it would be plenty of money to get us to Seattle and back. This was before the days of credit cards, and our folks were worried about us losing our cash or getting robbed along the way, so my dad took us to the bank and we each bought $100 worth of travelers' checks. If we lost those, we were told we could be reimbursed at any Western Union office.

It was a beautiful, warm summer morning on July 17, 1962, just before sunrise, when Rich and I backed down the driveway on our adventure. Rich's mom and dad had driven him over to our house, so all four parents were there to see us off. All four had looks of trepidation on their faces in the early morning light. It appeared as if they thought it might be the last time they would see either of us alive.

Rich and I couldn't get the grins off of our faces as we found our way to the 18th Street Expressway in Roeland Park, which connected up with the Kansas Turnpike near Bonner Springs. I started out driving and began giving Rich preliminary narrative instructions on operating a vehicle with a stick shift. Rich had his driver's license but had only driven a car with an automatic transmission. I had a hard time getting him to understand the purpose of the clutch, but I figured he would get it when I gave him the opportunity to practice once we got down the highway a stretch.

We took the Kansas Turnpike to Topeka. The 60 miles between Bonner Springs and Topeka was the only section of four-lane, divided highway on our whole trip. There were no interstate highways built across Kansas or Colorado or, for that matter, almost anywhere in the U.S. yet. We picked up US Highway 40 out of Topeka and continued our trek across Kansas. At Junction City, we turned onto Kansas State Highway 18. This was then a popular route to Colorado and angles northwest through several small Kansas towns and joins US Highway 24 in western Kansas. After several hours of driving, I decided it was time to give Rich a lesson in driving a car with a standard transmission. We must have been a comical sight as we lurched out of a gas station in central Kansas with Rich at the wheel. There was a lot of grinding of gears and cursing, and Rich repeatedly asked me to explain over and over again what the clutch was for. Almost every time we came to an intersection where we had to stop, Rich killed the engine by forgetting to step on the clutch as well as the brake. I got a little exasperated after a while and probably wasn't a very patient instructor. Rich might consider that a serious understatement.

At some point during the afternoon, I noticed some steam coming out around the radiator cap. When we checked the engine temperature gauge, we found it was pegged out. This should have been an ominous sign, but I don't think either of us was overly concerned at that point. We pulled to the shoulder of the road and shut off the engine. We opened up the engine cowl and sat on the running board until the engine cooled down enough to remove the radiator cap. We then emptied all of our canteens and other water containers into the radiator. While we were doing that, a couple of cars approached on the highway and stopped and asked us if we needed any assistance, but we waved them on. (In those days, few people would pass by a stranded motorist without stopping and offering help.) We babied the old car along to the next town where we stopped at a gas station and topped the radiator off from a garden hose, and we then continued on down Highway 18.

Sometime in the early afternoon, we cruised into the town of Stockton, Kansas. Rich had noticed on the map that there was a lake a few miles west of Stockton labeled Webster Reservoir. It looked like it was fairly close to the highway, and we both suspected there might be a place to camp there. As we drove through the town of Stockton, I noticed the radiator was again starting to emit some steam from the cap. I looked for a mechanic's garage and noted there was a small radiator shop located on a corner on the main street through town. I

180

pointed it out to Rich and told him I thought we should probably swing back into town and stop by there the next day. I thought we should have the cooling system of the car checked out before heading farther west.

We found our way to Webster Reservoir and, at the end of a two-rutted dirt road, located a beautiful grassy area near the water's edge that would serve as a perfect campsite. There was a large, lone cottonwood tree in the meadow. We drove the car out into the grass and parked near the tree on a flat section of ground that looked like a good spot, and there we pitched our tent.

After we got our camp all set up, some of the tension of the day seemed to fall away. Both of us had gradually become somewhat irritated with each other as the day wore on. I was frustrated with Rich because he just couldn't seem to get the idea of driving a car with a stick shift, despite my excellent instruction. He, on the other hand, was about at the end of his tolerance for my critical expressions of exasperation. The steaming radiator all day had added a degree of pessimism to this mix. So by the time we were all settled down in camp, we were both starting to relax and unwind a bit. We gathered firewood, prepared a fire pit, built a small campfire, and cooked dinner. I was the designated cook for the entire trip since Rich had never cooked anything in his life. Rich kept the fire stoked and did most of the cleanup afterwards.

By the time we got bedded down inside the tent, it was dark. It was eerily quiet since there were no other campers and, as far as we knew, no one around us for miles. We chatted about our day until both of us drifted off into a sound sleep to the soft, rhythmic sound of cicadas.

We were both awakened a little after midnight by strong winds buffeting the tent and the sound of distant thunder. The winds became stronger and stronger until it seemed like we were in the middle of a full gale. Lightning began to flash, intermittently illuminating the inside of the tent through the canvas walls. After a while, the lightning became so frequent it was almost continuous, and we could see each other and everything in the tent clearly as if it were a bright sunny day. Then the rain started. At this point we had to shout to hear each other over the continuous loud claps of thunder, the howling wind, and the pelting rain.

181

I had done a lot of camping as a kid at summer camp and as a Boy Scout. I had camped out on rainy nights a few times but had never been out in a storm like this. It was the first night Rich had ever camped out in his life. He had never slept without a solid roof over his head. We both had lived in the Midwest long enough to know tornados often accompanied severe thunderstorms such as this in western Kansas. With the rain now pouring down in torrents, the wind raging, the lightning illuminating the night, and the thunder crashing, we decided we should abandon ship and made a dash for the old car. We spent the rest of the night sitting straight up in the seat of the old 1938 Chevy with it rocking back and forth in the gale.

One thunderstorm after another seemed to make its way across Kansas that night, but when dawn finally arrived, it was all over. The sun came up in a beautiful clear sky. Rich and I had gotten little sleep, but we had survived the worst storm either of us ever remembered. Our campsite was a different story. Our tent was flat on the ground with one of the aluminum poles broken into two pieces. Our camping gear was scattered over about a half-acre of ground. Our sleeping bags were soaked. The big cottonwood tree near our campsite had survived the storm, but there were several other trees in the area that had the tops snapped off of them or had been completely uprooted.

We decided we would have to dry out our gear—mainly the tent and the sleeping bags—before we could pack it all back up. We came up with a plan. We would lay out all of the gear in the sun to dry, I'd drive the car into Stockton and get the cooling system checked out, and Rich would stay at our camp and organize everything for packing up when I returned. Neither of us thought this would delay us long. It was getting hot already, and the stuff should dry quickly. I figured I would be back by mid-to-late morning and we would be on the road again by noon. So I took off for Stockton and left Rich minding the store. I took the broken tent pole with me.

I found the radiator shop in town and parked in front of the open garage door. A middle-aged man walked out to meet me and asked me what he could do for me. I explained how the car was overheating and boiling off the water. He took the cap off of the radiator and said he needed to let it cool a little while, and then he wanted to look at the water in it. While we were waiting, he showed me around his shop. It looked like a typical maintenance garage with the exception of several large metal tanks for boiling out plugged radiators.

When he decided my car had cooled enough that he wouldn't get burned, he went out and stuck his finger into the top of the radiator. When he withdrew his finger, it was covered with a goopy, oily residue, indicating the radiator was all stopped up and badly in need of cleaning. He also showed me some areas on the radiator core that looked like small leaks. There wasn't any way around it, the radiator was going to have to come out and be boiled out in one of his tanks. While it was out, he would pressure test it and repair the leaks with solder.

This was not good news. He quoted me a price for the job, but it was a significant percentage of the money I had for the rest of the trip. When the owner of the shop saw the distress on my face, he suggested a much more palatable price if I would remove the radiator from the car and then re-install it after it was cleaned and repaired. He said he had all of the tools I would need and I could borrow them. We were now down to getting the whole job done for a few dollars. I could do that. It didn't concern me at all that I had never taken out and re-installed a radiator before. I had been taking things apart and putting them back together since I was small boy, so I was pretty sure I could just look at it and figure it out.

As I started disassembling things, I was wondering what Rich would think had happened to me. It was probably going to take me an hour or two to get the radiator out, it needed to be boiled for four hours, and then it would probably take me another hour or two to get it reinstalled. I had no way to get in touch with Rich and tell him about this development. He would just have to sit tight. He had no way to go anywhere, so I assumed he would be right where I left him when I got back.

Once I got the radiator pulled and it was boiling away in the vat, I started working on the broken tent pole. The owner of the radiator shop was turning out to be a very nice fellow and was quickly becoming one of my best friends. He helped me repair the tent pole with a jury-rigged splice. After that little job was done, I crossed the street to a little corner diner and had a hamburger at their lunch counter.

By the time I had reinstalled the radiator, hooked all the hoses back up, and arrived back at the campsite, it was two o'clock in the afternoon. Rich didn't even hear me driving across the grass toward the campsite. He was sound asleep on one of the cots with the bright sun shining directly on him. The remainder of our gear must have dried out because he had everything neatly folded and stacked. It was all ready to be packed into the trunk so we could take off down the road. He had even made sandwiches for our lunch (which was long past) and packed them in the cooler. When I woke him, he didn't seem to be too upset that I had been gone all day. He said something like, "Well, I had a pretty nice day, and I knew you'd come back." We loaded up quickly and hit the road. We knew, with such a late start, we wouldn't get many miles of road behind us that day.

We were almost to the Colorado state line, with me at the wheel, when Rich's exuberance got a little away from him. Rich had been taking Karate lessons for some time, and he suddenly decided to release some of his excitement of the moment by practicing a karate chop in the air in front of him. In class, he was taught to practice chops by checking the blow to his opponent just short of striking him. The idea was to allow practice without anyone getting injured but also to learn precise control of the movements. Unfortunately, Rich misjudged his chop and actually struck the windshield with the outside of edge of his hand using a knife-edged blow. The windshield on my antique car was, fortunately, divided into two separate sections by a center mullion. But the right half of the windshield cracked in every direction from the point of contact and looked a little like the roadmap lying in Rich's lap. I immediately uttered (more like screamed) some rather harsh words while Rich sat there with a stunned look on his face and his mouth agape. This was followed by a couple of minutes of complete silence as we both stared through the windshield at the road ahead of us. Then both of us began laughing hysterically until we were almost out of control. I actually thought I might have to pull over to the side of the road to recover.

The windshield on that old car was safety glass, so it didn't completely shatter, and it did not leak. It was on the passenger's side, so it didn't interfere with the driver's vision. We just left it the way it was until we got back to Kansas City at the end of the trip.

It seemed like the incident with the windshield just helped both of us sort of "roll with the punches" and not get too upset with any further difficulties on the rest of the trip. The hysterical laughing that followed probably helped in that regard as well.

By late afternoon, we were pulling into the little town of Limon, Colorado. There was no good place to camp, so we found a hotel and got a room for the night. I believe the hotel was the only one in town. It was an old building, but it was clean and neat. We paid $3 for our room for the night.

The next morning, we continued on US Highway 24 to Colorado Springs. We arrived there mid-morning and stopped at a small garage where we had the car checked over by a mechanic. The route we were planning through the Colorado Rockies involved traversing some high mountain passes, and the radiator trouble on the first day had made us realize there might be other things wrong with the car we didn't know about. We particularly wanted the brakes checked out. The mechanic looked the car over and informed us that the brakes were fine, but an engine compression check indicated we had low compression on several cylinders that he suspected was due to a leaky head gasket. Replacing it was a fairly major task, and we did not have the time or the funds to do anything about this problem. He told us the leak was reducing the power of the engine and also could be causing oil to get into the cooling system and plug up the radiator. This was disconcerting since we thought our radiator troubles were over after the repairs in Stockton. We thanked the mechanic, paid him a few dollars and headed west, still on US Highway 24.

Sometime in the afternoon, we arrived at the junction of Colorado State Highway 82. This road is now a paved road, but in 1962 it was only gravel and, even today, it is closed all winter. We took this gravel road over 12,095-foot Independence Pass to the little ski town of Aspen. The old 1938 Chevrolet climbed bravely up this rather frightening road, although we did have to stop several times to let the engine cool and refill the radiator. We were well prepared with lots of water. We had filled every container we had that morning including a canvas water bag we had bought in Colorado Springs at the suggestion of our mechanic friend. This was slung over the radiator cap and hung down across the grill. The water stayed relatively cool in that spot, and it was readily accessible for refilling the radiator. We refilled the bag from streams along the road many times.

Highway 82 via Independence Pass was the shortest route to Aspen when coming from the east, but when we finally got to the town, we were told the road was rarely used because it was unpaved and so difficult. Most travelers to Aspen took the longer, but much easier, route around to the west and then doubled back from western end of State Highway 82. We did not see one other vehicle going over Independence Pass that day.

We camped a few miles outside of Aspen that night in a pretty little spot next to a mountain stream. It was not a regular campground, but just a wide spot in the road with enough room to drive off into the grass. I cooked our dinner over a campfire, and Rich washed the dishes in the stream. Rich wasn't much of a cook, so this became our regular routine. My campfire cooking experience from my Boy Scout days was coming in handy. Our campsite was at a fairly high elevation, and both of us thought we were going to freeze to death during the night.

The next day we drove into Aspen and saw the chair lift was running to the top of Ajax Mountain—the big ski mountain—for summer tourists. We bought tickets and rode it to the top. We spent an hour or so looking at the spectacular views in every direction and ate lunch on the sun deck. On the ride back down, we saw a few people below us hiking up or down the mountain.

We picked up a few grocery supplies, and we then drove by the Alpine Lodge, a quaint little inn that had been converted from an old house. I wanted Rich to see it because it was the place Steve and I had bunked two years before on a ski trip with the Kansas City Bachelors Club (another crazy story I probably should have written about). We took a picture of my car in the drive to show Steve when we got back home.

We pulled out of Aspen in mid-afternoon and drove northwest through the towns of Glenwood Springs, Rifle, and Meeker. We found a campsite near Meeker that was indicated on our map and located at the end of a rough dirt road designated Highway 132. That road does not appear on the Colorado map today—at least as that highway number. Rich had been keeping a daily diary for our trip and, the next morning, wrote: "Dave lucked out—found the secret of warmth—bury yourself in sleeping bag till near suffocation."

We left Meeker for a long day of driving, heading north on what is now State Highways 13 and 789. We picked up US Highway 30 in southern Wyoming, took it west to US 191, and headed north to Pinedale, Wyoming. It was a tough day with lots of radiator trouble. We had to stop, let the engine cool, and refill the radiator several times.

We were flagged down by a stranded cowboy in the Red Desert of southern Wyoming who said he had walked 35 miles on back roads to reach the highway after his truck broke down. He wanted us to take him to the next town, but we didn't have any room in the car. He even offered us handfuls of cash he had in his pockets. He had no water and told us he was extremely thirsty. We gave him a cold Coke from our ice chest. We had to save the little water we had for the radiator. He thanked us and sat down and waited for the next vehicle to come along.

We stopped in Rock Springs to buy a few supplies when I realized, somewhere along the way, I had lost all of my Travelers' Checks. We went to a Western Union office to see if we could get them refunded, but no luck. We did some calculations and figured out Rich probably had enough money to get us through the rest of the trip.

At one point during the day, we crested a hill and almost ran into a herd of cattle being driven down the road by cowboys on horseback. There were several hundred head of cattle and it took us about 30 minutes to work our way through them.

We camped out that night at Little Half Moon Lake campground near Pinedale, Wyoming. Rich described it in his diary as a "mosquito-infested swamp." I don't think it was that bad, but that night I locked our only set of keys inside the car. It probably wouldn't have been too big a deal except for the fact the keys were in the ignition with the engine running, and it was after dark. We had bought some radiator flush chemical earlier in the day, and the instructions said to put it in and leave the engine running for 30 minutes. I thought it was a good idea to lock it so no one could sneak up and steal it while it was running. For some reason, it didn't occur to me that I would have no way to unlock the car myself and, also, that there probably wasn't another soul within 30 miles of us. In any case, Rich did a miraculous recovery by crawling into the trunk, removing the radio speaker from the rear deck, maneuvering his hand and arm up through the hole, and then fishing the keys out of the ignition with a hanger wire. This was done under my verbal instructions as I viewed his movements from the side window with a flashlight. It was quite a feat!

The following day, with the radiator newly flushed, we headed into Pinedale where, as good Catholic boys, we went to Sunday Mass. We then again made an attempt to get a refund on my lost travelers' checks, but…no luck. We headed north out of Pinedale for Jackson Hole, Wyoming, and then Grand Teton and Yellowstone National Parks. In Jackson Hole we parked the car and strolled around the central plaza for a few minutes before continuing on. We stopped a few times in Grand Teton to take pictures of the beautiful scenery, and we arrived at the south entrance to Yellowstone late in the afternoon. There was a campground just inside the entrance, and we pitched our tent at a site which was at the top of an embankment above the Snake River. We slept well that night to the river's rushing sounds. We camped there for three nights, using it as a base for exploring the park. I recently—in 2011—drove through the park and out the south gate. The area where we camped is no longer a campground. It has been converted to a picnic area.

Rich and I spent the next two days touring the park. We visited the beautiful and historic Old Faithful Inn and watched the Old Faithful Geyser erupt on schedule. As we walked back to the car from the Inn, we ran into a girl whom we recognized from our high school in Kansas City—Betty Gail Wortman. This seemed like an amazing coincidence in view of the fact there are hundreds of people there at any one time. As she walked past us on a sidewalk, both Rich and I casually said hi to her as if we had just seen her in the halls of our high school five minutes before. We were both too shy around girls to even consider a brief conversation with her and her parents.

On our second day in Yellowstone, we drove out of the park at West Yellowstone and continued another 30 miles or so into southwest Montana to see Quake Lake. The lake had been created by a massive earthquake just three years before—in 1959. I had no idea at the time that 43 years later I would build a log home just a few miles to the west of Quake Lake and spend my summers there in retirement.

We decided to make this the turnaround point for the trip. We were still about 750 miles shy of Seattle, and with all the car trouble we were having, we decided to abandon the idea of getting to the World's Fair and, instead, head for home. So after three nights of camping in Yellowstone, we pointed the Chevy south on U.S Highway 287. We made it to Rawlins, Wyoming, for the night. While driving through the town, we spotted a sign in the front yard of a little house advertising "Room for rent." The house was owned by an old widow, and we rented her basement room for $1 each. It was nice to get a warm bath after several days of camping.

The next morning, feeling fit and refreshed, we headed for Rocky Mountain National Park in northern Colorado. Just east of Rawlins we split off of US Highway 30 and headed south on what is now Wyoming State Highway 130 and then Wyoming 230. At the

Colorado line this turned into Colorado State Highway 125. We followed this to Granby, at the southwest corner of Rocky Mountain National Park, where we picked up US Highway 34. This highway is known as Trail Ridge Road through the park and ascends to over 12,000 feet above sea level at one point. It was the highest paved road in the United States then, and this was the main reason we included Rocky Mountain National Park on our return route. It was another big test for my crippled antique car, and we added lots of water to the radiator on the climb. As we ascended Trail Ridge Road that day, it began to rain hard, and we discovered at that point the windshield wipers were not working at all. The wipers on this old car were powered by a vacuum pump motor, and it had apparently failed. We pulled over onto a shoulder and waited until the rainfall lightened up and then continued along our way with somewhat limited visibility. We encountered snow—in mid-July—along the side of the road as we neared the top.

We passed through the little resort town of Estes Park a few miles before crossing the east boundary of the National Park. After exiting the park, we stayed on US Highway 34 through Loveland and Greeley and stopped for the night in the eastern Colorado town of Akron. This would be our last night on the road, and we had just enough money left from Rich's treasury to pay for a cheap hotel room and dinner at a café. The hotel was an old brick building, and our room had high ceilings, wood furniture, and a tilting panel above the door for venting from the hallway (this type of window was known as a "transom window" and was a common feature in many buildings before the days of air conditioning); it was a little austere but clean and comfortable.

Early the next morning, we accomplished our usual routine of filling up every water container we had to feed our thirsty radiator. We then headed east on US Highway 34 toward the Kansas state line. Somewhere in the vicinity of the state line, we picked out a north-south highway and jogged back south to US Highway 24. From that point on, our route was a reversal of our trip west through Kansas on the first day of the trip. We had to stop a few times under the hot Kansas sun to let the engine cool and top off the radiator, but we made it! We pulled into the driveway of our family home in Kansas City in the late afternoon with lots of stories to tell our folks and friends. The trip lasted 10 days from start to finish, but provided Rich and me a lifetime of treasured memories.

I still marvel today that our parents allowed us to undertake such a journey at our tender, young ages. I do think it was a brave—and a little crazy—decision for them to make, but I think it was a good one. The trip gave both Rich and me each a new sense of confidence and responsibility at a vulnerable stage in our lives when there are many directions to go on the road toward maturity and adulthood. I look back on this now and feel it was good for us both. One effect of this trip on me was to turn me into a road warrior for my whole adult life. This didn't seem to happen to Rich, but for me there are few things I enjoy more than cruising down a lonesome highway on a road trip. I love to travel by car all over the United States to see new places and to revisit places I have been. One of my favorite television commercials of the 1950s and early 1960s was the Chevrolet commercial with actress Dinah Shore enthusiastically singing, "See the USA in your Chevrolet....America's the greatest land of all..." That catchy tune still comes to my mind sometimes when I am exploring the back roads of America—and, more often than not, in a Chevrolet.

1962 – The Cuban Missile Crisis causes dangerous relations between the U.S. and the Soviet Union – The first person is killed trying to cross the Berlin Wall – Marilyn Monroe is found dead – Elvis Presley's "Return to Sender" is the most popular song –

Chapter 30

There was about a month of summer vacation left when we got back from our road trip. I was finally able to get a refund on my lost travelers' checks, but after I reimbursed Rich for my share of the trip expenses he had shouldered, I didn't have much cash left. My car needed some expensive major repairs that were a little beyond my mechanical expertise, so I needed a job to earn some money before school started. I still had a few lawns I took care of. This provided a little income, but it wasn't enough. I felt I needed a real job and wanted to find something I could do part-time after school during the school year. About this time, my mother told me about a friend of hers whose son had a part-time job working in the stockroom at Jack Henry's, an exclusive men's clothing store on the County Club Plaza. The woman's son had worked there for several years, but he was going off to college in September. So Jack Henry's was looking for a replacement for him. I applied and got the job right away.

The kid whom I was replacing worked with me in August and helped me get oriented and trained on the job. There were also two full-time stockroom employees who were in charge—both older men—Al Mesmer and Lee Tolly. Al was the senior employee for the department and seemed to be the boss. Lee was probably a little older but was under Al, and he was in charge when Al wasn't there. Both of these men knew everything about the operation of the stock room.

We worked exclusively in an underground basement below the sales floor. There were stairs and a ramp to a loading dock behind the building. The job involved receiving, unpacking, hanging, and tagging clothing which arrived from the manufacturers. All of the men's clothing sold by Jack Henry's was high quality and quite expensive – three-piece Hickey-Freeman suits and Countess Mara ties, for example. The suits had to be hung in a specific manner on custom wooden Jack Henry hangers. They were then arranged according to size on hanging carts which were on wheels. Before being moved to the elevator for transfer to the sales floor, they were priced and tagged. Again, the tags had to be carefully attached to the   sleeve of the coat in a precise manner. For items like shirts and ties, there was a machine that attached the price tag with a straight pin. The tag was required to be in a certain spot on each item, so proper insertion in the tagging machine was critical.

The stockroom was also the mail room. We had a Pitney Bowes postage meter, and all of the incoming and outgoing mail was handled and routed by our stockroom team. The store had a gift shop, and one of my jobs was to pack, wrap, and ship any gifts or clothing being sent. We had a long work table against one wall that was all set up for this chore with rolls of brown wrapping paper, packing materials, tape dispensers, and an assortment of cardboard boxes. We also had all the materials for fancy giftwrapping.

There was one funny incident that occurred a couple of weeks before Christmas. The manager of the gift shop came down to the basement to see me with five identical gift items he wanted to be giftwrapped and shipped. It was unusual for the manager to be making this request personally. He explained that the customer who had purchased the gifts was a woman who was a long-time customer of the gift shop, and her husband bought all of his suits from the store. I don't recall what the gifts were, but they were Christmas gifts for her five grown grandsons. The gift shop sold a selection of fine, high-end desk accessories such as letter openers, pen and pencil sets, barometers, etc., and the gifts for her grandsons were probably along those lines. The manager of the gift shop wanted to be sure I giftwrapped, packaged, and shipped these items with the utmost of care for his special customer. I pictured his customer as a distinguished looking gray-haired woman who was probably tastefully bejeweled in diamonds and most likely wearing a mink coat. I suspected her grandsons would be flying in from college soon—probably Harvard, Yale, Princeton, William and Mary, or Dartmouth—for the Christmas holidays. All five likely were polo players, on the tennis team, and members of the crew rowing team. With these mental images, I took this task on with serious attention to detail. I assured the manager I would wrap each item meticulously and get them on their way immediately.

I had never before had five identical items to wrap and ship at the same time, so I thought I could do this operation most efficiently in an assembly line fashion. So I took one of the items and used it to pick the appropriate size box and then lined up four more boxes of the same size. I then cut a sheet of gift-wrap paper to the size of one of the boxes and then four more sheets the same size. I did the same with a

194

decorative ribbon, final shipping boxes, and brown wrapping paper. I put the boxes all in a stack, the gift paper in a stack, the ribbons in a stack, and then filled out five address labels for the five different addresses the manager had provided. I placed the address labels in a stack. He had also provided five personal gift notes which had been handwritten to each grandson by their grandmother. I placed these in a stack on the work table with all of the other supplies. I then had all the supplies ready, and the wrapping and packaging would go quickly. I packed each gift carefully into a gift box and tossed one of the handwritten notes into each box. I placed a lid on each one and then gift wrapped each one with fancy paper and ribbon. They all looked beautiful! I then placed each one, with ample packing material, in a shipping box and applied the previously-cut brown butcher paper. The last step was to slap the shipping labels and postage on. This operation absolutely could not have been done more efficiently, and each of the packages looked neat and professional. I sent them out later that afternoon.

A couple of weeks after Christmas, the manager of the gift shop came storming down to the stock room looking for me. The elderly grandmother was up in the gift shop and was furious. Apparently when Grandson Landon opened his grandmother's Christmas gift, the note said, "Dear Bronson, you have always been my favorite…." When Grandson Bronson opened his gift, the note said, "Dear Spencer, you have always been my favorite…." As it turned out, not one of the five grandsons had gotten the correct card. When I explained my assembly line approach to wrapping the packages, I tried to make it sound like this was an easy mistake anyone could have made. The manager, however, was not amused and looked at me like I was a complete idiot. I didn't get fired for this little incident, but I had to take a lot of ribbing from Lee and Al for a while.

I held this job for my entire senior year of high school and worked several afternoons each week and on Saturday. The store wasn't open on Sunday as this was considered the "Lord's Day" and a day of rest for everyone. Almost all stores were closed on Sundays. My pay was based on the hours I worked each week at a rate of $1.25 per hour. I used my earnings almost exclusively to fix up my old Chevy.

I learned a lot from this first job as an actual employee. I'm still quite good at wrapping packages, and I attribute that to getting lots of practice at Jack Henry's. Also, if you could look into my clothes closet today, you would see that all of my shirts and slacks are hung neatly and beautifully on wooden hangers. My closet definitely meets Jack Henry's standards.

Chapter 31

The summer ended—suddenly it seemed—and I was back in school, attending my classes, working quite a few hours at Jack Henry's, and busy with lots of homework every night. I was still expected to do my share of the family chores on the weekends too. I managed to go to most of the high school football games with some of my friends that fall, but I didn't seem to have much of a social life beyond that. I made it to a few Friday night social "mixers" and "sock hops" held at the school, but I was still shy around girls and rarely asked anyone to dance. I was becoming self-aware by this time that I was quite a ways behind some of my contemporaries when it came to interacting with females. I had still been on very few dates in my life and must say I was fairly uncomfortable on all of those occasions.

At about this time, I started to consciously worry about my failure to enter the dating scene. It seemed all of the really attractive and popular girls in my class were spoken for. Each was usually "going steady" with one of the school's star athletes. I couldn't, in my wildest dreams, imagine being a romantic Casanova like all of these smooth talkers seemed to be. Besides, I wasn't much of an athlete. The few times I had tried out for a school team, I was quickly cut. This didn't do much for my confidence. I did quite well on the academic side, but it didn't seem like any girls cared about that at all. I was starting to wonder if I would ever have a wife and a family. That was a real concern since, back then, everyone was expected to grow up, get a job, get married, and have a family. A common worry for a teenage girl in those days was that she would end up an old maid; I found myself thinking the same way, and it was humiliating.

I actually had gone out on a few dates since I had been in high school, but the stress associated with each of these occasions was so great it hardly made the experience worth it. The first biggest hurdle was always getting up the nerve to ask a girl out in the first place. Inviting her face to face was out of the question. Calling her on the phone, though, had a number of associated problems too. There was only one telephone in our house, and it was located on the telephone stand in the dinette, just off the kitchen. So with seven family members, it was quite impossible to make the call with any degree of privacy. I just had to tell my mother, father, and four sisters what I was about to do and then order them to basically get lost. Even then, my conversation had to be guarded, since I knew at least one of them was right around the corner listening intently. By the time I got to this stage of shooing everyone away from the area of the telephone, I had already secretly searched the telephone book for the girl's number and was hoping I had picked out the correct one.

When these preparatory actions had been completed, I was finally ready to dial. As I began to dial, fear usually built up to a sharp crescendo, and I would usually hang up before the girl's phone had a chance for even one jingle. What was I so worried about? Well, what if she wasn't there and her mother answered and wanted to know who was calling? I had no desire to deal with that. If she was there and actually answered the phone herself, would I be able to hold it together and talk smoothly? I always practiced exactly what I planned to say over and over, but it still might not come out right. What if she didn't even know who I was? What if she laughed at me? What if she had a boyfriend I didn't know about? Despite all this fear of rejection, I always felt if she just said "no" I could simply hang up and never call her again. That would actually be kind of a relief. The result of all these concerns was that I probably dialed the girl's number 50 times before I finally got up the nerve to let it actually ring. If I ever actually got to talk to the girl and ask her out, she had no idea what I had been through up until that point.

Although the phone call and setting up the date was probably the scariest part of dating for me, there was a multitude of other major stressors involved. On the actual night of the date, I would most likely have to meet one or both of her parents; they would size me up and then make a decision of whether or not to trust their little darling to the likes of me. If they had only known how wimpy I was about all of this, I don't think they would have had a worry in the world about the safety and reputation of their precious child. Although I had heard stories about some pretty scary fathers out there, I don't recall any who issued any overt threats. I did have a few who made it quite clear what time their daughter was expected home, and, in those cases, I kept a close watch on the time when the hour of curfew neared.

None of the dates I went on even came close to sparking anything like a romance. For something magic to happen, I knew I would have to summon up the courage to hold the girl's hand or put my arm around her shoulder during a movie. The idea of doing

198

something like that weighed heavily on me to the point of occupying 100 percent of my conscious thought. During a movie, I frequently saw couples around me in the theater who were comfortably snuggled up with the guy's arm romantically draped over his date's shoulder. I sometimes completely lost track of a movie's plot while working to maneuver my arm over the back of my date's seat and attempting to make it look like a totally casual, natural, and unconscious motion. I would generally extend my opposite arm over an empty seat on the other side of me. Then if my date looked at me with a "what are you doing?" look, I could tip my head back, yawn, and pretend like I was stretching my arms. I never got to the next step of moving my arm from the back of the seat to actually touching the girl's shoulder.

As all of this was going on, the biggest potential event of the entire evening was clouding my mind with dread. This was the thought of the goodnight kiss when I delivered my date back to her doorstep. It could hardly be considered an actual date if there was no goodnight kiss. There were lots of worries about this bouncing around inside my brain all evening—even as I was trying to get my arm positioned to the back of her theater seat. Would the front porch light be on when we got back or would it be dark? Would her mother or, heaven forbid, her father be waiting for us and peer out the window when they heard the car drive up? Would the girl stop and face me, providing an opportunity to plant one on her? Maybe she would just turn her back, say goodnight, and hurry inside. If I did get the chance, what kind of kiss would it be—a quick peck on the cheek or right on the lips? If on the lips, should I lick my lips first or should they be dry? Should I tip my head to one side so our noses wouldn't bump into each other? What if we both tip our heads the same direction and our noses hit anyway? Should my eyes be open or my eyes be closed? What do I do with my arms and hands—put them down at my sides or passionately embrace her? How long should our lips be locked together? All of these worries seemed to overpower any bit of courage I was able to summon up at these times. I couldn't quite get there.

To top everything off, in those days the boy was expected to pick up the check and treat the girl to everything—a movie, a carnival ride, a pizza, gas for the car, whatever. It was unheard of for a girl to pay for anything on a date. That was the way it was. So I also had to spend my hard-earned money while I put myself through the extremely uncomfortable stresses of dating. By the start of my senior year in high

199

school, I hadn't been on many dates, and they were coming fewer and farther between.

I finally stopped pushing myself so hard to make something happen in the dating world and started doing more of what I really enjoyed—just spending time in our garage working on my car. And, just like magic, the stress was gone.

Chapter 32

I was able to distract myself from my social problem with girls by working on my car. I began working on the mechanical parts I understood and tried to learn about the areas I didn't understand. I wanted to restore my old 1938 Chevy coupe to like-new condition and possibly customize it into a hotrod. There was one window crank missing and a few other little trim items needing replacement, just to start with. I needed to prowl through some junk yards to see what I could find. That is how I met Mac McClain.

Mac owned *Roe Auto Salvage*, which was only a few miles from our neighborhood. It was named after the three Roe sisters, who were old spinsters and were all in their late 90s at the time. They still lived on a remaining corner of the land. The original Roe family had pioneered on the same land, but the land was now covered with acres and acres of wrecked vehicles. I am not sure whether the site of the business still belonged to the Roe sisters at that point or whether it belonged to Mac, but, in any event, that was the location of his thriving salvage yard. It was near the Roe sister's shopping center of Roeland Park. There was a gravel drive that meandered through the maze of "previously-owned" vehicles to a fairly large metal barn-like building in the center. This building was heated with a potbellied wood stove and served as Mac's office, parts department, body shop, and paint booth. Just outside of the building, there was a sandblasting pit and an area where he stocked bricks, patio blocks, gravel, sand, and other miscellaneous landscape supplies.

I got to know Mac pretty well when I was in high school, and we developed sort of a mutual admiration for each other. Mac was old enough to be my grandfather at the time—probably in his late 50s or early 60s. He was a tall, silver-haired, good looking guy with a calm, assured manner. He was powerfully built with strong arms and a ruddy complexion. He always sported a winning smile when I popped into his office. He wore gray coveralls and always had a railroad engineer's cap on his head. With the cap usually at a jaunty angle, his strong angular facial features, the white teeth, and the big smile, he always reminded me of the movie actor Kirk Douglas. Mac looked good even when he crawled out from under a car covered with dirt and grime. I think my mother was even a bit attracted by Mac's looks and personality when she had taken me there one day on one of my foraging expeditions. She told me later she had talked to him while I was out in the yard searching for a part, and he had told her he thought I was "a fine young man."

I didn't realize it right away, but Mac's home was just a few blocks from ours, and he had actually been one of my customers on my paper route when I was in grade school. I saw Mac driving into work one day in a beautifully restored Model T Ford and realized it was the same vehicle I had admired in his driveway several years before.

Mac's main business was restoring antique cars. He was a master mechanic and, during the restoration process, would completely tear a car apart down to the frame. He had an automotive paint booth and was an expert at body and paint. He worked on everything but specialized in Model T and Model A Fords. When he painted one of these, he painted each body part separately and then put it all together. When he finished one, it was museum quality and always original—exactly as the car had come out of the factory. Mac knew that teenage boys at the time loved to customize cars and build hotrods. I got a lot of lecturing from him when I started talking about having him install 1940 Chevy taillights on my 1938 Chevy. He clearly let me know he didn't approve of that at all and said it would decrease the value of my car significantly. He did say, though, he would do the job for me if I insisted that was what I wanted.

As we got to know one another better, Mac provided me with advice on a lot of other things as well. One afternoon I showed up to buy a couple of cinder blocks. They were 50 cents each. I needed to do some work under the rear end of the car and was going to use the cinder blocks to support the frame while I had the wheels off. Mac immediately told me he would only sell me those blocks if I could assure him I wasn't going to use them to support the car. He told me some horror stories about cinder blocks collapsing and crushing the person under the vehicle. He said if that is what I planned to do with them, he wouldn't sell them to me, but he would weld up some steel stands for me if that is what I needed. I left with the cinder blocks after assuring him my mother needed them and wanted me to pick them up for her. He was wagging his finger at me as I drove off.

I have an old scrapbook photo of my car up on the cinder blocks and my head underneath the left axle. The 50-cent cinder blocks worked fine and didn't collapse and drop the car on my head. I saved three dollars because the strong steel stands Mac wanted to build for me would have cost two dollars each.

Chapter 33

My fear of dating and girl phobia finally got cured in kind of a funny way. One day during the first month of my senior year, Sister Immaculata approached me and told me I had been selected as one of several delegates from our high school, Bishop Miege, to The National Catholic Youth Conference. The conference was going to be held in Milwaukee, Wisconsin, later that fall. I suppose I should have considered it a real honor to have been selected by the faculty as a representatives of our school, but I actually had feelings closer to the opposite. I doubted if the quarterback of the football team or any of the other "cool guys" who had steady girlfriends had been selected. This was probably because the religious faculty didn't consider them nearly as holy and saintly as I was. I felt I had little choice but to accept. I had known Sister Immaculata for many years and didn't have the heart to refuse her. She had always looked at me like she thought I was some kind of child saint, and I knew it would break her heart if I turned her down. I consoled myself with the thought that I would be excused from classes for a few days.

Our student delegation took the train from Kansas City to Milwaukee. There was a whole train car reserved for the Catholic youth from several dioceses attending the convention. Sister Immaculata and one other nun were along with the group from our school as our chaperons for the three-day conference. Once the train left the station, all of the kids in the car started moving around to different seats and becoming acquainted or, in some cases, renewing old acquaintances from other schools. A loud, festive, party-type atmosphere developed, and the chaperons seemed to just sit back and watch. I suddenly found myself sitting next to a fairly attractive and gregarious young lady from a school in North Kansas City. Her name was Cheryl. She had black hair, a pretty face, long black eyelashes, brown eyes, was medium height, and had a shapely figure. She was talking her head off while looking straight into my eyes, occasionally taking hold of my hand and touching my arm as she yakked away and gestured profusely. Cheryl sat next to me for most of the trip to Milwaukie. We talked and talked—about what, I have no recollection. She introduced me to all of her friends on the trip. She seemed quite popular and well liked. When she introduced me, she seemed to act as if I was now her boyfriend. I was in a state of shock and somewhat infatuated by her aggressive attention. I had never before had this kind of devotion lavished on me by a female.

We were in Milwaukee for three days. We all stayed in the same downtown hotel near the auditorium where the conference was held. The boys from our school all stayed in one room and the girls in another. Cheryl and her group had a room just down the hall. I can't remember anything about the conference itself, and I'm not sure I knew exactly what it was all about at the time. Cheryl sat in the seat next to me in the big arena each day and snuggled up as closely as possible, holding my hand or my arm. I'm sure the nuns were as aware as everyone else in our group that I suddenly had a girlfriend and that she wasn't a bit shy in showing her affection for me.

During the three days in Milwaukee, we were all under close surveillance by our chaperones. We were also under strict orders that no boys were allowed in the girls' hotel rooms or girls in the boys' hotel rooms. One night the North Kansas City group of girls decided to go to a movie at a theater down the street from the hotel. Cheryl asked me to go with her and her group of friends, and I went. I made the bold move of actually putting my arm around her shoulder during the movie, and she seemed to snuggle closer. I was so proud of myself with my new confidence. There was some fallout from my date to the movies though. Sister Immaculata and the other nun with us had done a room check that evening at the hotel and found everyone in our group was present and accounted for except for me. I had neglected to ask permission from them to go to the movie, and they were on the warpath. They quizzed me over and over again, asking repeatedly whether I had been in Cheryl's hotel room. I assured them over and over again I had not, but I think they were still suspicious. If they had only known how socially inept I was, they would have realized I was ages away from anything close to a bedroom experience with a girl. They were so upset about it that they reported it to our school principal, Father Sullivan, when we got back from the trip. I had to go to his office the following week and attempt to smooth the whole thing over.

Cheryl advanced the level of romance on the train trip back to Kansas City. She sat in the seat next to me all the way back. The last few hours of the trip were in the dark, and the lights in the car turned down low so people could sleep if they wanted to. Cheryl put her head on my shoulder and pretended to sleep. I was feeling somewhat overwhelmed by all this and felt a little intoxication from the wonderful smell of her perfume wafting up all around me. At some point she reached up and put her hand on the side of my face, turned my face toward her face, and kissed me sweetly on the lips. At this point my head was spinning and my heart was pounding. I couldn't believe all this was happening to the guy who, only three days before, had an almost paralyzing fear of girls. Things seemed to move along at a fairly rapid pace after that first kiss until it turned into a full-fledged make-out session. By the time our train pulled into the Union Station in Kansas City, I had turned into a kissing machine.

There were many trips to North Kansas City in the old '38 Chevy over the next three or four weeks. I took Cheryl on dates at least every Saturday night and sometimes on both Friday and Saturday. My mother asked me to invite her for dinner one night so the family could meet my new (and first-ever) girlfriend. She came to dinner all gussied up and poured out her charm on them. It didn't turn out too well when, over the next few days, everyone in my family— my mother, father, and four sisters—all told me they didn't like her. That did not deter me though.

Cheryl and I kept dating for a few weeks, but the romance for me suddenly cooled off just as fast as it had heated up at the start. I somehow found out that on nights she wasn't out with me she was out with one of several other "boyfriends," including one of my classmates at Bishop Miege. One of my friends told me he had heard this guy bragging about what a "good make" Cheryl was. I was hurt by this and was in quite a funk for a while. It was a blow to my ego more than anything else since I never felt like I was falling in love with this aggressive girl. I dealt with this new information by dumping her. I simply stopped calling her. She called our house a few times after that, but I told everyone in the family to tell her I wasn't home. All of my sisters were shocked she did this since it was almost unheard of in those days for a girl to call a boy on the phone.

One afternoon, a couple of weeks after I had last seen her, she came walking up the driveway to our house. Nick Davis and I were in the garage underneath my '38 Chevy doing some kind of work on it at the time. Cheryl was contrite and said she would sure like to see me soon. She looked sad, and I actually felt kind of sorry for her. I said very little to her as she sat on a stool in the garage and watched us work. At one point Nick realized we needed a tool from his garage, two blocks up the street. Nick's dad was home, and we sent Cheryl up to his house to pick up the tool we needed. When she came back with it, I thanked her, she left, and I never saw her again. I think Mom, Dad, and my sisters had seen right through Cheryl the night she had dinner with us. My mom told me the next day that she didn't like her and that she was one of those "boy-crazy girls." I think Mom was right. But little did Mom know how much her boy needed a boy-crazy girl to pull him out of his shell at that point in his life.

Chapter 34

In spite of my scandalous behavior at the National Catholic Youth Conference, I was nominated that fall for another high office. Miss Hellinger, a young teacher assigned as faculty moderator for the production of the yearbook, chose me as one of the two co-editors for this annual publication. I surmised she must not have had any recent chats with Sister Immaculata, or she wouldn't have been talking to me about this. Miss Hellinger was my English teacher, and she was another teacher who seemed to think I had potential. I thought a lot of her too, but, regardless of that, I received the news of this honor with tempered enthusiasm. I told her I had to think about it for a few days and would get back to her.

Miss Hellinger later confided to me that she couldn't believe I wasn't absolutely thrilled to be chosen for such a position and thought any other student would consider it a great honor. A number of factors were at work here causing my hesitation. I was still on the high end of the shyness curve for one thing and didn't like to be put in any position of attention. I was also thinking about my job at Jack Henry's, and I knew the work on the yearbook would require a lot of time after school and cut into the hours I wanted to work at my part-time job. I was hesitant to take on a job I didn't think I could devote full attention to and produce a quality product. Even today, I still hesitate to accept a job at all if I think I can't give it one 100 percent.

My solution to this problem was to ignore the whole thing. When I didn't get back to her as promised, I was hoping she might find some other victim to take the job of co-editor. After a few days had gone by, she found me. She was a little cranky at this point and made it clear she wanted an answer from me. I told her about my part-time job, and she said the staff could work around that because I was her first choice and she still wanted me to do it. So, with considerable apprehension, I finally accepted her offer.

I met with my co-editor, a girl named Patrice Kramf, early in the fall. I knew Patrice as a quiet, serious girl who had always been a good student. I liked her and thought we would work well together. As I worked with her through the year, I discovered she had a terrific sense of humor. This is something I never would have guessed about her. At that first meeting, together with Miss Hellinger, we put together a list of students to invite to our staff. We notified each of these kids; then we set up another meeting for the entire staff after school one day in which we discussed the basic organization of the book and, later, assigned students to work on the various sections.

Our advisor and moderator, Miss Hellinger, told us we needed a theme for the book. This totally stumped us all for a while, but then, in order to get things moving right along, she announced she had something in mind that might work. The school was undergoing a large expansion that year to add more classrooms and a gymnasium, and construction was going on all year. With this in mind, she thought "Growth and Progress" might be a good theme for the book. She then went on to describe how we might have two-page spreads between sections of the book which would depict the architect's blueprints. The theme, she thought, could be easily carried through and applied to student growth and progress in academics, athletics, and other extra-curricular activities. Patrice and I, as well as the rest of the staff, had no other suggestions for a theme, so "growth and progress" was it. I was wondering at this point why Miss Hellinger couldn't just be the editor. She seemed to know what she was doing.

The staff started meeting one or two afternoons each week in a classroom after school. There was little pressure to work at it seriously that fall since the deadline was a long way off. Also, we didn't have a lot of material to work with until the academic year was a little further along and we'd had a chance to accumulate some stories and photographs. I spent little time at these early meetings and continued with my work schedule after school at Jack Henry's. I occasionally stopped by the work sessions to see how things were going, but I rarely helped much with anything before I zipped off to my job. I wasn't taking much responsibility as a co-editor, but Patrice and Miss Hellinger seemed to be perfectly capable without me. I didn't think there was much I could add by being at all of these meetings, and I didn't want to give up my hours at work. I reminded myself that I never wanted to be an editor anyway and had accepted the position reluctantly. Besides, it didn't seem like Patrice, Miss Hellinger, or anyone else on the staff cared much whether I was there or not. As it turned out I was wrong about that.

After Christmas vacation and we had begun the second semester of our senior year, the after-school work session became more frequent. Before long, the staff was working every day after classes in order to get the book finished by the printer's deadline in late April. One afternoon when I was dutifully checking in on the group before heading off to Jack Henry's, Miss Hellinger told me she and Patrice would like to speak to me privately in another classroom. They made it clear that day that the two of them, and the entire staff for that matter, were quite disappointed in me. My apparent lack of interest and dedication to the group had been obvious to all, and I was becoming a frequent target for rather scathing and critical remarks during their long work sessions. Miss Hellinger was particularly disappointed I believe since she had chosen me as a co-editor, and it was becoming glaringly apparent she had made a bad choice. I had caused a morale problem among the yearbook staff, and I had to do something about it.

I was feeling pretty ashamed of myself by the time I got home that evening. I began to wonder why Miss Hellinger and Patrice had to practically slap me across the face to make me aware I had, up to this point, been a total slacker. The next day at work, I told Al and Lee I would only work Saturdays in the stockroom until the yearbook was on its way to print. After that, I was at every single work session of the yearbook staff. In fact I was frequently the first one to arrive and the last one to leave. There was initially the problem of getting me up to speed. I had no idea how to cut, paste, and organize a page layout. When I say "cut and paste," I mean literally cut and paste. This was long before the days of personal computers and word processing. We cut out text items, pictures, and photographs and then pasted them on to pages which would be copied with a commercial copying machine later at the printer's.

There was a lot of grumbling and sarcastic remarks from some of the staff over having to teach me everything. I'm not sure they even wanted me there for a while since they were all so angry with me. Patrice, my co-editor, was not shy in expressing herself in this regard and poked a few wry comments at me. This attitude finally changed though as they all realized I had started taking my responsibility seriously. By the time we sent the last pages off to the printer, everyone on the staff seemed to have accepted me back, and we were having a lot of fun as we worked on it every afternoon. Working with all the girls on the yearbook staff did wonders to ease my discomfort in social situations with girls.

Chapter 35

I was accelerating rapidly into adulthood during that senior year of high school and had learned a lot of good lessons for life, but early in the spring semester, something happened that made it seem like I was approaching the speed of light—I fell head over heels in love.

One of my classmates, who knew I was working on the yearbook, informed me of a rumor that Miss Hellinger had a cute sister who was a high school senior at another Kansas City high school; I waited for an opportunity to ask her about this. It wasn't long after that, late one afternoon, when Miss Hellinger needed a ride home to her apartment after one of our yearbook work sessions. I offered to drive her home in my old '38 Chevy and, on the way, used the opportunity to ask her about her sister. She confirmed the fact she did indeed have a sister, named Sharon, who was just my age, and she didn't think Sharon had a regular boyfriend. We then started plotting a way for me to meet Sharon.

Miss Hellinger told me Sharon was a cheerleader for her school, Bishop Hogan High. Basketball season had just started, and I came up with the idea of going to one of her basketball games and finding her at the halftime or end of the game and introducing myself. That way we could sort of size each other up before considering an actual date. I didn't want Sharon to think I was going to her basketball game just to meet her though. I was afraid that might make me look desperate for a girlfriend. So I asked Miss Hellinger to tell Sharon I was a scout for our basketball team and was attending her game at the request of our coach to gather information on the players the Bishop Miege team would later face. I wanted her to know I wanted to meet her, but I preferred she think it was only because the opportunity arose since I was going to be there anyway.

The following weekend, Hogan High was scheduled to play St. Pius X in North Kansas City, so I planned to do my "scouting" that Saturday night. One potential worry was that St. Pius X was also the school of my former kissing mentor, Cheryl. I was hoping she wouldn't be there. I thought I might avoid being seen by blending into the crowd on Hogan's side of the gymnasium court.

I got to the game and found a good spot in the bleachers on the Hogan side near the pep club girls where I had a good view of the cheerleaders, who were down on the floor directly in front of this group. I don't know how I figured out which of the cheerleaders was Sharon. Miss Hellinger may have shown me a picture possibly. In any event, if she had told me just to look for the most beautiful girl I had ever seen, I would have picked her out immediately. I don't think I took my eyes off of her during the whole game. My classmate who had heard she was cute was definitely right. She was much more than cute to me—she was absolutely gorgeous! It was hard for me to imagine actually getting a date with this girl, but I was sure going to try.

I waited until the game was over to make my move. It was difficult keeping her in sight as the crowd quickly clambered down the bleachers onto the court. Once I reached the floor, it was even harder to keep her in sight. I zigged, I zagged, and I shouldered my way through the crowd, occasionally losing sight of her. She had a dark purple and white cheerleader's uniform on, her school colors, and so it wasn't too difficult to spot her again. Sharon's sister, Miss Hellinger, had told her to expect to meet me there and that I planned to introduce myself, but she was talking animatedly with her friends and didn't look like she was waiting for me or expecting me at all.

I finally got to her and her little circle of friends. I tapped her tentatively on the arm, and she turned and looked at me. I had a clipboard clutched against my chest with a tablet on it with player's names, numbers, and all kinds of scribbling. The whole basketball scout idea seemed kind of stupid now, but I was keeping up the charade. We didn't say much to each other, and that first encounter probably lasted less than a minute, but my heart felt like it was pounding its way through my chest wall. I asked her if I could call her sometime; she said that would be fine and gave me her phone number. We said goodbye, and that was it. I made a beeline for the door, hoping I wouldn't run into Cheryl before I got out of there. Luck was with me, and I didn't see Cheryl or any of her friends.

The next day was a beautiful, clear, cold wintery day. I was full of hope. I decided I would call Sharon that afternoon. Our meeting at the game the night before was so brief and the whole atmosphere so filled with distractions that I thought if I waited too long to call her, she wouldn't remember she had even met me. When I went to Sunday mass that morning, I prayed I wouldn't blow this. I got home at about noon and called. I was so nervous I was afraid my voice was two or three octaves higher than normal and warbling. I bravely asked her if she would like to go out for a coke with me that very afternoon.

I picked Sharon up at her house at 3:00 PM in my old '38 Chevy for this first date. She seemed crazy about my old car; I liked that. I opened the door for her, she hopped in, and we were off to Winstead's Drive-in Restaurant on The Plaza. On the way, I was amazed at how easily our conversation flowed. On the few dates I had been on there had always been embarrassing long gaps in the conversation when neither of us knew what to say. So I had been worried about what I would say to keep the conversation rolling with this girl I had just met. It was not a problem. I have no idea what Sharon and I talked about that day, but we were both laughing and talking comfortably the whole afternoon.

When I dropped Sharon off back at her house a couple of hours later, I asked her if she would like to go to a movie with me the following weekend. She accepted. Now I had a real date lined up. Things were happening fast, and my head felt like it was spinning on my drive back home. I thought I was the luckiest guy in the world.

That next Friday night, Sharon and I went to a movie and then back to Winstead's. The carhop came and hooked a tray over the edge of my window and then took our orders. We somehow managed to find lots of things to talk about while we waited for her to return with two cherry cream cokes—a Winstead specialty. Sharon had a curfew of 11:00 PM, so we left in time to get her back to her house safely before the deadline. I had worried all week about whether or not to try a good night kiss at the door. It was considered a bit forward to do this on the first, or even the second, date. So I had made the decision not to do something so intimate and possibly scare her off right away, but when I took her up to the front porch that night, the plan suddenly changed. She turned to face me and moved her lips toward mine, and we just naturally gave each other a very brief kiss. Then she disappeared quietly through the front door. It was all spontaneous, natural, romantic, and sweet—perfect!

Sharon and I went out almost every weekend after that. Some weekends we were together on both Friday and Saturday nights. We went to movies, out for a hamburger, or occasionally we just went for an afternoon drive. Sometimes on a nice day, we took a picnic to a park.

On a couple of our dates I took her up into the Air Traffic Control Tower at Kansas City Municipal Airport to watch airplanes take off and land. There was little airport security in those days, and I had discovered there was a phone at the base of the tower I could pick up to ring the supervisor. I'd ask if we could come up and tour the tower, and he'd buzz the door open for us. I had always loved airplanes, and this was one of my favorite things to do. I don't think Sharon liked watching the airplanes as much as I did, but I do think she enjoyed it, and it was something different to do. As we watched the airplanes from the dark tower cab, I put my arm around her and stood as close to her as I could get.

One beautiful Sunday afternoon I called Sharon to go out for a while, but she said she couldn't go because she had a project due for her science class the next week. She was doing a study on air pollution and was planning to go out to several areas of the city and take air samples. I told her I'd be right over to drive her around and help her with the project. When I got to her house, she brought out a strange looking apparatus which was a twisting maze of glass tubes plumbed to a couple of vats with some kind of chemical in them and, at one end, a bulb syringe was attached. We spent the afternoon driving to different parts of the city and using this contraption to "sniff" the air. She carefully wrote down each location in a notebook and the test results at each place. Apparently the liquids were supposed to change color if certain pollutants were present, but nothing at all happened. At one stop, instead of aspirating a sample of air into her tester, Sharon managed to squirt the chemical out of it and all over our faces and clothes. We almost laughed ourselves sick over that but hoped the liquid was not toxic and would make us truly sick. I think her science project was a total flop, but I had a wonderful time that afternoon just being with her.

I brought Sharon over to our house one night to meet my family and have dinner with us. Mom, Dad, and my sisters all thought she was great. They loved her. But the next day my mom had a little talk with me about not getting too serious with a girl at such a young age. She reminded me I had four years of college ahead of me and possibly another four years in medical school after that. She said I should not just date one girl, but "play the field," and eventually I would find someone who was just perfect for me.

I didn't listen to Mom's advice that day. I thought I had found the woman of my dreams and had no interest in any other girls. Sharon and I continued to date throughout the remainder of my senior year of high school. I became so obsessed with her that she was in my mind almost every waking moment and in my dreams at night. I could hardly stand waiting for the weekends to see her, and I started making an occasional afternoon trip to Hogan High to pick her up after school and take her home. Both of us had lots of homework to do, so we didn't spend much time together on these occasions, but just seeing her was enough to get me through until the weekend. I was definitely in love.

The romantic feelings of my heart during those days were inflamed further by some of the music we listened to—mostly on AM radio. It was a musical era of wonderful love songs—*Put Your Head on My Shoulder* by Paul Anka; *Dream* by the Everly Brothers; *Misty* by Johnny Mathis. There were many more of these that put the magic moments and feelings of teenage love to words and music. Many of these wonderful songs captured my dreamlike rapture perfectly and added another layer to it.

Although I was dating Sharon exclusively, I was never sure she was exclusively dating me. There were a few times that spring when I asked her out and she told me she was busy and couldn't go. I wasn't sure whether she just said that because she thought we were seeing a little too much of each other and she needed a break, or because she actually had a date with someone else. I never asked her if she was going out with anyone else, and if she was, I don't think I really wanted to know it. I never felt threatened with the idea anyway since I felt close to her and I was pretty sure the feeling was mutual.

As the end of the year approached I sensed Sharon was starting to pull back from me a bit. She didn't actually say anything, but I could feel it. I think she maturely realized we would each be going separate ways after high school and knew that continuing a long-distance romance was unlikely and, for her at least, also undesirable; the way I felt at that point was totally, if unrealistically, the opposite. I felt closer to her than ever. I didn't want to let her go. I couldn't imagine being without her.

One night near the end of the school year, we sat in my car in her driveway at the end of an evening out. We frequently sat, cuddled up closely together, in the car after a date to postpone the moment of

217

saying goodbye as long as possible. I felt Sharon's feelings for me had already started to cool a little bit, but on this particular night I made a mistake that seemed to chill our relationship a little further: I told her I loved her. But instead of getting the reply from her that I had hoped for, she just said, "no you don't." This is not what I wanted to hear from her. I went on to tell her I thought she was perfect in every way. Her response to this was to laugh and ask me why I thought she was perfect. But I still didn't shut up. I tried to express all of my feelings for her in words that seemed totally inadequate, but she didn't really want to hear it at all. I think she already had a pretty good idea of how I felt and had started to feel a little overwhelmed by it. Now she was getting confirmation, and it scared her. What I had hoped for on this particular night was that she would also tell me she loved me. But what I got was not what I wanted. I had taken a big risk that night and lost.

Sharon and I continued to date after that through the end of the school year and then, sporadically, throughout the following summer until we both left Kansas City for college in the fall; after that night, though, our relationship changed. My feelings for her hadn't changed, but I had become possessive and smothered a wonderful relationship. We still had fun together, but her closeness to me had cooled and was gone forever. I was suffering a deep, anguishing pain.

It was years later that I heard the expression: *If you love something, let it go. If it comes back to you, it's yours forever. If it doesn't, then it was never meant to be.*

At that time in 1963 I was badly hurt and thought I would never fall in love again; I was wrong about that. I guess it is true that *time does heal all wounds,* but in this case, the time involved was several painful years.

Chapter 36

During that spring of my senior year, as I was walking around in a love-induced daze, Namo's (grandma Fearon's) health started deteriorating. We knew Namo had high blood pressure and an enlarged heart. Dr. Gist told her that shortly after Dabo died, eight years earlier. She had gone to see him because she had shortness of breath whenever she exerted herself. He had started her on a diuretic and some digitalis leaf. The medication seemed to help a little, but now, as my graduation from high school approached, Namo was getting much worse.

After Dabo died, we all worried about Namo living by herself in her apartment, so Mom suggested she find a roommate. She put the word out at church, and in no time we found a little old lady to move in with her who seemed to be the perfect companion. Her name was Margaret Shaw, a spinster who had retired after supporting herself her entire life working as a bookkeeper. Margaret was a frail, tiny person who had about the sweetest disposition of anyone I had ever met. She told us she had grown up in an orphanage and didn't know exactly how old she was. She seemed much older than Namo, moved carefully and slowly around, and had a quiver to her voice when she talked. She couldn't hear well and was almost totally blind. Whenever Namo came over to our house, Margaret came with her, and we all started calling her "Aunt Margaret." Aunt Margaret was another devout Catholic, and it seemed as though she was saying the rosary almost all day every day. Namo and Margaret became best of friends.

After I got my car, Namo and Aunt Margaret called me frequently to take them to church on Sundays, drive them to the grocery, or to run errands. They timed their trips for weekends, after school, or while I was on summer vacation from school. It was a little tricky getting them into the car. They each had a cane, so I would set the canes on the ground while I helped them, one at a time, up onto the running board. Aunt Margaret usually slid into the seat first and sat in the middle with the floor shift between her knees, while Namo preferred to ride "shotgun." After I got them in, I handed them their canes, which they propped up between them. Aunt Margaret always seemed more shaky than normal during these outings. I think she was nervous, but I was never sure if it was because she hadn't ridden in a car much or because of having a fairly inexperienced teenage driver. Namo seemed to thoroughly enjoy the ride whenever I took them anywhere and didn't seem a bit nervous. We must have been a rather comical sight—two white-haired old ladies driving down the road sitting abreast in a 1938 Chevy coup with a skinny little blond-haired kid at the wheel.

By April of that year, 1963, Namo had gotten so short of breath she couldn't sleep lying down. She had to prop herself up with pillows and, even then, was gasping for breath at times. Dr. Gist had done all he could for her, and said she needed to be on oxygen. So we decided to move her to our house so we could take care of her. My sister Judy had moved to New York where she was based as an airline stewardess (the proper term for flight attendant in those days) for Trans World Airlines, so Judy's old bedroom became the sick room. We rented a hospital bed that could be raised, lowered, and adjusted in many ways to get Namo into comfortable positions to breathe. We got an oxygen tank and had it regularly serviced. We quickly discovered we needed two tanks, so she would always have a spare when one ran out. Everyone in the family participated in Namo's care, but I was the monitor of the oxygen and adjusted the flow rates according to Dr. Gist's orders, and I made the switch to the standby tank when a tank ran low.

With Namo being on the second floor of the house, Mom said we needed to figure out a way for Namo to be able to call for help during the day when no one else was upstairs. I told her I would take care of that and rigged up an alarm button for her to push in the event of an emergency. I went to the hardware and bought a big, round electric bell with a clangor. It looked just like the loud bell on the outside of St. Agnes School that was sounded at the end of recess. I bought a doorbell transformer, a doorbell button, and some electrical wire. I brought my supplies home and got to work in my basement workshop. I mounted the bell and transformer on a scrap of lumber. I placed this assembly on the floor of the downstairs hall near an electrical outlet. I mounted the button on another scrap of wood and attached it to one of the bedrails on Namo's hospital bed. I ran about 25 feet of wire over the banister and down to the hall to connect the button to the bell circuit. I then hooked up a wire to supply power from the outlet in the hall to the transformer. When I tested the alarm system, I found it was extremely loud. It seemed even louder than the recess bell on the side of the school. In fact, you could hear it all over the house, from the basement to my attic room. You could even hear it if you were out in the garage.

I showed Namo the button and told her if she had an emergency and needed someone right away to just push the button and one of us would come right up. That evening, one of the girls brought a dinner tray to Namo's room and got her all set up to eat. Then the entire family sat down at the dining room table for our evening meal. We were about half through eating when the alarm bell went off with its deafening blare. All six of us went charging up the stairs and through the door of the sick room. Several of us almost got jammed in the doorway as we all tried to get through at once. We were all asking Namo what was wrong since she didn't seem to be in any more distress than usual. She said, "I'm all through with my dinner, and I was wondering if one of you would take my tray back to the kitchen now."

Namo didn't like the big green oxygen tank standing about five feet tall next to her bed. She said it scared her to see it there. I asked her if it would help if I dressed it up for her. She thought that was a great idea. I put one of my old shirts on it, tied a neckerchief around its neck, and put one of my baseball caps on top. I then added my Groucho Marx glasses with the fake nose and mustache. When I finished, I wasn't sure whether I'd made the tank less scary or more scary, but Namo loved it. She laughed so hard I had to turn up her oxygen until she calmed down. For the next few weeks my sisters and I kept changing the outfit and adding new little touches to Oxygen Man.

On May 2, Namo's condition deteriorated rapidly. She asked that we transfer her to the hospital because she didn't want to die in Judy's bedroom. We called an ambulance, and Mom rode with her to St. Mary's Hospital. Namo died the next morning on May 3, 1963. We had a funeral mass at Guardian Angel, and then she was laid to rest next to Dabo in St. Mary's Cemetery.

Aunt Margaret outlived Namo by many years. After Namo's death we moved her into a Catholic nursing care facility. In her new home, she learned to read brail and was able to enjoy reading again. We all visited her regularly over the ensuing years and occasionally brought her to our house for Sunday dinner. We were Aunt Margaret's only family.

Chapter 37

As graduation day approached, the senior boys began talking about having a big celebration party—a stag party—a beer bash. Charlie Richardson's family had a small farm near the town of Stanley, Kansas, which was only about a 30-minute drive south of Kansas City on US Highway 69. Charlie volunteered to host a campout on his folk's property, and everyone seemed to agree this would be a great spot for a weekend of debauchery. Charlie never told us whether or not he had asked his parents about this idea or whether he had their permission. Regardless of this, the event was scheduled for a Saturday, one week before graduation. The party was to start in the afternoon and continue all through the night and into Sunday, and, from the sound of things, it seemed there would be almost 100% attendance. That meant about 75 happy campers were going to be heading for Stanley that weekend.

I don't think anyone in my class, at that point in our lives, had much experience with drinking alcohol. I had tried a beer a couple of times and had gotten a kick out of the way it made me feel kind of silly. I didn't know anyone who had tried hard liquor by then, and illicit drug use in our high school was nonexistent. No one had ever heard of marijuana in those days. We were all quite innocent of any significant vices.

In Kansas, it was not legal at the time to purchase or consume alcohol before the age of 21 unless it was only "three-two beer" (3.2% alcohol). In that case, the minimum age was 18. So for those of us who hadn't turned 18 yet, our previous experimentations had been illegal. The beer for the party had to be bought by the guys who had already turned 18, and the rest of us would chip in and pay them back.

I didn't want to miss out on this big weekend event, but I had one problem. I had a date scheduled with Sharon that Saturday night. I really wanted to go to the party, but I couldn't stand the thought of losing even one evening with her. I didn't want to cancel our date. I talked with Charlie and asked him if I might just come down to the farm after my date with Sharon instead of getting there in the afternoon with everyone else. He told me there were two other guys who also couldn't stand to be away from their honeys for one evening and were planning to arrive late also. So I got together with those two guys—Dave Bussjaeger (Buzzy) and Bernie Bialek—and we decided we would all meet that night after our dates and take my 1938 Chevy down to Stanley.

It was after 11 o'clock by the time I had gotten Sharon safely home and picked up Buzzy and Bernie. At Buzzy's house, we loaded our sleeping bags and two cases of Schlitz Beer, which he had hidden under some bushes by the street, into the trunk of my Chevy. We cruised out of town—sitting three abreast—on US Highway 69. A few miles outside of town, I pulled off to the side of the road and we each got a can of beer out of the trunk for the road.

There was little traffic as we sped south on the highway sipping our beer. No one had ever told any of us there might be a danger associated with drinking and driving. Road signs which said "If you drink—don't drive" didn't start appearing until many years later. I think all three of us had ridden in a car with our parents after they had consumed a few cocktails, and I had even seen my parents driving while sipping on a "roady." So we didn't really give it much thought that evening. Throwing down a beer now and then was one of the rites in the passage to adulthood. Operating a motor vehicle while consuming alcohol (or after) was no big deal—especially since it was only three-two beer.

It seemed like we had only been on the road for 30 or 40 minutes when Bernie announced we were getting close to Stanley and should start looking for the turnoff to Charlie's farm. We didn't have a map or any written directions, but Bernie had been to the farm once during the day and was confident he could direct me right to it. As we made a left turn off the highway onto a gravel road, Bernie admitted he wasn't real sure we were on the correct road. He directed me through several turns at various intersections until I had no idea which direction we were going or which way it was back to Highway 69. Bernie had told Charlie he was sure he could find the road the farm was on, but that he couldn't remember exactly what the gate looked like. Charlie suggested that once we got on the road to the farm we just drive down it honking our horn, and one of the guys would come out and stand by the gate to direct us in. That might have worked if Bernie could have found the correct road, but we were totally lost.

We continued to cruise down one country road after another in hopes Bernie would eventually see some landmark that jogged his memory. After a while, it seemed we had been on every gravel road

224

within 100 square miles and had travelled some of the same roads several times. The roads were all gravel but were smooth, well maintained, and fairly wide. The Kansas farm country in this area was also generally flat. As the time ticked away and we meandered all over the countryside, all three of us became more than a little impatient to find the party. I drove a little faster and a little faster as I started sipping my second beer. All of the roads had been straight, generally following the section lines defining the farmlands, and I could see intersections of the crossroads well before I got to them.

We finally got on a long, straight road we hadn't been on before. Bernie thought it looked familiar and said he thought this was the one. I sped up to about 45 miles per hour as we approached the bottom of a slight hill. This was the first stretch we had been on that wasn't totally flat. I crested the top of the rise, and, as the headlights dropped to illuminate the downhill ahead, we could see the road ended abruptly in a T'd intersection with a bridge over a creek to the right. Bernie and Buzzy both yelled at me. I stomped on the brakes and spun the steering wheel to the right, hoping I could guide us through the superstructure of the bridge and not slam into the end of it. It was too late. The car entered a sliding skid to the left with dust and gravel flying in every direction. We were now facing 90 degrees to the right of the road we had been on, pointed at the entrance to the bridge and lined up with the direction of the side road, but we weren't going forward anymore—we were sliding sideways. The car slid off the side of the road just before the bridge and rolled several times down a steep embankment toward the bottom of a ravine next to the creek bed. There were loud thuds and the sounds of crunching metal and breaking glass as the car tumbled. Then, all of the noise and motion stopped abruptly as the car stopped rolling and lay on its left side with the top facing down the incline. An eerie quiet settled over the whole scene as the headlights illuminated a tangle of tall grass and brush, viewed sideways through a shattered windshield.

We untangled our bodies from one another and climbed out into the darkness through the right (top) door. We checked each other over and found Bernie had a cut on the top of his head that was bleeding a little, but, other than that, we were all just a little bruised and scraped. I had, ironically, installed seatbelts in the car just a few weeks before, but none of us were using them.

We quickly decided we had better get rid of the rest of the two cases of beer in case the police came. Not that we thought we'd be in any trouble for drinking and driving, but Bernie and I weren't 18 yet, so were under the legal age to be in possession of beer. We walked up the creek a ways and hid it under some brush. Buzzy planned to come back and get it sometime if he could ever find the place again.

After a while we realized that no one knew about this accident and there wouldn't be anyone coming for us. Buzzy kept a cool head, surveyed the area, and announced that he thought we could drive the car down the field a bit—the opposite direction from the bridge—to a point where the field sloped gently up to the level of the road. But first we had to get the car back up on all four wheels. The adrenaline must have been really flowing through our bodies. We all three got on the downhill side of the car, grabbed the edge of the roof, and put our backs into it. To our amazement, we flipped it back <u>UP</u> the hill and onto all four wheels. Buzzy was strong as an ox. So Bernie and I conceded later that the successful effort was probably 90 percent from his incredible heave since Bernie and I were both skinny little shrimps.

All of the four fenders were crushed against the tires, but we walked around the car and pulled on each one of them until all four tires had some clearance. I decided to hand the keys to Buzzy and let him try to get the car back on the road. He seemed to be thinking more rationally than I at that point, and, for the first time, I wondered if the alcohol might be having some influence on my thinking and judgment. Buzzy jumped in and started it right up. He maneuvered it down into the field and then parallel to the road until he got to a place where the slope was more gradual. He was then able to power it through a ditch and up onto the gravel.

We never made it to our senior boys bash. We somehow found our way back to the highway. We were quiet on the ride back to town. The top of the car was partially caved in, and all the fenders were crushed. There was mud and straw stuck all over the outside of the car, all of the glass was shattered, but the car amazingly tracked straight down the road and seemed to drive normally.

By the time we arrived back in Kansas City, the eastern sky had a pink glow—the beginning of a new day.

AFTERWARD

The class graduation was a formal cap-and-gown ceremony held in the old Saint Agnes grade school gymnasium. Dad took eight-millimeter movies as we all paraded up to get our diplomas. Bernie and Buzzy still sported a couple of Band-Aids as they walked by and squinted under dad's glaring light bar. We had come up with a cockamamie story about a farmer in a pickup truck running us off the road as the explanation for the wreck. Bernie and Buzzy swore never to reveal to anyone the humiliating and embarrassing details of what really happened that night. I am not sure my parents or anyone else really believed us, but we stuck to it, and they seemed happy we were all still alive. I sold the car to a young fellow who owned a body shop, and he planned to completely repair and restore it.

I got a job that summer operating a tractor and mowing the right-of-ways for the county highway department. This was thanks to our good neighbor and my wonderful friend, Carl Standiford, the Chairman of the Board of County Commissioners of Johnson County. Carl seemed always to love and respect me no matter what trouble I got into. I had that highway department job every year for each summer vacation during college for the next four years.

My relationship with Sharon continued to cool even further after the car crash. I suspected she didn't believe I had been truthful with her about what really happened. I think she lost some respect for me after that, and I could tell the magic we once had was fading. But the harder I tried to win her back, the more aloof she seemed to become. I pined away that summer and suffered terribly from what I could see I was losing. It was a long time before I finally got over her.

The rest of my life has been a continuing and wonderful adventure. I met the love of my life, became a physician, a commercial airline pilot, a woodworker and furniture maker, a husband, a father, a grandfather, and – finally – a happy retiree who is now starting to write about it all.

Made in the USA
Monee, IL
25 July 2020